Joe,

Here'r a little light reading...

Gary

The U.S. Wealth Transfer Tax
and the Non-Citizen

The U.S. Wealth Transfer Tax and the Non-Citizen

ISBN: 978-0-9882183-5-2

TABLE OF CONTENTS

INTRODUCTION

This concise treatise introduces students to the U.S. estate and gift tax imposed on non-citizens. The book explains some of the pertinent death and gift tax issues facing resident and non-resident foreign nationals. The study of foreign tax has been one of my most fulfilling pursuits. I hope the book inspires law students to consider practice in the area.

CHAPTER 1
THE U.S. ESTATE AND GIFT TAX

Overview

Since 1916, the United States has imposed an "Estate Tax"[1] on the U.S. assets of foreign decedents and on all assets of U.S. citizens and residents. The Estate Tax covers transfers of wealth at death. The U.S. also imposes a "Gift Tax"[2] on gratuitous lifetime transfers. Gift Tax covers the value of gifts made during life. Non-resident non-citizens are taxed only on gifts of U.S. based assets.[3]

Since 1977, the Gift Tax and the Estate Tax have been integrated for U.S. citizens and residents. The value of both taxable gifts and taxable estate assets may be offset to the extent of the "unified credit" against both Estate and Gift Tax. Lifetime gifts of property (to the extent exceeding the $15,000 annual exemption for each donee)[4] are taxable but reduce the grantor's taxable estate (at death).[5] Tax on lifetime gifts may be offset by the unified credit, but lifetime use of the credit reduces the credit available at death. The estate of a U.S. decedent is afforded the remaining "unified credit" against the Estate Tax.

The unified credit "exempts" from taxation the value of property up to the "applicable exclusion amount."[6] For calendar year 2021, the exclusion amount for U.S.

---

[1] Internal Revenue Code §2001 (hereinafter "IRC").

[2] IRC §2501.

[3] IRC §2511.

[4] IRC §2503 (applicable to U.S. residents and non-resident non-citizens("NRNCs")).

[5] Beginning on January 1, 1977, the tax was calculated on the combined value of an individual's "taxable estate" (generally assets owned or controlled, less certain deductions allowed by the IRC), and an individual's "adjusted taxable gifts" (i.e., gifts not included in the "taxable estate").

[6] IRC §2010(c)(2).

citizens and residents is \$11,700,000 per individual.[7] Gift or Estate Tax is only owed by U.S. residents and citizens if the aggregate value of all lifetime gifts (exceeding \$15,000 per donee per year) and all testamentary bequests (i.e., gifts at death) exceed the unified credit.

Currently, the rate of tax for both Gift Tax and Estate Tax is 40% of the value of property transferred.[8]

Non-Resident Non-Citizens

The Estate Tax exemption for non-resident non-citizens ("NRNCs") is only \$60,000.[9] The NRNC may not apply the \$60,000 exemption amount against taxable lifetime gifts.[10] Gift Tax is, therefore, due on all lifetime gifts exceeding the \$15,000 annual exemption.

Gifts to one's U.S. citizen spouse are, however, not taxable (for both U.S. and non-U.S. grantors). The exemption for lifetime gifts to non-citizen spouses is, however, limited to \$149,000 annually.[11] A few U.S. tax treaties include a gift tax marital deduction for transfers to noncitizen spouses. If a treaty applies, the limited annual exclusion may be avoided. See page 125 below, regarding Estate and Gift Tax Treaties.

---

[7] The applicable exclusion amount is indexed for inflation on an annual basis.

[8] Although IRC §2001(c) provides a "rate schedule" for the imposition of the tax, the highest marginal rate is imposed beginning with estates valued over one million dollars. As the current exemption amount is in excess of eleven million dollars, the Estate Tax essentially functions as a "flat tax" at the top marginal rate.

[9] IRC §2102(b)(1) (the \$60,000 exemption amount translates into the actual tax credit amount of \$13,000).

[10] IRC §2505(a) (which omits reference to nonresident noncitizens and applies the Estate Tax credit to taxable lifetime gifts by citizens or residents of the United States).

[11] IRC §2523(i)(2) (the \$100,000 is annually adjusted for inflation).

The rate of Estate and Gift Tax on NRNCs is the same as that applied to U.S. grantors. If applicable, U.S. estate and gift tax treaties diminish the Estate and Gift Tax imposed on non-citizens.

Tax Basis

The tax treatment of property inherited by an heir can be very distinct from the tax treatment of property received as a gift. The tax basis received in property (gifted or inherited) governs the tax impact of a later sale of the property. Recipients of (i) property inherited from a U.S. citizen or resident or (ii) U.S. situs property inherited from an NRNC, receive a "stepped-up" income tax "basis" on the inherited property. The "step-up" adjusts the tax basis of property inherited to the fair market value of the property (as of the date of the decedent's death).[12]

If for any reason the property is valued lower than the donor's tax basis at the time of inheritance, the decedent receives a "step-down" basis in the property.

The step-up in tax basis of inherited property allows the heirs to avoid having to pay (in the event of a subsequent sale of the property) tax on any prior appreciation. In contrast, the recipient of a lifetime gift receives a tax basis equal to the lower of (i) the tax basis held by the grantor or (ii) the fair market value of the property at the time of the gift.[13] If the expected "step-up" to fair market value is substantial, it may be prudent to defer certain gifts until death.

---

[12] IRC §1014(a)(1).
[13] IRC §1015(a).

Burnet v. Brooks
Supreme Court of the United States, 1933.
288 U.S. 378, 53 S. Ct. 457.

OPINION

Proceeding by David Burnet, Commissioner of Internal Revenue, opposed by Ernest Brooks and others, as executors of the will of Ernest Augustus Brooks, to review a decision of the United States Board of Tax Appeals. The Circuit Court of Appeals affirmed the decision of the Board of Tax Appeals, and David Burnet, Commissioner of Internal Revenue, brings certiorari (287 U. S. 594, 53 S. Ct. 222, 77 L. Ed. __). Reversed, and cause remanded.

On Writ of Certiorari to the United States, Circuit Court of Appeals for the Second Circuit. Judge: Mr. Chief Justice HUGHES delivered the opinion of the Court.

Respondents contested the determination of the Commissioner of Internal Revenue in including in the gross estate of decedent certain intangible property. Decedent, who died in October, 1924, was a subject of Great Britain and a resident of Cuba. He was not engaged in business in the United States. The property in question consisted of securities, viz., bonds of foreign corporations, bonds of foreign governments, bonds of domestic corporations and of a domestic municipality, and stock in a foreign corporation, and also of a balance of a cash deposit. [1] Some of the securities, consisting of a stock certificate and bonds, were in the possession of decedent's son in New York City, who collected the income and placed it to the credit of decedent in a New York bank. Other securities were in the possession of Lawrence Turnure & Co., in New York City, who collected the income and credited it to decedent's checking account, which showed the above-mentioned balance in his favor. None of the securities was pledged or held for any indebtedness. Finding these facts, the Board of Tax Appeals decided that the property should not be included in the decedent's gross estate for the purpose of the federal estate tax (22 B. T. A. 71), and the decision was affirmed by the Circuit Court of Appeals. 60 F.(2d) 890. This Court granted certiorari, 287 U. S. 594, 53 S. Ct. 222, 77 L. Ed. __.

The provisions governing the imposition of the tax are found in the Revenue Act of 1924, c. 234, 43 Stat. 253, 303-307, and are set forth in the margin. [2] Two questions are presented: (1) Whether the property in question is covered by these provisions; and (2) whether, if construed to be applicable, they are valid under the Fifth Amendment of the Federal Constitution. The decisions below answered the first question in the negative.

First. The first question is one of legislative intention In the case of a nonresident of the United States, that part of the gross estate was to be returned and valued "which at the time of his death is situated in the United States." In interpreting this clause, regard must be had to the purpose in view. The Congress was exercising its taxing power. Defining the subject of its exercise, the Congress resorted to a general description referring to the situs of the property. The statute made no distinction between tangible and intangible property. It did not except intangibles. It did not except securities. Save as stated, it did not except debts due to a nonresident from resident debtors. As to tangibles and intangibles alike, it made the test one of situs, and we think it is clear that the reference is to property which, according to accepted principles, could be deemed to have a situs in this country for the purpose of the exertion of the federal power of taxation. Again, so far as the intention of the Congress is concerned, we think that the principles thus impliedly invoked by the statute were the principles theretofore declared and then held. It is quite inadmissible to assume that the Congress exerting federal power was legislating in disregard of existing doctrine, or to view its intention in the light of decisions as to state power which were not rendered until several years later. [3] The argument is pressed that the reference to situs must, as to intangibles, be taken to incorporate the principle of mobilia sequuntur personam and thus, for example, that the bonds here in question though physically in New York should be regarded as situated in Cuba where decedent resided. But the Congress did not enact a maxim. When the statute was passed it was well established that the taxing power could reach such securities in the view that they had a situs where they were physically located. As securities thus actually present in this country were regarded as having a situs here for the purpose of taxation, were are unable to say that the Congress in its broad description, embracing all property "situated in the United States," intended to exclude such securities from the gross estate to be returned and valued.

The general clause with respect to the property of nonresidents "situated in the United States" is found in the provisions for an estate tax of the Revenue Act of 1916, §203 (b), 39 Stat. 778, and was continued in the Revenue Acts of 1918, §403 (b), 40 Stat. 1098; of 1921, §403 (b), 42 Stat. 280; and of 1924, §303 (b), 26 USCA §1095 note, the provision now under consideration. Before the phrase was used in the act of 1916, this Court, in passing upon questions arising under the inheritance tax law of June 13, 1898, §29, 30 Stat. 464 (in a case where the decedent had left "certain federal, municipal and corporate bonds" in the custody of his agents in New York), recognized that the property would not have escaped the tax, had it been imposed in apt terms, in the view that the property was intangible and belonged to a nonresident. Eidman v. Martinez, 184 U. S. 578, 582, 22 S. Ct. 515, 46 L. Ed. 697. While that statute was found to be inapplicable, as the property had not passed, within the limitations of the statute, "by will or by the intestate laws of any state or territory," the opinion conceded the power of Congress "to impose an inheritance tax upon property in this country, no matter where owned or transmitted." Id., page 592 of 184 U. S., 22 S. Ct. 515, 516, 521, 46 L. Ed. 697. We see no reason to doubt that it was with this conception of its power that the Congress enacted the later provisions for an estate tax in the case of nonresidents. And before the Revenue Act of 1921 was passed, we had stated the principles deemed controlling in De Ganay v. Lederer, 250 U. S. 376, 39 S. Ct. 524, 525, 63 L. Ed. 1042, in construing the provision of the Income Tax Law of 1913, 38 Stat. 166, imposing a tax upon the net income "from all property owned in the United States by persons residing elsewhere." The decision was upon a certified question with respect to the income of a citizen and resident of France from stocks, bonds, and mortgages secured upon property in the United States, where the owner's agent in the United States collected and remitted the income and had "physical possession of the certificates of stock, the bonds and the mortgages." The Court said: "The question submitted comes to this: Is the income from the stock, bonds, and mortgages, held by the Pennsylvania Company [the agent], derived from property owned in the United States? A learned argument is made to the effect that the stock certificates, bonds, and mortgages are not property, that they are but evidences of the ownership of interests which are property; that the property, in a legal sense, represented by the securities, would exist if the physical evidences thereof were destroyed. But we are of opinion that these refinements are not decisive of the congressional intent in using the term 'property' in this statute. Unless the contrary appears, statutory words are presumed to be used in their ordinary and usual sense, and with the meaning commonly attributable to them. To the general understanding and with the common meaning usually attached to such descriptive terms, bonds, mortgages, and certificates of stock are regarded as property. By state and federal statutes they are often treated as property, not as mere evidences of the interest which they represent." Having no doubt "that the securities, herein involved, are property," the Court proceeded to the question, "Are they property within the United States? It is insisted that the maxim 'mobilia sequuntur personam' applies in this instance, and that the situs of the property was at the domicile of the owner in France. But this Court has frequently declared that the maxim,

7

a fiction at most, must yield to the facts and circumstances of cases which require it, and that notes, bonds, and mortgages may acquire a situs at a place other than the domicile of the owner, and be there reached by the taxing authority." Then, describing the location of the certificates of stock, bonds and mortgages in question in the possession of the agent in Philadelphia, the Court concluded that the securities constituted "property within the United States within the meaning of Congress as expressed in the statute under consideration." The reference in the statement of this conclusion to the authority of the agent to sell, invest, and reinvest was by way of emphasis and is not to be taken as importing a necessary qualification. The Court, answered the certified question in the affirmative. Id., pages 380-383 of 250 U. S., 39 S. Ct. 524, 525, 63 L. Ed. 1042.

Under the Revenue Act of 1916, the Commissioner of Internal Revenue ruled "that Congress has the power and evidenced an intention" in that act "to impose a tax upon bonds, both foreign and domestic, owned by a non-resident decedent, which bonds are physically situate in the United States," and that "such bonds must be returned as a portion of his gross estate." T. D. 2530. The regulations promulgated by the Treasury Department under the Revenue Act of 1918, interpreting the words "situated in the United States," contained the following: "The situs of property, both real and personal, for the purpose of the tax is its actual situs. Stock in a domestic corporation, and insurance payable by a domestic insurance company, constitute property situated in the United States, although owned by, or payable to, a nonresident. A domestic corporation or insurance company is one created or organized in the United States. Bonds actually situated in the United States, moneys on deposit with domestic banks and moneys due on open accounts by domestic debtors constitute property subject to tax." Regulations No. 37, art. 60, T. D. 2378, 2910, 3145. This provision, in substance, as to bonds and moneys due (other than insurance moneys and bank deposits which were made the subject of a special statutory provision), was repeated in the regulations under the Revenue Act of 1921, as follows: "Bonds actually within the United States, moneys due on open accounts by domestic debtors, and stock of a corporation or association created or organized int he United States, constitute property having its situs in the United States." Regulations No. 63, art. 53, T. D. 3384. We find no ground for questioning the intention of the Congress, when in the Revenue Act of 1924 it re-enacted the provision as to the property of nonresidents "situated in the United States," to impose the tax with respect to bonds physically within the United States and stock in domestic corporations. Brewster v. Gage, 280 U. S. 327, 337, 50 S. Ct. 115, 74 L. Ed. 457.

The argument is pressed that the regulations above quoted are silent as to stock owned by nonresidents in foreign corporations when the certificates of stock are held within the United States. We think that the omission is inconclusive. It may be more fairly said that the express terms of these regulations did not go far enough, rather than that, so far as they did go, they failed to express the legislative intent. In the view which identifies the property interest with its physical representative, no sufficient reason appears for holding that bonds were intended to be included, and not certificates of stock, if these were physically in the United States at the time of death. See De Ganay v. Lederer, supra; Direction Der Disconto-Gesellschaft v. United States Steel Corporation, 267 U. S. 22, 28, 29, 45 S. Ct. 207, 69 L. Ed. 495. The regulations adopted under the Revenue Act of 1924 expanded the provision as to the "situs of property of nonresident decedents" so as to include stock in foreign corporations when the certificates were held here, by providing: "Real estate within the United States, stocks and bonds physically in the United States at date of death, moneys due on open accounts by domestic debtors, and stock of a corporation or association created or organized in the United States, constitute property having a situs in the United States." Regulations No. 68, art. 50, T. D. 3683. The Revenue Act of 1926, sec. 303(b), 44 Stat. 73 (26 USCA §1095 note) re-enacted the provision as to property of nonresidents "situated in the United

States," and the regulation under that act expressly embraces "certificates of stock, bonds, bills, notes, and mortgages, physically in the United States at date of death" as property "having a situs in the United States," in addition to the clause relating to stock of domestic corporations. Regulations No. 70, art. 50. And these provisions have been continued. Id. 1929 edition.

We do not find that the qualifying provisions of sections 303 (d) and (e) of the Revenue Act of 1924, 26 USCA §1095 (d, e) are inconsistent with the departmental construction. Section 303 (d) provided that "stock in a domestic corporation owned and held by a nonresident decedent shall be deemed property within the United States." Respondents point to the absence of a similar provision as to bonds and as to stock in foreign corporations and invoke the maxim expressio unius est exclusio alterius. But the argument seems to prove too much. It is not to be supposed that the Congress intended that stock owned by a nonresident in a domestic corporation, where the certificates of stock were held in the United States, were to be subject to the tax, and that bonds of the same corporation similarly owned and physically in the United States, were to be excepted. See T. D. 2530. We think that the government's construction of the provision is the more reasonable one, that the place where the stock was held was not an element in the application of section 303 (d), and that this provision was designed to insure the inclusion of the stock of a domestic corporation in all cases whether the certificates were physically present in the United States or not. Compare Corry v. Baltimore, 196 U. S. 466, 473, 474, 25 S. Ct. 297, 49 L. Ed. 556.

Section 303 (e) provided: "The amount receivable as insurance upon the life of a non-resident decedent, and any moneys deposited with any person carrying on the banking business, by or for a nonresident decedent who was not engaged in business in the United States at the time of his death," are not to be deemed "property within the United States." The Revenue Act of 1918, §403 (b) (3), 40 Stat. 1099, had provided that the amount receivable as insurance, where the insurer is a domestic corporation, should be regarded as property within the United States, and this was repealed by the substituted provision of the Revenue Act of 1921, §403 (b) (3), 42 Stat. 280, to the contrary effect; the latter being carried forward in the Revenue Act of 1924. It is a matter of common knowledge that American life insurance companies were engaged in business abroad, and no clear inference with respect to the question now under consideration may be drawn either from the original provision or from its repeal. [4] But the significance of the remaining clause of the act of 1921, re-enacted in 1924, is apparent. This provided for the exclusion from the gross estate of bank deposits in this country, in the circumstances stated; deposits which, as constituting property of nonresidents situated in the United States, had theretofore been subject to the estate tax. [5] The Congress evidently thought it necessary to make this express exception, in order to exclude such deposits from the tax, but did not provide any exception with respect to bonds and certificates of stock physically here.

As to decedent's deposit balance in the instant case, the Board of Tax Appeals did not make an explicit finding that Lawrence Turnure & Co., with whom the decedent had a checking account, was "carrying on the banking business." The Board thought that the point was not material. 22 B. T. A. page 87. If that firm was engaged in the banking business, the statute required the exclusion of the deposit balance from the gross estate. As to the securities, in view of the legislative history and departmental construction, we find no basis for holding that the statute, if valid in this application, did not require their inclusion.

Second. The question of power to lay the tax. As a nation with all the attributes of sovereignty, the United States is vested with all the powers of government necessary to maintain an effective control of international relations. Fong Yue Ting v. United States, 149 U. S. 698, 711, 13 S. Ct. 1016, 37 L. Ed. 905; Knox v. Lee, 12 Wall. 457, 555, 556, 20 L. Ed. 287. "We should hesitate long," we said in Mackenzie v. Hare, 239 U. S. 299, 311, 36 S. Ct. 106, 108, 60 L. Ed. 297, Ann. Cas.

1916E, 645, "before limiting or embarrassing such powers." So far as our relation to other nations is concerned, and apart from any self-imposed constitutional restriction, we cannot fail to regard the property in question as being within the jurisdiction of the United States; that is, it was property within the reach of the power which the United States by virtue of its sovereignty could exercise as against other nations and their subjects without violating any established principle of international law. This view of the scope of the sovereign power in the matter of the taxation of securities physically within the territorial limits of the sovereign is sustained by high authority and is a postulate of legislative action in other countries. The subject was considered by the House of Lords in Winans v. Attorney-General, [1910] A. C.27. The question was as to the liability to estate duty, under the British Finance Act, 1894, of bonds and certificates when these were physically situated in the United Kingdom at the death of the owner, who was a citizen of the United States and domiciled here. The securities were payable to bearer, marketable on the London Stock Exchange, and passed by delivery. The executors insisted that "the property did not pass by the law of the United Kingdom but by the law of the deceased's domicile"; that "the presence in the United Kingdom of the documents of title to the property did not create a liability to estate duty"; that "all the debtors on the bonds and certificates were at the time of the death and all material times outside the United Kingdom and beyond its jurisdiction"; that "the marketability of a piece of paper in the United Kingdom was not sufficient to make the debt of which it was evidence liable to estate duty"; and that "the property was not situate in the United Kingdom." The House of Lords was not convinced by these contentions. The Lord Chancellor observed that "the property received the full protection of British laws-which is a constant basis of taxation-and can only be transferred from the deceased to other persons by the authority of a British Court." Id., p. 30. Lord Atkinson referred to the status of the securities under international law. "Being physically situated in England at the time of their owner's death," said his Lordship, "they were subject to English law and the jurisdiction of English courts, and taxes might therefore prima facie be leviable upon them.

There does not appear, a priori, to be anything contrary to the principles of international law, or hurtful to the polity of nations, in a state's taxing property physically situated within its borders, wherever its owner may have been domiciled at the time of his death." Id., p. 31. And Lord Shaw of Dunfermline summed up the application of the British acts as follows: "In the case of an English citizen all his property 'wheresoever situate,' subject to the exception in the act, is aggregated, and into that aggregation-to confine oneself to the matter in hand-all personal property situate out of the United Kingdom must come, unless legacy or succession duty would not have been payable in respect thereof. In the case of the foreign citizen no taxation, of course, falls, except upon property situate within the United Kingdom, and I know no reason either under the law of nations, by the custom of nations, or in the nature of things why property within the jurisdiction of this country, possessed and held under the protection of its laws, should not, upon transfer from the dead to the living, pay the same toll which would have been paid by property enjoying the same protection but owned by a deceased British subject." Id., pp. 47, 48. In this view, the securities were held to be subject to the estate duty.

In Direction Der Disconto-Gesellschaft v. United States Steel Corporation, 267 U. S. 22, 45 S. Ct. 207, 208, 69 L. Ed. 495, a somewhat analogous question of jurisdiction arose in relation to the title to shares of stock of an American corporation, which were owned by German corporations, and the certificates of which had been seized in London by the British Public Trustee appointed to be custodian of enemy property during the late war. As was found to be usual with shares which it was desired to deal in abroad, the shares had been registered on the books of the American corporation in the name of an English broker or dealer who had indorsed the certificates in blank. The German corporations had bought the shares and held the certificates in London. Their suit here suit here was to establish title, to cancel outstanding certificates, and to have new certificates issued to them. They based their claim on the proposition that seizure of the certificates in Great Britain did not constitute a seizure of the shares; that the presence of the certificates did not bring the shares within the territorial jurisdiction of Great Britain. This Court took a different view and sustained the title of the British Public Trustee. The Court thus stated the basis of its ruling: "New Jersey having authorized this corporation like others to issue certificates that so far represent the stock that ordinarily at least no one can get the benefits of ownership except through and by means of the paper, it recognizes as owner anyone to whom the person declared by the paper to be owner has transferred it by the indorsement provided for wherever it takes place. It allows an indorsement in blank, and by its law as well as by the law of England an indorsement in blank authorizes anyone who is the lawful owner of the paper to write in a name, and thereby entitle the person so named to demand registration as owner in his turn upon the corporation's books. But the question who is the owner of the paper depends upon the law of the place where the paper is. It does not depend upon the holder's having given value or taking without notice of outstanding claims but upon the things done being sufficient by the law of the place to transfer the title. An execution locally valid is as effectual as an ordinary purchase. Yazoo & Mississippi Valley R. R. Co. v. Clarksdale, 257 U. S. 10, 42 S. Ct. 27, 66 L. Ed. 104. The things done in England transferred the title to the Public Trustee by English law." The Court thought it "so plain that the Public Trustee got a title good as against the plaintiffs by the original seizure" that it was deemed unnecessary to advert to the treaties upon which the Public Trustee also relied or upon the subsequent dealings between England and Germany. Id., pages 28, 29 of 267 U. S., 45 S. Ct. 207, 208, 69 L. Ed. 495.

As jurisdiction may exist in more than one government, that is, jurisdiction based on distinct grounds-the citizenship of the owner, his domicile, the source of income, the situs of the property-efforts have been made to preclude multiple taxation through the negotiation of appropriate international conventions. These endeavors, however, have proceeded upon express or implied recognition, and not in denial, of the sovereign taxing power as exerted by governments in the exercise of jurisdiction upon any one of these grounds. For many years this subject has been under consideration by international committees of experts and drafts of conventions have been proposed, the advantages of which lie in the mutual concessions or reciprocal restrictions to be voluntarily made or accepted by powers freely negotiating on the basis of recognized principles of jurisdiction. In its international relations, the United States is as competent as other nations to enter into such negotiations, and to become a party to such conventions, without any disadvantage due to limitation of its sovereign power, unless that limitation is necessarily found to be imposed by its own Constitution.

Respondents urge that constitutional restriction precluding the federal estate tax in question is found in the due process clause of the Fifth Amendment. The point, being solely one of jurisdiction to tax, involves none of the other considerations raised by confiscatory or arbitrary legislation inconsistent with the fundamental conceptions of justice which are embodied in the due process clause for the protection of life, liberty, and property of all persons; citizens and friendly aliens alike. Russian Volunteer Fleet v. United States, 282 U. S. 481, 489, 51 S. Ct. 229, 75 L. Ed. 473; Nichols v. Coolidge, 274 U. S. 531, 542, 47 S. Ct. 710, 71 L. Ed. 1184, 52 A. L. R. 1081; Heiner v. Donnan, 285 U. S. 312, 326, 52 S. Ct. 358, 76 L. Ed. 772. If in the instant case the federal government had jurisdiction to impose the tax, there is manifestly no ground for assailing it. Knowlton v. Moore, 178 U. S. 41, 109, 20 S. Ct. 747, 44 L. Ed. 969; McCray v. United States, 195 U. S. 27, 61, 24 S. Ct. 769, 49 L. Ed. 78, 1 Ann. Cas. 561; Flint v. Stone Tracy Co., 220 U. S. 107, 153, 154, 31 S. Ct. 342, 55 L. Ed. 389, Ann. Cas. 1912B, 1312; Brushaber v. Union Pacific R. R. Co., 240

U. S. 1, 24, 36 S. Ct. 236, 60 L. Ed. 493, L. R. A. 1917D, 414, Ann. Cas. 1917B, 713; United States v. Doremus, 249 U. S. 86, 93, 39 S. Ct. 214, 63 L. Ed. 493. Respondents' reliance is upon the decisions of this Court with respect to the limitation of the taxing power of the states under the due process clause of the Fourteenth Amendment. Farmers Loan & Trust Co. v. Minnesota, 280 U. S. 204, 50 S. Ct. 98, 74 L. Ed. 371, 65 A. L. R. 1000; Baldwin v. Missouri, 281 U. S. 586, 50 S. Ct. 436, 74 L. Ed. 1056, 72 A. L. R. 1303; Beidler v. South Carolina Tax Commission, 282 U. S. 1, 51 S. Ct. 54, 75 L. Ed. 131; First National Bank of Boston v. Maine, 284 U. S. 312, 52 S. Ct. 174, 76 L. Ed. 313. They insist that the like clause of the Fifth Amendment imposes a corresponding restriction upon the taxing power of the federal government.

The argument is specious, but it ignores an established distinction. Due process requires that the limits of jurisdiction shall not be transgressed. That requirement leaves the limits of jurisdiction to be ascertained in each case with appropriate regard to the distinct spheres of activity of state and nation. The limits of state power are defined in view of the relation of the states to each other in the Federal Union. The bond of the Constitution qualifies their jurisdiction. This is the principle which underlies the decisions cited by respondents. These decisions established that proper regard for the relation of the states in our system required that the property under consideration should be taxed in only one state, and that jurisdiction to tax was restricted accordingly. In Farmers' Loan & Trust Company v. Minnesota, supra, the Court applied the principle to intangibles, and referring to the contrary view which had prevailed, said (page 209 of 280 U. S., 50 S. Ct. 98, 99, 74 L. Ed. 371, 65 A. L. R. 1000): "The inevitable tendency of that view is to disturb good relations among the states and produce the kind of discontent expected to subside after establishment of the Union. The Federalist, No. VII. The practical effect of it has been bad; perhaps two-thirds of the states have endeavored to avoid the evil by resort to reciprocal exemption laws." It was this "rule of immunity from taxation by more than one state," deducible from the decisions in respect of various and distinct kinds of property, that the Court applied in First National Bank v. Maine, supra, page 326 of 284 U. S., 52 S. Ct. 174, 176, 76 L. Ed. 313

As pointed out in the opinion in the First National Bank Case, the principle has had a progressive application. In Louisville & Jeffersonville Ferry Company v. Kentucky, 188 U. S. 385, 23 S. Ct. 463, 47 L. Ed. 513, the question related to a ferry franchise granted by Indiana to a Kentucky corporation which Kentucky attempted to tax. Despite the fact that the tax was laid upon a property right belonging to a domestic corporation, the Court held that the Fourteenth Amendment precluded the imposition. Id., page 398 of 188 U. S., 23 S. Ct. 463, 47 L. Ed. 513. In Union Refrigerator Transit Company v. Kentucky, 199 U. S. 194, 26 S. Ct. 36, 50 L. Ed. 150, 4 Ann Cas. 493, the principle was applied to the attempted taxation by Kentucky of tangible personal property which was owned by a domestic corporation but had a permanent situs in another state.

The Court decided that where tangible personal property had an actual situs in a particular state, the power to subject it to state taxation rested exclusively in that state regardless of the domicile of the owner. By Frick v. Pennsylvania, 268 U. S. 473, 45 S. Ct. 603, 69 L. Ed. 1058, 42 A. L. R. 316, the rule became definitely fixed that as to tangible personal property the power to impose a death transfer tax was solely in the state where the property had an actual situs, and could not be exercised by another state where the decedent was domiciled. See First National Bank v. Maine, supra, page 322 of 284 U. S., 52 S. Ct. 174, 76 L. Ed. 313. The decision in Farmers' Loan & Trust Company v. Minnesota, supra, overruling Blackstone v. Miller, 188 U. S. 189, 23 S. Ct. 277, 47 L. Ed. 439, carried forward the principle by applying it to intangibles. The Court was of the opinion that "the general reasons declared sufficient to inhibit taxation of them [tangibles] by two states apply under present circumstances with no less force to intangibles with taxable situs imposed by due application of the legal fiction. Primitive conditions have passed; business is now transacted on a national scale. A very large part of the country's wealth is invested in negotiable securities whose protection against discrimination, unjust and oppressive taxation, is matter of the greatest moment." 280 U. S. pages 211, 212, 50 S. Ct. 98, 100, 74 L. Ed. 371, 65 A. L. R. 1000.

But it has been as decisively maintained that this principle, thus progressively applied in limiting the jurisdiction of the states to tax, does not restrict the taxing power of the federal government. The distinction was clearly and definitely made in United States v. Bennett, 232 U. S. 299, 34 S. Ct. 433, 436, 58 L. Ed. 612. The question arose under section 37 of the Tariff Act of August 5, 1909, 36 Stat. 112, imposing a tax upon the use of foreign built yachts, owned or chartered by citizens of the United States. The levy of the tax with respect to a yacht owned by a citizen of the United States, domiciled here, but which was not used within the jurisdiction of the United States and had its permanent situs in a foreign country, was resisted under the due process clause of the Fifth Amendment. The objector invoked the doctrine, already established, which denied to a state, under the Fourteenth Amendment, jurisdiction to tax personal property which had a permanent situs in another state. Union Refrigerator Transit Company v. Kentucky, supra. Under that doctrine, as we have seen, it made no difference that the owner of the property was a citizen of, or domiciled in, the state which attempted to lay the tax. The argument was pressed that the federal statute should not be so construed as to apply to the use of a yacht wholly beyond the territorial limits of the United States, since if so interpreted it would be repugnant to the Constitution. But the Court thought that to apply that rule of interpretation would be to cause "an imaginary doubt" as to the constitutionality of the statute, and would render it necessary to give the statute "a wholly fictitious and unauthorized meaning." We found nothing "of such gravity in the asserted constitutional question" as to justify departing from the evident legislative intention.

Speaking through Chief Justice White, and fully recognizing the principle applicable to the taxing power of the states, the Court observed that the argument involved a misapprehension, not as to what had actually been decided, but "in taking for granted that because the doctrine stated has been applied and enforced in many decisions with respect to the taxing power of the states, that the same principle is applicable to and controlling as to the United States in the exercise of its powers." "The confusion results," the Court continued, "from not observing that the rule applied in the cases relied upon to many forms of exertion of state taxing power is based on the limitations on state authority to tax resulting from the distribution of powers ordained by the Constitution. In other words, the whole argument proceeds upon the mistaken supposition, which is sometimes indulged in, that the calling into being of the government under the Constitution had the effect of destroying obvious powers of government instead of preserving and distributing such powers. The application to the states of the rule of due process relied upon comes from the fact that their spheres of activity are enforced and protected by the Constitution, and therefore it is impossible for one state to reach out and tax property in another without violating the Constitution, for where the power of the one ends the authority of the other begins." "But this," the Court added, "has no application to the government of the United States so far as its admitted taxing power is concerned," for that power "embraces all the attributes which appertain to sovereignty in the fullest sense.

Because the limitations of the Constitution are barriers bordering the states and preventing them from transcending the limits of their authority, and thus destroying the rights of other states, and at the same time saving their rights from destruction by the other states, in other words, of maintaining and preserving the rights of all the states, affords no ground for constructing an imaginary constitutional barrier around the exterior confines of the United States for the purpose of shutting that government off from the exertion of powers which inherently belong to it by virtue of its sovereignty." Id., pages 305, 306 of 232 U. S., 34 S. Ct. 433, 437, 58 L. Ed. 612.

13

This distinction between the limitations of state jurisdiction to tax and the broad authority of the federal government, was restated and applied in Cook v. Tait, 265 U. S. 47, 55, 56, 44 S. Ct. 444, 68 L. Ed. 895, and was again explicitly recognized in Frick v. Pennsylvania, supra, page 491 of 268 U. S., 45 S. Ct. 603, 69 L. Ed. 1058, 42 A. L. R. 316.

The distinction cannot be regarded as limited to tangible property. It has equal application to intangibles. It does not rest upon the question whether the property is of the one sort or the other, but upon the fact that the limitation of state jurisdiction to tax does not establish the limitation of federal jurisdiction to tax. If the federal government may rest its jurisdiction to lay its tax upon the fact of the citizenship and domicile in this country of the owner of tangible property, wherever that property may be situated, although the state may not impose a like tax with respect to property having a permanent location outside the state, the federal government cannot be regarded as restrained in its power to tax securities owned by a nonresident, but physically in this country, merely because the state is debarred from laying such a tax with respect to a nonresident of the state. The decisive point is that the criterion of state taxing power by virtue of the relation of the states to each other under the Constitution is not the criterion of the taxing power of the United States by virtue of its sovereignty in relation to the property of nonresidents. The Constitution creates no such relation between the United States and foreign countries as it creates between the states themselves.

Accordingly, in what has been said, we in no way limit the authority of our decisions as to state power. We determine national power in relation to other countries and their subjects by applying the principles of jurisdiction recognized in international relations. Applying those principles we cannot doubt that the Congress had the power to enact the statute, as we have construed and applied it to the property in question. The securities should be included in the gross estate of the decedent; the inclusion of the balance of the cash deposit will depend, under the statute, upon the finding to be made with respect to the nature of the business of the concern with which the deposit was made.

The judgment is reversed, and the cause is remanded for further proceedings in conformity with this opinion. It is so ordered.

Mr. Justice BUTLER is of opinion that the statute does not extend to the transfer of the foreign or other securities effected by the death of decedent, Ernest Augustus Brooks, a British subject resident of, and dying in, Cuba, and that the conclusions of the Board of Tax Appeals and Circuit Court of Appeals are right, and should be affirmed.

CHAPTER 2
DETERMINING U.S. ESTATE TAX STATUS

The impact of the Estate Tax depends on whether an individual decedent is a U.S. citizen, a U.S. resident or a NRNC. Status as a citizen, resident or NRNC is significant because the Estate Tax is far more expansive as applied to citizens and residents (as opposed to NRNCs).

Definition of U.S. Citizenship

U.S. citizenship may be obtained by birth or naturalization.[14] Citizenship is granted by the 14th Amendment to the United States Constitution. "All persons born or naturalized in the United States, and subject to the jurisdiction thereof, are citizens of the United States and of the state wherein they reside."[15] For purposes of birthright citizenship, the definition of "United States" includes the fifty states, Puerto Rico, Guam, the Virgin Islands, and the Commonwealth of the Northern Mariana Islands.[16] Birthright citizenship is unrelated to intent and applies even when neither parent is a U.S. citizen or resident.[17] The rule operates independently of citizenship rules of other countries[18] and extends to people born in the United States who never reside (or intended to reside) in the U.S.[19] As such, it is possible to inadvertently acquire U.S. citizenship, due purely to the timing of parental travel.

---

[14] United States v. Wong Kim Ark, 169 U.S. 649, 702 (1898).
[15] U.S. Const. amend. XIV, §1.
[16] 8 USC §1101(a)(38).
[17] United States v. Wong Kim Ark, 169 U.S. 649 (1898).
[18] Perkins v. Elg, 307 U.S. 325, 329 (1939).
[19] An individual can renounce their citizenship, most commonly by making a renunciation before a U.S. diplomatic or consular officer abroad. 8 USC §1481(a)(5).

Non-Citizens: Residency and the Concept of Domicile

The Internal Revenue Code speaks of U.S. "residents" and "non-residents" regarding the Estate and Gift Tax. The Code, however, contains no definition of "resident" or "residency" applicable to the imposition of Estate or Gift Tax. Instead, Estate Tax regulations require a determination of whether an individual has established "domicile" in the U.S.[20]

The regulations state that "a person acquires domicile in a place by living there, for even a brief period of time, with no definite present intention of later removing therefrom".[21]

To establish an individual as domiciled in the U.S. (i.e., a "resident" for Estate and Gift Tax purposes), two elements must be proven. The first is physical presence in the U.S. The second is the individual's intent to remain in the United States. As this second element requires a case-by-case examination of intent,[22] categorization can be unpredictable.[23]

The intent to establish domicile is a state of mind, proven by facts and circumstances. Factors include: (i) the time spent in the U.S. and abroad; (ii) the financial investment and location of the decedent's home; (iii) the place of business operations; (iv)

---

[20] Treas. Reg. §20.0-1(b)(1) (discusses the scope of regulations as applied to the estates of citizens or residents).

[21] *Id.*

[22] Carrasco- Favela v. INS, 563 F.2d 1220 (5th Cir. 1977). *See also* Mas v. Perry, 489 F. 2d 1396 (5th Cir. 1974), *cert. denied*, 419 U.S. 842, 95 S. Ct. 74, 42 L. Ed. 2d 70; Garner v. Pearson, 374 F. Supp. 580, 589-90 (M.D. Fla. 1973).

[23] Bowring v. Bowers, 24 F.2d 918 (2d Cir. 1928) (holding that, despite evidence indicating the taxpayer's desire and intention to return to England, he had established a residence "of no transient character and... so substantial as to be of a permanent nature" and thus determined the taxpayer to be a resident alien).

U.S. visa and immigration status; (v) the reason for spending time in the U.S. (i.e., healthcare, tourism or asylum); (vi) the residence of friends and family; (vii) the place of religious and social affiliations; (viii) the residence reflected in legal documents; (ix) place of voter registration and driver's license and (x) residence status disclosed on tax filings.[24]

The U.S. income tax rules for determining residency are distinct from the Estate Tax rules.[25] An individual may therefore be a resident for income tax purposes but not for Estate Tax purposes and visa versa.

Once domicile is established (for Estate Tax purposes), it is presumed to continue until shown to have changed.[26] If an individual previously established U.S. domicile, the burden will be on the party asserting non-U.S. domicile to prove a change in status.[27] Several court cases address the issue.

In *Estate of Khan v. Commissioner*[28] the decedent, a citizen of Pakistan, was held to be a U.S. resident at the time of his death. The decedent had substantial ownership interests in a ranching business and a residential real estate enterprise in California (both of which were initially purchased by the decedent's father). The decedent applied for a U.S. social security number and green card to preserve subsidies given by the U.S. Department of Agriculture to the decedent's farming operation. Although the decedent spent the vast majority of his life in Pakistan, died without knowing English, and spent

---

[24] *See* Estate of Valentine v. Comm'r, 21 B.T.A. 197 (1930), *acq.* X-1 C.B. 4., 67; Jellinek v. Comm'r, 36 T.C. 826 (1961), *acq.* 1964-1 C.B. 4.; Estate of Bloch-Sulzberger, 6 T.C.M. 1201, 1203 (1974); Estate of Nienhuys, 17 T. C. 1149, 1159 (1952); Estate of Paquette, 46 T.C. M. (CCH) 1400, T.C.M. (P-H) ¶ 83,571 (1983).
[25] IRC §7701(b) (discusses the definition of residency for purposes of Title 26 U.S.C., other than Subtitle B, Estate and Gift Taxes).
[26] Estate of Nienhuys v. Comm'r, 17 T.C. 1149 (1952).
[27] *Id.*
[28] Estate of Khan v. Comm'r, 75 T.C.M. (CCH) 1597, 1998 T.C. M. (RIA) ¶ 98,022.

fourteen of his last eighteen years exclusively in Pakistan (all of which suggest no intention to permanently reside in the U.S.), the U.S. Tax Court treated him as a resident for Estate Tax purposes.

The court placed substantial weight on the fact that (i) the vast majority of the decedent's business assets were located in the U.S., (ii) the decedent had obtained a green card and social security number, and (iii) the decedent had applied for a U.S. re-entry permit prior to his last trip to Pakistan (although he never returned to the U.S.). The Tax Court noted that the decedent would have returned to the U.S. but for a debilitating medical condition. Curiously, the court also seemed to give weight to the fact that the taxpayer's family had a history of immigrating to the United States. This family history factor may be a cause for concern from a planning perspective because the intentions of other individuals were apparently imputed to the taxpayer.[29]

Conversely, in the case of *Estate of Paquette v. Commissioner*,[30] a Canadian citizen split his time between Quebec, Canada and Florida. Although, at the time of his death, the taxpayer owned no physical residence in Canada, the Tax Court determined that he was a non-resident for U.S. Estate Tax purposes. The Court based its determination on the facts that the decedent (i) chose to reside in Florida instead of Canada for health reasons (the cold weather adversely impacted his medical condition), (ii) maintained investment accounts in Canada, (iii) voted in Canada, (iv) maintained a Canadian driver's license, (v) registered his vehicle in Canada and (vi) executed his will in Canada. This case stands for

---

[29] Although the taxpayer in this case actually sought to be treated as a resident, this case may be viewed as a "trap" for those intending to avoid residency.

[30] Estate of Paquette v. Comm'r., 46 T.C.M (CCH) 1400, T.C.M. (P-H) ¶ 83,571 (1983).

the proposition that the location of a physical residence does not by itself create a presumption of domicile; rather, "it is merely one of several factors which must be examined to ascertain [a] decedent's intent."[31]

Likewise, in the case of *Forni v. Commissioner*,[32] the taxpayer was a citizen and resident of Italy. The taxpayer's wife died with property located in the U.S. As a result of a Presidential Order issued during World War II, the trust company which held the wife's assets was prohibited from releasing the property to the taxpayer.[33]

The taxpayer had moved to the U.S. claiming residency, but correspondence with his U.S. attorneys revealed he had no intention of staying in the U.S. longer than necessary to free the assets (and return to his native Italy). The Tax Court held that the decedent lacked the requisite intent to change his domicile and remained a non-resident for U.S. Estate Tax purposes.

---

[31] *Id.*
[32] Forni v. Comm'r., 22 T.C. 975 (1954).
[33] *Id.* at 977.

Jellinek v. Commissioner,
United States Tax Court, 1961.
36 T.C. 826.

Drennen, *Judge:*

Respondent determined deficiencies in income tax against petitioners for the taxable years 1952, 1953, 1954, and 1955 in the respective amounts of $4,458.69, $4,155, $4,225.17, and $3,550.12.

The sole issue is whether petitioner Rudolf Jellinek (hereinafter referred to as Rudolf) was a nonresident alien during the period 1952 through 1955.

The evidence consisted of a stipulation of facts with exhibits attached and the depositions of the two petitioners taken in Vienna, Austria, on written interrogatories and cross-interrogatories.

FINDINGS OF FACT.

The stipulated facts are found as stipulated. Petitioners are, and at all times during the period here involved were, husband and wife. They filed timely joint Federal income tax returns, Form 1040, for the taxable years 1952, 1953, 1954, and 1955 with the district director of internal revenue at Newark, New Jersey. On each such return petitioners reported that their home address was "c/o C. A. Greenleaf, 488 Liberty Road, Englewood, New Jersey."

On their returns for the above years, petitioners reported the following compensation received, which was the only income reported:

Year	Employer	Where employed
1952	{Paramount International Films, Inc	Germany
	{Paramount Films of Germany, Inc	Germany
	{Paramount International Films, Inc	Germany
1953	{Paramount Films of Germany, Inc	Germany
	{Toffenetti Restaurant C	New York City
	{Charles Antell, Inc	Baltimore, Md
	{Paramount International Films, Inc	Germany
1954	{Paramount Films of Germany, Inc	Germany
	{Stern Bros	New York City
	{Paramount International Films, Inc	Germany
1955	{Paramount Films of Germany, Inc	Germany
	{Vincent Guarneri	New York City

Year	Wages	U.S. income tax withheld
	$5,200.00}	
1952		$4,688.32
	20,243.26}	
	5,200.00}	
		4,688.32
	20,343.26}	
1953		
	702.50	105.50
	172.80	35.20
	5,200.00}	
		4,221.10
1954	20,343.26}	

20

```
                           822.95                116.91
                         5,200.00}
                                               4,221.10
         1955            17,371.78}
                          1,423.00                259.00
```

Petitioners did not report any itemized deductions and did not claim the standard deduction on any return for the years 1952 through 1955. For each of those taxable years petitioners computed net or taxable income as reported on their joint returns by subtracting $1,800, representing the credit for personal exemptions for each of them and their one child, from the total income reported.

With each of the returns filed for the above years petitioners attached Treasury Department Form 1116 entitled "Statement in Support of Credit Claimed by Individual For Taxes Paid or Accrued to a Foreign Country or a Possession of the United States." This form was filed each year to support petitioners' claim for credit for the German tax on wages and the Berlin emergency contribution (Notopfer) which had been collected in each year from the salary paid Rudolf by Paramount. On each Form 1116 it was reported that Rudolf was a resident of Germany.

Rudolf paid German tax on wages and the Berlin emergency contribution (Notopfer) on the compensation paid him by Paramount in the taxable years involved in the following amounts (expressed in dollars):

Year	Total German tax paid
1952	$7,426.45
1953	7,059.40
1954	6,974.20
1955	6,219.20

On their returns for the above years petitioners claimed a *credit* for tax paid to a foreign country in the following amounts:

Year	Credit claimed
1952	$7,426.45
1953	7,059.40
1954	6,833.17
1955	5,751.46

In the statutory notice giving rise to this proceeding, respondent allowed in each year the total German taxes paid as *deductions* from petitioners' adjusted gross income but disallowed the claimed *credit* for foreign taxes paid.

Rudolf was born June 13, 1892, in Vienna, Austria. Melitta was born in 1910 in Prague, Czechoslovakia. Prior to World War II, Rudolf was a citizen of Czechoslovakia. In 1948 or 1949 he ceased to be a Czech citizen and in 1957 became a citizen of Austria. During the intervening years he was a stateless person. During the years Rudolf was a stateless person he traveled on a passport issued by the International Refugee Organization (IRO).

At the time of trial petitioners lived in Vienna, Austria. Rudolf was working in Vienna as assistant to the manager of American Films Export Association, which is connected with Paramount Pictures, Inc. He had been connected with Paramount since 1925. From 1945 to 1956, when he was transferred to Vienna, Rudolf was general manager for Germany for Paramount or its related companies. His office was in Frankfort, Germany. Sometime before 1951 petitioners rented and furnished a 5-room house in Neu Isenburg, Germany, near Frankfort. Rudolf paid 500-marks-per-month rent for the house and he maintained this house until he was transferred to Vienna.

Paramount asked Rudolf to come to the United States in October 1951 and paid for his trip to New York. Melitta entered the United States on September 19, 1951, at New York City. Rudolf came to the United States for the first time on October 19, 1951. He received an American immigrant visa in Frankfort. On this visit Rudolf brought only enough clothing for the trip by air and he and Melitta stayed at a hotel in New York City. He left his cook and a pet dog in the rented house in New Isenburg.

Under date of October 24, 1951, Rudolf completed and filed a United States Department of Justice form entitled "Application for a Certificate of Arrival and Preliminary Form for a Declaration of Intention," in which he reported that his place of residence was Hotel Bancroft, 40 West 72d Street, New York City; that he entered the United States for permanent residence on October 19, 1951; that since such lawful entry for permanent residence he had not been absent from the United States; that his last place of foreign residence was Frankfort, Germany; and that he desired to declare his intention to become a United States citizen in the United States District Court for the Southern District of New York. A Department of Justice form entitled "Certificate of Arrival" was issued for Rudolf and recited that he was admitted to this country for permanent residence.

When Rudolf came to New York in October 1951 he intended to become a citizen of the United States. He discussed the possibilities of working in this country with Paramount but he determined that it was not possible to get a job here. He thought there was a legal requirement that he stay in the United States for 2½ or 3 years in order to become a citizen. After determining that he could not find immediate employment in this country Rudolf decided he could not stay long enough in the United States to meet the residence requirements for citizenship. He did not buy a house or rent an apartment in the United States.

On December 11, 1951, petitioners left New York City by plane for Frankfort. Before he left, Rudolf completed and filed a Department of Justice form entitled "Application for Permit to Reenter the United States." This application form showed that it was to be used by an "alien lawfully admitted to the United States for permanent residence." On this form Rudolf reported his and Melitta's address as 40 West 72d Street, New York City; that the name and address of his employer was Paramount International Films, Inc., 1501 Broadway, New York City; that he intended to be absent from the United States for 1 year, during which time he was going to visit Germany and other European countries as a representative for Paramount International Films, Inc.; and that his address abroad was to be "Frankfort on Main, Friedrich Abert Strasse 48, Germany." A permit to reenter the United States dated November 28, 1951, was issued to Rudolf. This permit was to expire November 28, 1952. Melitta and Rudolf were in Neu Isenburg until August 1952 when she left Europe and brought their son, George, to school in the United States. Melitta stayed in this country from August 1952 until about April 1953 when she returned to Neu Isenburg.

By letter dated August 18, 1952, Rudolf made formal request to the Immigration and Naturalization Service for a 6 months' extension of his permit to reenter the United States. In this letter, which was a sworn statement by Rudolf, he stated: This request for an extension has been made necessary by the fact that my continuous presence in Germany is required by my employers, Paramount International Films, Inc. I am employed by this corporation as a sales executive.

In support of his request, Rudolf enclosed a letter written to him by the continental supervisor for Paramount International Films, Inc., in Paris. The supervisor indicated that this letter was in reference to our conversation about your intended return to the United States in order to comply with immigration laws and in order not to overstay the time-limit on your Re-Entry Permit. Rudolf's permit was extended from November 28, 1952, to May 28, 1953.

Rudolf returned to New York City on March 2, 1953. He brought only personal clothing with him and stayed in a hotel in New York City. Furniture and other personal belongings were left in Neu Isenburg. Before he was to leave the United States he made application for a second permit to reenter this country. In the second application Rudolf indicated that he was an alien lawfully admitted to the United States for permanent residence; that he had arrived in the United States for permanent residence on October 19, 1951; that he had last arrived in the United States on March 2, 1953, at New York City; that his and Melitta's address was 488 Liberty Road, Englewood, New Jersey; that he was going abroad on March 31, 1953, as a representative for his employer, Paramount International Films, Inc.; and that his address abroad would be

"Friedrich-Eberstrasse 48, Frankfurt-Main, Germany."

On March 16, 1953, Rudolf was granted a second permit to reenter the United States. This permit was to expire March 18, 1954.

Rudolf left New York City on March 31, 1953 and arrived in Frankfort the next day. By letter dated January 19, 1954, which was a sworn statement, Rudolf made formal request for a 12 months' extension of his second permit to reenter the United States. This request was in substantially the same form as his request for extension of his first permit. On February 18, 1954, Rudolf's second permit to reenter the United States was extended to March 18, 1955.

Melitta again came to the United States in March 1954 and remained in this country through November 1956, when she became a citizen of the United States. She returned to Europe in December 1956 and has remained there living with Rudolf to date.

Rudolf came to New York City again on March 4, 1955, and stayed until March 25. On March 7, 1955, he completed and filed a third application for a permit to reenter the United States. In this application he again indicated that he was an alien lawfully admitted to the United States for permanent residence; that he had arrived for permanent residence on October 19, 1951; that his last arrival was on March 4, 1955; that his address was "c/o Paramount Pictures, 1501 Broadway, New York City"; and that he was going abroad on business for about 2 years for Paramount International Films, Inc.

On March 8, 1955, a third permit to reenter the United States was issued to Rudolf. This permit was to expire March 9, 1956.

On March 25, 1955, Rudolf left New York City to return to Frankfort.

On January 12, 1956, Rudolf wrote the Immigration and Naturalization Service and by sworn statement made request for a 12 months' extension of his permit to reenter the United States. He again stated that his employer needed him in Germany and submitted a letter from the continental supervisor for Paramount International Films, Inc., in Paris, in support of his request. Rudolf's sworn statement and the letter which he attached were much like the ones previously submitted to obtain extensions of his permits to reenter the United States.

In February 1956 Rudolf was transferred to Vienna by his employer. His permit to reenter the United States was permitted to expire, and Rudolf was granted Austrian citizenship in 1957 and was issued an Austrian passport.

Petitioners have been living together in Vienna since Melitta's return to Europe in December 1956. They have not lived apart from each other during the years discussed above because of marital difficulties. At the time the depositions were taken Melitta would have liked to come to the United States permanently, but she could not since Rudolf was in Vienna. Rudolf had no intention of becoming a citizen of the United States at that time.

Petitioners' son, George, attended Staunton Military Academy, Staunton, Virginia, and later the University of Alabama for a few months. He then joined the United States Air Force. He married in 1958. In 1960 he was attending the Latin American Institute in New York City.

Rudolf was physically present in the United States only during the periods October 19 to December 11, 1951, March 2 to March 31, 1953, and March 4 to March 25, 1955. He stayed in a hotel in New York City on each of these occasions and at no time did he maintain an apartment or home in the United States. No part of Rudolf's income for the taxable years 1952 through 1955 was from sources within the United States.

OPINION.

On their joint returns filed for the years 1952 through 1955, petitioners computed the Federal income tax on their entire net or taxable income and claimed a *credit* against the tax for taxes paid to West Germany on Rudolf's income earned in Germany. Respondent disallowed the credit, determining in the notice of deficiency that petitioners were resident aliens of the United States during each of the years involved, but allowed a *deduction* of the German taxes paid in computing net or taxable income for each year. Petitioners do not claim error in the disallowance of the credit for foreign taxes and do not take issue with the determination insofar as it relates to Melitta, but do maintain that Rudolf was a nonresident alien during each of the taxable years and that his income from sources without the United States is nontaxable. [2] Respondent agrees that Rudolf was an alien and that none of his income was derived from sources within the United

States during the years in question, so the issue is narrowed to whether Rudolf was a resident or nonresident during the taxable years. If Rudolf was a nonresident alien in those years, his income was nontaxable for United States income tax purposes. Under section 212(a) of the 1939 Code and section 872(a) of the 1954 Code the gross income of a nonresident alien includes only the gross income from sources within the United States.

Petitioner's argument is that even though Rudolf intended to become a citizen of the United States when he first came here in October of 1951, he abandoned that intention soon after arriving when he found he could not get a suitable job here, and that he never established a residence or became a resident of the United States. They also contend that even if Rudolf became a resident in 1951, he abandoned that residence when he left the United States in December 1951 and never reestablished residence in this country.

Respondent's position is that when Rudolf first came to this country in 1951 with the intention of becoming a citizen and permanent resident of this country, he became a resident alien at that time, and did not abandon that residence by his absences from this country during the years 1952 through 1955, as evidenced by his keeping valid reentry permits in existence during the entire periods he was absent from this country until he was transferred to Austria in 1956.

In support of his position respondent relies on section 39.211, Regs. 118, defining "nonresident alien individuals" and providing rules of evidence for determining whether an alien has acquired residence in the United States, on I.T. 4057, 1951-2 C.B. 93, and on *L. E. L. Thomas*, 33 B.T.A. 725 (1935), and *Walter J. Baer*, 6 T.C. 1195 (1946). I.T. 4057 and both of the cited cases deal with situations where it was assumed or admitted that the alien had once acquired residence in the United States and the question was whether such residence had been abandoned. As we pointed out in *Joyce de la Begassiere*, 31 T.C. 1031 (1959), affirmed per curiam 272 F. 2d 709 (C.A. 5, 1959), cases involving the question of whether a person with an established residence in a place ceases to be a resident of that place because of absence are not in point in determining whether a person has established residence in the first place. See also *Florica Constantinescu*, 11 T.C. 37 (1948).

The first question we must decide here is whether Rudolf ever became a resident of the United States, because if he did not his income is not taxable. Section 39.211-2, Regs. 118, provides in part that a "nonresident alien individual" is a person whose residence is not within the United States, that an alien actually presents in the United States who is not a mere transient or sojourner is a resident of the United States for purposes of the income tax, and that whether he is a transient is determined by his intentions with regard to the length and nature of his stay. Section 39.211-4 of the regulations establishes rules of evidence for determining whether an alien has acquired residence, and provides first that an alien, by reason of his alienage, is presumed to be a nonresident alien. It provides further that such presumption may be overcome by-(2)(i) proof that the alien has filed a declaration of his intention to become a citizen of the United States under the naturalization laws, or (iii) proof of acts and statements of an alien showing a definite intention to acquire residence in the United States or showing that his stay in the United States has been of such an extended nature as to constitute him a resident.

The quoted provisions of the regulations merely indicate the type of proof that will be considered in determining whether the presumption of nonresidence has been overcome and does not, in our opinion, purport to mean that the filing of a declaration of intention alone would establish residence. As we said in *Joyce de la Begassiere, supra* at 1036: It is obvious from the above definitions [of "resident" in various dictionaries] that a nonresident alien cannot establish a residence in the United States by intent alone since there must be an act or fact of being present, of dwelling, of making one's home in the United States for some time in order to become a resident of the United States. Some permanence of living within borders is necessary to establish residence.

The term "residence" for purposes of determining whether an alien is a nonresident under section 211 *et seq.* of the 1939 Code and section 871 *et seq.* of the 1954 Code is not statutorily defined. However, this and other courts have had occasion to consider the question of residence in those cases in which the issue has been whether a United States citizen was a resident of a foreign country or countries for purposes of section 116(a) of the 1939 Code, as amended by section 148 of the Revenue Act of 1942, as well as in those cases in which the issue has been whether an alien is a resident or nonresident of the United States. The criteria for determining a taxpayer's residence have been held to be the same under both issues. See, e.g.,

Seeley v. *Commissioner*, 186 F. 2d 541 (C.A. 2, 1951), affirming in part and reversing in part 14 T.C. 175 (1950); *Downs* v. *Commissioner*, 166 F. 2d 504 (C.A. 9, 1948), affirming 7 T.C. 1053 (1946), certiorari denied 334 U.S. 832 (1948), rehearing denied 335 U.S. 837 (1948); *Weible* v. *United States*, 244 F. 2d 158 (C.A. 9, 1957); *Jones* v. *Kyle*, 190 F. 2d 353 (C.A. 10, 1951); *Swenson* v. *Thomas*, 164 F. 2d 783 (C.A. 5, 1947); *Henningsen* v. *Commissioner*, 243 F. 2d 954 (C.A. 4, 1957), affirming 26 T.C. 528 (1956); *Donald H. Nelson*, 30 T.C. 1151 (1958); *Joseph A. McCurnin*, 30 T.C. 143 (1958); *Leigh White*, 22 T.C. 585 (1954); *David E. Rose*, 16 T.C. 232 (1951); *C. Francis Weeks*, 16 T.C. 248 (1951); *Herman Frederick Baehre*, 15 T.C. 236 (1950); *Audio Gray Harvey*, 10 T.C. 183 (1948); *Arthur J. H. Johnson*, 7 T.C. 1040 (1946); *Yaross* v. *Kraemer*, 83 F. Supp. 411 (D. Conn. 1949); *White* v. *Hofferbert*, 88 F. Supp. 457 (D. Md. 1950).

From the decided cases, the legislative history of the provisions of the law, and the Commissioner's regulations and rulings some criteria have been established to help determine whether a citizen of the United States is a resident of another country and whether an alien spending some time in the United States has become a resident of the United States. It would be of little value to restate those here, however, because it is settled that the determination of residence must be based upon the facts and circumstances of each particular case. Suffice it to say that although "residence" does not require a permanent home, *Ceska Cooper*, 15 T.C. 757 (1950), *Herman Frederick Baehre, supra*, or even a definite and settled abode, *Swenson* v. *Thomas, supra*, it does require that the taxpayer have some degree of permanent attachment for the country of which he is an alien, *Joyce de la Begassiere, supra, Rolf Jamvold*, 11 T.C. 122 (1948), and it has been said that it is this degree of permanence of an individual's attachment for a country in which he is at some time physically present which determines whether he is a domiciliary, a resident, or a transient of that country; see *Seeley* v. *Commissioner, supra.*

We think the evidence in this case indicates that Rudolf never accomplished the establishment of residence in this country even though he may have had it in mind to do so when he first came to this country in 1951. It appears that he came here at the invitation of his employer and with hopes that he could find such employment in the United States that would permit him to live here and become a citizen. That this was only a tentative plan, however, is evidenced by the fact that he did not give up his home in Frankfort but left his furniture, personal effects, and a pet dog there and continued to employ a cook at his German home. This tentative plan failed to materialize when Rudolf found he could not find suitable employment in the United States. For the short period of less than 2 months that he was in New York in 1951 he stayed in a hotel. This was only a temporary arrangement until he could determine whether he would take up residence in this country. Rudolf took no steps to acquire a home or place to live in the United States; he took no part in any community activities and made no effort to become a part of any community; there was no "permanence of living within borders" so far as Rudolf was concerned. It appears that Rudolf's intent to establish residence in the United States was at all times conditional upon his finding suitable employment here and when the condition was not met the intent was abandoned before the fact of residence was ever accomplished.

If Rudolf did not become a resident on his first trip to the United States it seems clear that he did not do so later. The evidence is that Rudolf was present in the United States on only two occasions, each time for less than 1 month, after he left New York in December of 1951, and that these visits were to see his wife and son. On neither of these occasions did he make any effort to acquire a home in this country or to follow up his declaration of intention to become a citizen. He stayed in a hotel on each occasion and brought with him only the clothes necessary for his trip. He maintained his office and his home in Frankfort, and paid German taxes on his income throughout the period here involved. He became a citizen of Austria, his native country, soon after he was transferred there in 1956.

Respondent stresses the fact that Rudolf filed a declaration of intent to become a United States citizen when he first arrived and thereafter kept reentry permits alive at all times until he was transferred to Vienna, and claims that these facts are inconsistent with Rudolf's testimony that he abandoned his hopes of living in America soon after he arrived here. We do not think Rudolf's filing of a declaration of intent within a few days after he arrived in New York is inconsistent with his testimony. Admittedly he came here hoping to become a resident and citizen of the United States. But the filing of the declaration alone did not make him either. And the fact that he obtained reentry permits which stated that he had entered the United States for permanent residence is not inconsistent with his testimony that he kept the reentry permits alive so he could get to this country to see his wife and son. The record indicates no other purpose in his two subsequent trips to the United States; and the statements in the requests for permits that he had originally entered the United States for permanent residence were simply statements of fact.

It is true that petitioners filed joint United States income tax returns for each of the years here involved, which is not permissible for a nonresident alien, but it is also true that attached to each of those returns was a statement wherein Rudolf stated that he was a resident of Germany.

While the documentary and other evidence relied on by respondent indicates that Rudolf originally intended to become a resident of this country and actually entered the country with that thought in mind, and may also support an inference that he kept hopes of eventually becoming a resident alive until he was transferred to Vienna, such evidence does not establish the fact of actual residence in this country, which we believe is necessary before an individual becomes a resident alien for tax purposes. Furthermore, we think the conclusion is much more consistent with the admitted facts that Rudolf never abandoned his residence in Frankfort and never took any steps to actually acquire the status of a resident of the United States.

We conclude that Rudolf did not become a resident of the United States in 1951 or at any time thereafter during the years involved and consequently was a nonresident alien within the meaning of section 212 of the 1939 Code and section 872 of the 1954 Code. Compare *Joyce de la Begassiere, supra*; *Richard H. Lovald*, 16 T.C. 909 (1951); *Florica Constantinescu, supra*; *Commissioner* v. *Patino*, 186 F.2d 962 (C.A. 4, 1950), affirming 13 T.C. 816 (1949). It follows that Rudolf's income during these years was not taxable.

Decision will be entered under Rule 50.

Estate of Nienhuys v. Commissioner
United States Tax Court, 1952.
17 T.C. 1149.

Arundell, Judge:

The respondent determined a deficiency in estate tax in the amount of $291,822.72. The propriety of the determination depends in large part upon whether the respondent was correct in holding that the decedent was a resident of the United States at the time of his death. Other issues deal with the value of properties of the decedent that were located in The Netherlands and other foreign countries at the date of death, including shares and accrued dividends thereon in American corporations. The issue as to properties in foreign countries and accrued dividends turns upon the question of the value of the Dutch guilder at the optional valuation date elected by the executrix in the estate tax return.

FINDINGS OF FACT.

1. *Domicile Issue*

The decedent, Jan Willem Nienhuys, died on April 8, 1946, at the age of 68 years in Southern Pines, North Carolina. He died testate, leaving two wills. One was executed in The Netherlands in 1935 and was established in The Netherlands as his last will and testament. The other was executed in the State of New York in 1942 and related only to property located in the United States. It was admitted to probate in a surrogate's court in New York in May 1946, and letters testamentary thereunder were issued to the decedent's widow, Alida M. Nienhuys.

The executrix under the United States will of the decedent filed a nonresident alien estate tax return with the collector for the second district of New York on June 3, 1947. She elected in that return to have the gross estate valued under the optional valuation date or dates in accordance with the provisions of Internal Revenue Code section 811 (j).

The decedent was survived, in addition to his widow, by four sons, all of whom had attained majority prior to the time of the decedent's death.

The decedent was born in Amsterdam, The Netherlands, in 1878, and throughout his life and at the time of his death he was a citizen of The Netherlands. His widow is a Dutch citizen. She and the decedent were married in The Netherlands in 1905.

In January 1940, and for some years prior thereto, the decedent owned, and he and his family occupied, a spacious residence on a large tract of well landscaped ground in Bloemendaal, which was a good residential community within commuting distance of Amsterdam. The house was well furnished and contained paintings of considerable value. The decedent and his wife entertained extensively and had frequent house guests. The decedent owned two other houses in Bloemendaal, and a farm.

In 1907 the decedent became president of the Amsterdam Tobacco Trading Company, which had been founded by his father in 1894. That company dealt in leaf tobacco, and specialized in the sale of tobacco grown in Sumatra and Java, which tobacco was used in the manufacture of cigars. Prior to 1940, the Sumatra and Java tobaccos had been sold at auctions held in Amsterdam. In that year the tobacco growers did not ship their product to The Netherlands because of the war then being waged in parts of Europe. In order to obtain a supply of tobacco for his company, and for an American company, the decedent decided to go to Sumatra where the tobacco was to be sold. He and his wife flew to Sumatra in January 1940, and at that time they intended to return to Holland in March or April. They had round-trip tickets. After attending to business matters, they did some visiting, and started the return journey on a Dutch plane on May 7, 1940. Because of the invasion of Holland by Germany on May 10, 1940, the plane, acting on orders, terminated the flight at Alexandria, Egypt. After considerable difficulty, due to shortage of funds and delay in obtaining passport endorsements, the decedent and his wife obtained passage on an Egyptian boat to Marseilles, France. They landed in Marseilles without funds. Although the decedent had a letter of credit, he could not raise funds on it because at that time no one knew the value, if any, of the Dutch guilder. At that time, the decedent planned to return to Holland by way of Paris and England. The decedent cabled a business acquaintance, Henry M. Duys, in New York, for funds. Mr. Duys cabled funds and suggested that the decedent and his wife come to the United States. They decided to act on the suggestion, obtained visitors' visas, sailed from Genoa, and landed in the United States on June 20, 1940.

On arrival in the United States, the decedent and his wife first stayed as guests with Mr. and Mrs. Duys. They subsequently rented furnished apartments in New York City. Beginning in the latter part of 1941, they leased an unfurnished apartment on Long Island, which they furnished with light, inexpensive furniture that they intended to send to their son and daughter-in-law in the Dutch East Indies when the war ended. While living on Long Island, the decedent collected literature put out by American firms on modern kitchens. He intended to install such a kitchen in a house that he planned to build for occupancy by himself and his wife on their return to Holland.

When the decedent arrived in the United States in 1940, he had a credit balance of some $21,000 with H. Duys & Co., Inc., a New York corporation, which had been associated with the decedent's company in Holland in the purchase and sale of leaf tobacco, and in which the decedent owned some stock and was vice president thereof. Due to wartime restrictions on the funds of nationals of enemy and enemy-occupied countries, the decedent was permitted to draw only limited amounts of money from his credit balance. Under his visitor's visa, he was limited in his acceptance of gainful employment. In order to overcome these restrictions, the decedent went to Canada in the early part of 1941, and reentered the United States as a Netherlands quota immigrant. After his reentry to the United States under the immigration visa, the decedent was employed on a salary basis by H. Duys & Co., Inc.

The decedent filed annual resident Federal income and New York State income tax returns for the period from April 20, 1941, to the date of his death. The decedent's net income from sources within the United States for each of the years 1941 to 1945, inclusive, was:

```
1941--$16,587.73   (for the period from April 20, 1941 to
                    December 31, 1941)
1942--$31,556.92   (before deduction of $60,000 for a war loss
                    represented by personal property in The
                    Netherlands, which was later disallowed)
1943--$34,912.12
1944--$37,531.38   (before deduction of $35,000 for a war loss
                    represented by real property in The Netherlands,
                    which was later disallowed)
1945--$45,540.85
```

When the decedent left Holland in 1940, he gave a limited power of attorney to one of his sons. When he was unable to return to Holland, a court in that country issued to the son a full power of attorney to manage the decedent's affairs. The son made no changes in the decedent's investments, but he destroyed the certificates representing the decedent's stock in H. Duys & Co., Inc., in order to keep them from falling into enemy hands. New certificates were issued in 1945 and were kept in this country. The son sent to a New York investment house some stock certificates covering investments of the decedent in other companies. Such certificates were in the United States at the time of the decedent's death. The son paid all Dutch taxes that were owing by the decedent; and he paid the household servants. The son also paid his father's dues in clubs and societies in Holland, and in 1945 the decedent requested the son to continue to make such payments.

The decedent's home in Bloemendaal was requisitioned by the Germans in 1943 for use as an officers' club. Both the house and the surrounding grounds suffered damages while the property was occupied by the Germans. The son above mentioned arranged for his parents to stay with relatives on their return to Holland pending their decision as to the restoration of their home or the construction of a new one. The decedent's wife organized the Netherlands Aid Society, both were active in that organization, and the decedent was its treasurer. They did not join any church in this country. The decedent joined the golf club at Forest Hills. The decedent and his wife did very little entertaining in this country. Most of their guests were Dutch sailors.

Upon liberation of The Netherlands from the hands of the enemy in 1945, the decedent made inquiry as to the possibility of returning to his home. He did not return at that time because of the policy of the Dutch government not to permit the return of its nationals who were abroad due to the shortage of food and fuel in Holland.

During the summer of 1945, the decedent was not feeling well. He wanted to return to Holland but, upon being advised of the fuel shortage, he was afraid of spending a cold winter in Holland and planned to return there the following spring. He was hospitalized in New York in the fall of 1945 where his illness was diagnosed as being due to a cancerous condition. In the winter of 1945, the decedent and his wife went to Pinehurst and then to Southern Pines, North Carolina, where the decedent died. His body was cremated, and his ashes were taken to Holland.

At all times after the decedent arrived in the United States in 1940, he desired to and intended to return to Holland and to resume his business and social activities in that country. He never applied for naturalization as a citizen of the United States.

The decedent's domicile at the time of his death was in The Netherlands, and he was a nonresident of the United States within the meaning of the Federal estate tax statutes.

2. *Valuation of Duys & Co. Stock*

At the time of his death, the decedent owned 1,096 shares of the common stock of H. Duys & Co., Inc. (herein called Duys & Co.). [pg. 1154] His estate owned those shares on the optional valuation date, April 8, 1947.

Duys & Co. was incorporated under the laws of the State of New York on December 19, 1916. On April 8, 1947, it had outstanding 7,917 shares of 7 per cent preferred stock, 6,000 shares of common stock, and 2,853 shares of common A stock. Each class of stock had a par value of $100 per share. The preferred stock was redeemable at $110 per share. The common stock was held as follows:

Name	No. of shares
Henry M. Duys	1,484
John H. Duys, Jr	706
Jan W. Nienhuys, Deceased	1,096
Jacobus Nienhuys	809
F. Van Tienhoven-Nienhuys	347
C. J. Van Tienhoven	200
E. Veltman-Nienhuys	437
E. A. Veltman	111
Ethel Holst-Knudsen	405
Luella D. Jacobs	405

The holders of the common stock were all members of the Nienhuys and Duys families. The common stock has never been listed on any exchange or sold on any public market.

The 1,096 shares of Duys & Co. common stock owned by the decedent amounted to 18.266 per cent of the number of shares of such stock that were outstanding. The value of those shares was reported in the estate tax return as $115 each, a total of $126,040 at April 8, 1947.

Duys & Co. is a grower of and dealer in leaf tobacco. The business was founded in 1900 by the father of the present president of the company and the father of the decedent under an arrangement by which a joint account was created for dealing in this country in Sumatra and Java tobacco. The financing of the venture was supplied by the Nienhuys family which was to receive one-half of the profits. The joint venture was succeeded by a partnership. The present corporation took over the business upon organization. The Nienhuys family acquired one-half of the common stock of the corporation.

Of the 7,917 outstanding shares of preferred stock of Duys & Co., the decedent owned 741. He owned none of the common A shares. The preferred stock had no voting rights except upon default of dividends amounting to 21 per cent. No dividends thereon were in default at April 8, 1947. The common A shares had no voting rights. The common shares had all voting rights at April 8, 1947. The common and common A shares were entitled to share equally in dividends and on liquidation.

The principal business of Duys & Co., aside from its growing operations, was that of middleman. It bought and sold tobacco on its own account and on commission. It did not do any manufacturing. Prior to 1940, Duys & Co. acquired the tobacco to meet its requirements at the auction sales in Holland. It was the practice for a member of the Duys family to go to Holland in the period that auction sales were held there, and he, in conjunction with the decedent, purchased Sumatra and Java tobacco, both herein called Sumatra tobacco, for Duys & Co. The 1939 crop of Sumatra tobacco was sold in Sumatra in 1940 at auction sales attended by the decedent on behalf of his Holland company and Duys & Co. The 1940 crop was sold at auction on Staten Island, New York, in 1941. The 1941 crop was allocated in 1942 by the Imperial Tobacco Company among users of Sumatra tobacco. Duys & Co. acquired some of each of the 1939, 1940, and 1941 crops. No Sumatra crops were grown during the war after the crop of 1941 due to the occupation of the South Pacific islands by enemy forces. The first crop marketed after the war was that of 1948 which was a small crop. The Imperial Tobacco Company conserved its inventories of prewar Sumatra tobacco and allocated such tobacco among dealers during the war.

At April 8, 1947, the prospects for Duys & Co. to reenter the Sumatra tobacco business appeared to be hopeless. During the war period, the Imperial Tobacco Company, which represented the Sumatra growers had been formed. It entered the selling field in the United States and sold directly to some of the customers of Duys & Co.

When the supply of Sumatra tobacco was cut off, Duys & Co. turned to other means of procuring its needs. It leased lands in the Connecticut River Valley and acquired a farm of about 40 acres in that valley. It raised tobacco there, known as Connecticut shade tobacco, which is grown under cheesecloth. Due to adverse weather conditions, including hailstorms, some crops were failures. It also raised some tobacco in that valley in the open which was a filler tobacco as distinguished from the wrapper tobacco grown under shade. In the Connecticut operations it was necessary for Duys & Co. to finance the farmers who planted and tended the crops.

On April 8, 1947, Duys & Co. had a wholly owned Cuban subsidiary, which dealt in Cuban tobacco and financed farmers in Cuba in the growing of tobacco. The bulk of the Cuban tobacco handled by the Cuban company is filler tobacco, which is less costly than wrapper tobacco, and is sold in volume at a small profit. The Cuban company sold tobacco in Havana direct to Cuban cigar manufacturers. Any surplus was sold by Duys & Co. in New York. Some low-grade Cuban tobacco was sold for use in making Cuban cigarettes. Duys & Co. financed one Cuban farmer who raised wrapper tobacco which was sent to New York for sale. Cuban operations were subject to the hazard of hurricanes.

Duys & Co. was also a jobber in Florida and Puerto Rican tobaccos, and it dealt in other miscellaneous tobaccos.

During the decade from 1938 to 1947, the selling prices of all kinds of tobacco handled by Duys & Co. increased very substantially. Unit prices of representative tobaccos handled by Duys & Co. on March 31, 1938 and 1947, were as follows:

Type of tobacco	Price per pound Mar. 31, 1938	Price per pound Mar. 31, 1947
Puerto Rico	$0.40	$0.92

Cuban unstripped	_____	.22	.82
Cuban stripped	_____	.56	1.67
Scrap	_____	.32	.87
Connecticut shade	_____	.63	3.69

The average retail price of inexpensive cigars in that period increased from 4.6 cents to 8.8 cents. The per capita consumption of tobacco used in cigars in that period was relatively stable and in each of the years 1938 and 1947 was .97 pounds. The number of factories manufacturing cigars in the United States has declined from 1915 when the number was 15,732, to 1938 when there were 3,834, and again to 1927 when there were 2,228. In the years 1915 to 1947, the year of peak production was 1920 when 8,097,000,000 cigars were produced. In 1938, production amounted to 5,015,000,000, and in 1947 the number was 5,488,000,000.

Gross sales of Duys & Co. of various tobaccos, and net profits after taxes, were as follows:

Fiscal year ending March 31	Sumatra tobacco	Connecticut tobacco	Cuban tobacco
1938 _____	$1,415,348.29	$427,359.41	$1,069,539.53
1939 _____	2,552,216.84	247,052.02	708,688.20
1940 _____	2,373,698.88	136,791.93	857,747.75
1941 _____	2,433,454.02	79,247.27	616,339.83
1942 _____	3,016,090.44	58,727.64	779,651.10
1943 _____	2,017,132.24	40,558.85	1,153,796.32
1944 _____	1,674,326.18	74,743.64	3,134,086.07
1945 _____	1,266,801.28	793,880.40	4,719,408.45
1946 _____	632,994.93	1,423,991.62	4,148,400.48
1947 _____	203,682.28	1,772,449.20	5,645,337.24

	Other misc. tobaccos	Total Sales	Net profit after taxes
1938 _____	$309,204.79	$3,221,452.02	$54,012.91
1939 _____	269,204.06	3,777,161.12	119,331.00
1940 _____	922,188.08	4,290,426.64	174,182.24
1941 _____	435,313.95	3,564,355.07	153,422.72
1942 _____	503,442.98	4,357,912.16	287,198.00
1943 _____	428,603.83	3,640,091.24	161,323.14
1944 _____	1,025,021.73	5,908,177.62	459,341.74
1945 _____	1,147,572.59	7,927,662.72	380,986.94
1946 _____	1,348,609.42	7,553,996.45	288,302.88

1947 _____   1,360,903.76   8,982,372.48   206,105.07

Net earnings per share of Duys & Co. after all taxes, and dividends per share on the common and common A stock for each of the fiscal years ended March 31, 1938 to 1947, inclusive, were:

Fiscal year ended Mar. 31	Net profit per share	Dividend per share
1938	<1>$ 0.16	
1939	7.18	$ 3
1940	13.34	4
1941	11.07	6
1942	26.18	10
1943	11.96	10
1944	45.63	11
1945	36.77	13
1946	26.31	13
1947	17.02	13

<1>Loss.

Duys & Co. largely financed its operations through bank loans. During the years 1938 to 1947, its annual borrowings from banks ran as high as $1,600,000.

Henry M. Duys has been an officer of Duys & Co. since its organization. He became president in 1940 and held that office on April 8, 1947. At that time, he made all major policy decisions affecting the business of the corporation, including the borrowing of funds, quantities of tobacco to be purchased, and the payment of dividends. He had able assistants in various departments of the business, but no one with over-all responsibility. He was 62 years of age on April 8, 1947. The corporation did not carry insurance on his life.

The value on April 8, 1947, of the common stock of H. Duys & Co., Inc., that was owned by the decedent at the date of death was $172.68 per share.

3. *Valuation of Property Outside the United States; Accrued*

Dividends

At the date of death, the decedent owned a number of corporate stocks and bonds, and also securities issued by various governments. Some of the corporate stocks and bonds were those of corporations organized in the United States and some were issues of foreign corporations.

In the estate tax return filed by the executrix, the several stocks owned by the decedent, the certificates for which were in The Netherlands, were listed as having no value because of foreign exchange control restrictions. In determining the deficiency in estate tax, the respondent included in the gross estate the several items summarized below as being assets located in The Netherlands:

Item	Value in guilders
Stocks and bonds	1,733,599.71
Less stocks and accrued dividends included in U. S. assets	101,646.90
Net value stocks and bonds	1,631,952.81
Mortgages	52,034.42

32

Miscellaneous property	338,454.98
Bank accounts	57,718.44

Total (in guilders)	2,080,160.65

The above total was translated by the respondent into United States dollars by applying thereto the official rate of exchange of $0.37695 per guilder, which resulted in an addition to the gross estate of the amount of $784,116.56. The corporate stocks which were included in United States assets were valued at market quotations in the United States on the optional valuation date, except as to certain stocks which had been redeemed prior to that date and those were valued at the redemption price in United States dollars. The value of accrued dividends on stocks which were included by the respondent in United States assets was determined by converting the guilder value thereof into United States dollars by application of the official rate of exchange of $0.37695 per guilder. As to some of the United States stocks, the certificates were held by the Dutch Administration Offices which had issued its certificates therefor to the decedent.

Among the properties included in gross estate by the respondent were stocks of three foreign corporations, the certificates for which were in England and Switzerland which had a value of 16,784.22 Dutch guilders. Also included by the respondent were deposits in banks in England, Switzerland and France which had a total value at the optional valuation date of 1,077.44 Dutch guilders. The mortgages that were owned by the decedent were mortgages on property located in Holland. The item of miscellaneous property consisted of claims against Dutch nationals and the Dutch government in the amount of 114,714.48 guilders, and tangible personal property consisting of furniture, furnishings, and paintings of the value of 223,740.50 guilders.

The stocks of American corporations which were represented by certificates issued by the Dutch Administration Offices had a value at April 8, 1947, of 88,805 guilders, and accrued dividends on those stocks had a value of 12,841.90 guilders.

Life insurance proceeds under a group life insurance policy issued by a United States insurance company were included in the gross estate by the respondent at a value of $5,000. The proceeds of the policy were payable to the decedent's widow.

By Royal Decree of October 10, 1945, known as the "Foreign Exchange Decree, 1945," and regulations promulgated thereunder, the Dutch government imposed comprehensive restrictions on the sale or disposition of personal property by Dutch nationals and residents of Holland. Under the Foreign Exchange Decree, the personal property in the estate of the decedent which was outside of the United States could not have been sold at the optional valuation date for an amount in United States dollars equal to its value in guilders converted into such dollars at the official rate of exchange.

On April 8, 1947, the value of a Dutch guilder was 10 cents in currency of the United States.

OPINION.

Arundell, *Judge:*

The Domicile Issue

The parties are in agreement on the basic premise that the amount of the estate tax on the estate of the decedent is dependent, in part, upon whether or not the decedent was domiciled in the United States at the date of his death. This agreement of the parties is in accordance with the respondent's regulations which provide that "A resident is one who, at the time of his death, had his domicile in the United States. All persons not residents of the United States as above defined, are nonresidents." Section 81.5, Regulations 105.

The parties are also in agreement on the fact that the decedent was born in The Netherlands and throughout his life, and at the time of his death, was a citizen of The Netherlands. In view of the agreement of the parties on these points, our immediate question is whether the decedent's domicile at the time of death was in the United States as determined by the respondent.

We start with the fundamental principle that "a domicile once acquired is presumed to continue until it is shown to have been changed." *Mitchell* v. *United States*, 88 Wall. 350. There is no question about the decedent having been domiciled in The Netherlands prior to the year 1940 when he left there on a business trip and his return thereto was prevented by the invasion of his country by enemy forces. In the light of the presumption of continued Dutch domicile, the facts must be examined to determine whether in or after 1940 any events occurred which result in overcoming that presumption. The opinion in the case of *Mitchell* v. *United States, supra*, gives as guides these principles:

To constitute the new domicile two things are indispensable: First, residence in the new locality; and, second, the intention to remain there. The change cannot be made except *facto et animo*. Both are alike necessary. Either without the other is insufficient. Mere absence from a fixed home, however long continued, cannot work the change. There must be the *animus* to change the prior domicile for another. Until the new one is acquired, the old one remains. These principles are axiomatic in the law upon the subject.

The quoted principles are the basis of the respondent's approach to the problem. He states in his brief that "The two components, *factum* and *animus*, must concur in order to effect a change of domicile." Although the decedent's failure to return to Holland in 1940 was forced upon him by circumstances beyond his control, the fact is that he did reside in the United States for nearly six years. Thus, the first of the two components that are relied on by the respondent-the *factum* -must be recognized as having existed.

As to the second factor-"the *animus* to change the prior domicile"- there is not only no sufficient evidence to overcome the presumption that Holland continued to be the country of his domicile, but there is abundant evidence to establish that no new domicile was acquired in the United States.

We have set out some of the facts upon which is based our ultimate finding that the decedent's domicile was in The Netherlands. An examination of all of the evidence, particularly the testimony of persons who were well acquainted with the decedent, leaves upon our minds a clear picture of a man who was unhappy about his enforced absence from his domicile and who intended to return to that domicile when circumstances made it possible and practicable to do so. He had an established business in Holland, which had been founded by his father, and which he wanted to carry on. His association with Duys & Co. was that of an employee, which was a far cry from the executive position of directing the business of his own corporation. He had in Holland a large home on extensive grounds, in which he and his wife had entertained on a large scale. In this country he lived in small apartments which were not at all suited to his customary way of living. The respondent points out that the decedent had sufficient income to have warranted the decedent's occupancy of more sumptuous quarters. His failure to do so is in keeping with his expressed view that his stay in the United States was only temporary. Other members of his family were in Holland and the decedent was concerned about their welfare. There is no evidence that he had any relatives in this country.

The respondent calls attention to certain statements made by the decedent in forms pertaining to his quota immigration visa. In reply to a question as to his "present permanent residence address" the decedent gave the address of the New York apartment that he was occupying at that time. One of the forms that the decedent signed contained the printed statement that "I intend to remain _____." Under the blank space were the words: "(Permanently or length of time)." The decedent inserted the word "permanently" in the blank space. The statements in the forms were made in the early part of the year 1941, at which time no one could prophesy with any assurance the length of the decedent's enforced absence from his homeland which was then in enemy hands and his Government was in exile. The forms did not provide space for any extended explanation. Even so, if we consider the statements as indicating actual residence in the United States, they do not establish domicile upon which "the incidence of estate and succession taxes has historically been determined." *Bowring* v. *Bowers*, 24 F. 2d 918, certiorari denied 277 U. S. 608; *Frederick Rodiek, supra.* "Residence without the requisite intention to remain indefinitely will not suffice to constitute domicile." Section 81.5, Regulations 105.

Neither do we regard with any significance the decedent's filing of resident income tax returns. Residence has a different meaning in the income tax provisions of the Code than it has in those relating to estate tax. For income tax purposes, an alien in the United States "who is not a mere transient or sojourner is a resident" and must file returns. Section 29.211- 2, Regulations 111, quoted with approval in *Commissioner* v. *Nubar*, 185 F. 2d 584.

The evidence supports the presumption of continuance of original domicile and overcomes the presumption of the correctness of the respondent's determination. It is accordingly held that the respondent erred in his determination that the decedent was a resident of the United States at the time of his death.

Value of Stock of H. Duys & Co., Inc.

The decedent owned 1,096 shares of the common stock of Duys & Co. at the time of his death. The shares were reported in the estate tax return at a value of $126,040, which is at the rate of $115 per share at the optional valuation date. The respondent determined a value of $189,257.28, or $172.68 per share, and by amendment to his answer he alleges that the shares had a value of $312,360, i. e., $285 per share, and claims a consequent increase in the deficiency.

Duys & Co. was a closely held corporation. All of its common stock was held by the Duys and Nienhuys families. In 1947 all voting rights were in the common stock.

As is usual in cases of valuation of stock of closely held corporations, each party has introduced evidence of the existence of factors which, standing alone, supports his position. The petitioner places stress on factors which would tend to make the stock unattractive to prospective investors and to depress the value. Examples of these are that the stock owned by the decedent was a minority interest-some 18 per cent of the common-and could not control corporate policy. Its operations were confined to growing, purchasing and selling leaf tobacco for use in cigars. It did not do any manufacturing in which respect it differed from some of the better known tobacco companies, nor did it deal in cigarette tobacco except as to a minor part of its Cuban tobacco. The operating and financial policies of the corporation were dictated by one man, Henry M. Duys, who was 62 years of age at the optional valuation date. The corporation did not carry insurance on the life of Mr. Duys.

The major basis of the business since its inception in 1900 had been the importation and sale of Sumatra and Java tobacco, and that part of the business was sharply curtailed if not entirely lost when enemy forces overran the Pacific islands in World War II. Its enforced change to the growing of domestic tobaccos was a costly and precarious venture.

On the other hand, the respondent points to the financially successful operations of the business over a long period of years, with emphasis on operations in the 10-year period covered by the fiscal years ended March 31, 1938 to 1947, inclusive. Although no far-eastern crops of tobacco were grown in the war period after the crop of 1941, Duys & Co. was able to procure some Sumatra and Java tobacco from the inventory of another company throughout the war period. During the period of scarcity of far-eastern tobacco, domestic cigar manufacturers became accustomed to using Connecticut shade tobacco for wrappers and were satisfied to use that tobacco. Dealings in Connecticut tobacco resulted in a loss of some $1,600 in 1941, but thereafter such dealings were profitable, with a profit of over $364,000 in 1946 and $276,000 in 1947. Operations in other tobaccos, including those of Puerto Rico, Cuba, and Florida, throughout the 10-year period resulted in an over-all profit in each of those years. Income per common share, with the exception of 1938, was substantial, ranging from a low of $7.18 to a high of $45.63. In the valuation year, 1947, earnings per common share amounted to $17.02. While the number of cigar factories had decreased considerably over a period of years prior to 1947, the per capita consumption of cigar tobacco had remained steady in the 10 years ending in 1947 and the number of cigars produced in 1947 was 470,000,000 greater than in 1938.

We have examined and weighed all of the evidence bearing on the value of the common stock of Duys & Co. Based upon our consideration of that evidence, and a weighing of the factors established by it, we have reached the conclusion and have found as an ultimate fact that the value of the common stock at April 8, 1947, was $172.68 per share. The evidence does not establish a lower value contended for by the petitioner or a higher value asserted by the respondent by amendment to his answer. The respondent's inclusion of the stock in gross estate at a value of $172.68 per share is sustained.

Valuation of Property Outside the United States; Accrued Dividends

The respondent has included in the gross estate the value of personal property that he determined was located in The Netherlands, including stocks in American corporations. It developed at the hearing that certificates for some stocks in foreign corporations, and some bank accounts of the decedent, were located in foreign countries other than The Netherlands. Based upon our conclusion that the decedent was not a resident of the United States, the greater portion of the personal property located outside the United States is not to be included in the gross estate. For estate tax purposes, stock of domestic corporations owned by a nonresident not a citizen of the United States is deemed to be property within the United States. Internal Revenue Code section 862 (a). Code section 861 (a) (1) requires an apportionment of deductions in such a case as this. For these reasons it is necessary to determine the value of such of the decedent's shares of stock in American corporations as were not included in the estate tax return and also the value of other of the decedent's properties, other than real estate.

There is no dispute between the parties as to the value in Dutch guilders of the decedent's property in The Netherlands and other foreign countries, and the shares in American corporations and accrued dividends thereon represented by certificates issued by the Dutch Administration Offices. The parties present the question to be decided as to such properties as one to be determined by the effect on such value of the blocking restrictions imposed by the government of The Netherlands under the 1945 decree on transactions involving foreign exchange. This presentation of the question stems from the fact that the estate tax, like its companion gift tax, is based on the value of property measured in terms of United States dollars. *Estate of Anthony H. G. Fokker*, 10 T. C. 1225, *Morris Marks Landau*, 7 T. C. 12.

Both parties take extreme views as to the effect of the decree of The Netherlands government. The petitioner contends that under the decree the property could not have been sold for United States dollars and therefore it had no value for estate tax purposes. The respondent's position is that the official exchange rate of $0.37695 per guilder should be used, as the valuation date is subsequent to the date of the liberation of The Netherlands and foreign trade had revived at the valuation date.

The evidence, as we analyze it, does not support the position of either party to the extent that each, respectively, claims. While Holland had been liberated from the hands of the enemy, and we assume that there had been a revival of foreign trade, at least to some extent, nevertheless there was in effect the governmental decree imposing restrictions on the sale of property of Dutch nationals in foreign exchange. The effect of such restrictions must be taken into account in determining value. *Morris Marks Landau, supra.* The evidence establishes that at the optional valuation date the decedent's estate could not have realized in dollars the full guilder value of the blocked properties converted at the official rate of exchange. There is evidence that as to stocks in American corporations owned by Dutch nationals, the certificates for which were in this country, the market price was only about one-half of the guilder value at the official exchange rate.

The petitioner's evidence establishes to our satisfaction that the respondent erred in converting guilder values into dollar values at the official exchange rate. However, it is not convincing that the properties involved in this issue had no value at all. The foreign exchange decree does not purport to be an absolute prohibition on transactions involving foreign exchange. The decree made it illegal to dispose of property in foreign trade "otherwise than by virtue of a license." There is no evidence that the decedent's estate made any effort to procure a license. There is evidence that property of Dutch nationals could not have been sold for free United States dollars, but there is also evidence that some foreign transactions were permitted if the proceeds were offered to The Netherlands Bank in exchange for guilders. While this no doubt involved some financial sacrifice on the part of the Dutch national, we cannot find as a fact that the property in the decedent's estate could not have been converted into United States dollars at some figure. The existence of the foreign exchange controls imposed by The Netherlands makes it difficult to fix an exact value for the property outside the United States, but some value must be determined under the estate tax provisions of the taxing statute. *Ithaca Trust Co.* v. *United States*, 279 U. S. 151. Our best judgment, based upon all the evidence, is that the decedent's property in The Netherlands should be valued at the optional valuation date by converting the guilder value into United States dollars at the rate of $0.10 per guilder.

Life Insurance

As the decedent was not a resident of the United States, the proceeds of the policy of insurance on his life are not includible in the estate. Code section 863 (a).

Administration Expenses

The parties have stipulated as to the deduction allowable to the estate for attorneys' fees and related expenses and disbursements incurred in the administration of the estate and in this proceeding or on a review,

```
Decision will be entered under Rule 50.
```

Khan v. Commissioner
United Sates Tax Court Memorandum Decisions, 1998.
75 T.C.M. (CCH) 1597, 1998 T.C.M. (RIA) ¶ 98,022.

WRIGHT, Judge:

MEMORANDUM FINDINGS OF FACT AND OPINION

Respondent determined a deficiency of $179,278 in petitioner's Federal estate tax. After concessions by petitioner, the sole issue for decision is whether decedent, Barkat A. Khan, was a resident of the United States at the time of his death. If decedent was a resident of the United States at the time of his death, petitioner is subject to the Federal estate tax imposed on the estates of U.S. residents under section 2001 and is entitled to the unified estate and gift tax credit of $192,800 allowed under section 2010. If decedent was a nonresident at the time of his death, petitioner is subject to the Federal estate tax imposed on the estates of noncitizen nonresidents under section 2101 and is entitled to a unified credit of $13,000 under section 2102(c)(1).

FINDINGS OF FACT

Some of the facts have been stipulated, and they are so found. The stipulation of facts and the exhibits attached thereto are incorporated herein by this reference.

Decedent, Barkat A. Khan, died in Pakistan on February 25, 1991. Decedent's son Mohammed Aslam Khan (Aslam) is the executor of decedent's estate and resided in Butte City, California, when the petition was filed in this case.

Decedent was born in India in 1910. In 1947, the area of India in which decedent lived became part of the newly formed Pakistan. At that time, decedent became a citizen of Pakistan and was a citizen of Pakistan at the time of his death.

In 1912, decedent's father, Namat Khan (Namat), left India and immigrated to the United States. Decedent and his mother, however, remained in India. Decedent farmed a 15-acre parcel of land in India. In 1935, decedent married Hussain Bibi Khan in India. They had four children, including two sons, Aslam and Ashiq Ali Khan (Ashiq), and two daughters, Ahmed Bibi and Sarwaree Bibi. All four children were born in India or Pakistan.

During his lifetime, decedent spoke only Punjabi. He did not speak English and could not read or write any language.

When decedent's father, Namat, immigrated to the United States in 1912, he joined his brother Babu Khan (Babu) in Butte City, California. Babu had immigrated to the United States in 1901. Soon after Namat immigrated to the United States, two more of his brothers, Adalat Khan (Adalat) and Munshi Khan (Munshi), also came to the United States. Namat and his three brothers established a farming and real estate business in Glenn County, California.

In 1935, Namat formed another farming partnership (Fazal-Namat Ranch partnership) near Butte City, California, with Fazal Mohamed (Fazal). Fazal was unrelated to Namat and had immigrated from India to the United States in 1924.

Two of Namat's brothers, Adalat and Munshi, died before 1953. They were not survived by any descendants, and following their deaths, Namat and Babu controlled the family business.

Namat died in November of 1958 while visiting his wife and family in Pakistan. Namat's estate primarily consisted of his 50-percent interest in the Fazal-Namat Ranch partnership, plus interests in residential rental apartments and commercial properties located in Chico and Cridley, California. Namat left three-fourths of his estate to decedent and one-eighth to each of decedent's cousins, Chrag Mohamed Khan (Chrag) and Mohammed Ali Khan (Mohammed Ali). Although the Fazal-Namat Ranch partnership technically terminated upon Namat's death, Fazal, as the surviving partner, continued to manage the business of the ranch with court approval for a period of 5 years.

In 1958, shortly after Namat's death, decedent's son Aslam came to the United States. Aslam attended high school and college. He joined Babu in running the family business and worked part time for the Fazal-Namat Ranch.

In 1963, Aslam married Sarwaree Begum, who also had immigrated to the United States from India. Aslam and Sarwaree have three daughters.

In July of 1965, Babu died leaving no descendants. During Babu's lifetime, he had given interests in properties in California to decedent's sons, Aslam and Ashiq. Those interests included real property interests in Chico, California, and stock in Yuba Plaza, Inc., a corporation formed to develop a regional shopping center. At the time of his death, Babu's estate consisted of farmland and a rental dwelling in Imperial County and his remaining stock in Yuba Plaza, Inc. In his will, Babu left one-half of his estate to decedent's son Aslam and one-sixth each to Chrag, Mohammed Ali, and Hushmat Bebe, all of whom were citizens of Pakistan. Aslam was the executor of Babu's estate. Aslam was the only family member in the United States and continued to operate the family business in partnership with an unrelated individual.

In 1969, Aslam received a bachelor's degree in agriculture from Chico State University and became a full-time trainee under Fazal. The relationship between Aslam and Fazal eventually deteriorated. As lam stopped working with Fazal and enrolled at Chico State University to study for a master's degree in agriculture.

In April of 1971, decedent came to the United States for the first time on a temporary visitor visa. At that time, decedent was 61 years of age. Decedent's wife, son Ashiq, and two daughters remained in Pakistan. Decedent lived with his son Aslam and Aslam's family while in the United States. Late in 1971, Aslam developed severe health problems, and he lost most of his eyesight. Although decedent's temporary visa allowed him to stay in the United States for only 6 months, decedent obtained extensions that permitted him to stay in the United States until March of 1974.

Fazal died on April 28, 1972, while decedent was in the United States. Fazal left his interest in the Fazal-Namat Ranch partnership to his wife and five nephews. Decedent sought and was granted an extension of his visa into 1974 in order to resolve problems with the dissolution of the Fazal-Namat Ranch partnership. The dissolution of the partnership required partitioning of the partnership property. The partnership farmed approximately 2,000 acres of irrigated rice land, some of which were leased. The property included valuable leases, land, machinery, equipment, a storage/dryer complex, and the headquarters. The division of the land required creating easements for roads, drainage, irrigation, and airstrips. Land used for growing rice must be leveled periodically at a cost of approximately $200 per acre. As a result, the acreage that had been most recently leveled was more desirable than the rest.

In July of 1973, Aslam obtained a permanent resident visa. Decedent requested an extension of his visa beyond April of 1974. His request was denied, and he returned to Pakistan on February 4, 1974.

After decedent returned to Pakistan, he attempted to obtain a permanent resident visa. Robert Kutz (Kutz), who has been the Khan family's attorney since 1954, wrote a letter dated September 26, 1975, to the U.S. Consul General in Lahore, Pakistan, "with respect to the anticipated applications for permanent residency visa to the United States of [decedent] and his wife Hussain Bibi." The stated purpose of the letter was to advise the Consul General that decedent owned a substantial amount of property in California and was capable of financially supporting himself and his wife in the United States. The Immigration and Naturalization Service, however, informed decedent that he would not be granted a permanent resident visa until his son Aslam became a U.S. citizen.

On November 15, 1976, the Fazal-Namat Ranch partnership was formally dissolved. Although the partnership was formally dissolved, not all of the property division was made at that time.

On November 15, 1976, decedent, Aslam, Ashiq, and decedent's cousins, Chrag and Mohammed Ali, formed a partnership called Namat & Aslam Khan Farms. They placed the assets distributed to them from the Fazal-Namat Ranch partnership in the new partnership in order to keep the farm operating. Although they formed the new partnership, they immediately began discussing partitioning the land and machinery because Chrag and Mohammed Ali wanted their own separate farms. At the time, decedent, Ashiq, Chrag, and Mohammed Ali were in Pakistan. Aslam managed the partnership's 1,300-acre rice farming operation because he was the only partner then residing in the United States.

Fred Lucchesi (Lucchesi) is a public accountant. Lucchesi prepared the tax returns for the Fazal-Namat Ranch partnership, the Namat-Aslam Ranch partnership, and the partners of those partnerships until

1982 when he sold his practice to Harrison-Dailey Accountancy Corp. (Harrison-Dailey). Because of Aslam's poor health, Aslam requested that Lucchesi continue to do the bookkeeping and compile all tax information to be provided to Harrison-Daily.

John Woodmansee (Woodmansee) is a certified public accountant associated with Harrison-Daily who began preparing tax returns for the Khan family in 1982. Although Woodmansee prepared decedent's tax returns, Woodmansee never met decedent and met with Aslam only on four or five occasions. Lucchesi provided Woodmansee with the information necessary to prepare decedent's tax returns. Woodmansee did not review the returns with decedent or any other member of the Khan family. After the returns were completed, Lucchesi would pick up the returns and take them to Aslam. Aslam was not able to read the returns because of his poor eyesight. Lucchesi did not review the returns in detail with decedent or Aslam. Lucchesi merely told Aslam where to sign the returns and whether there was any tax owed or a refund due. Aslam signed decedent's returns pursuant to a power of attorney. Lucchesi then placed the signed returns in envelopes and mailed them. For taxable years before and including 1984, Aslam filed Forms 1040NR, U.S. Nonresident Alien Income Tax Returns, for decedent.

In June of 1982, Aslam became a naturalized U.S. citizen. After obtaining his U.S. citizenship, Aslam planned to have his entire family come to the United States.

In March of 1984, Aslam went to Pakistan and met with decedent and the other Pakistani partners in an attempt to resolve differences among the partners. In July of 1984, the U.S. Department of Agriculture began requiring recipients of rice program subsidies to have Social Security numbers. Although Aslam had a Social Security number, decedent, Mohammed Ali, and Chrag had only temporary tax identification numbers. In 1984, decedent and Ashiq applied for immigrant visas. Ashiq's priority date was June 11, 1984. By letter dated September 4, 1984, the American Vice Consul in Lahore, Pakistan, informed Ashiq:

Although this office had received satisfactory evidence establishing your entitlement to immigrant classification, a waiting period of an indeterminate length of time must be anticipated before further consideration can be given to your application. This is necessary because there are more applicants for visas than there are immigrant visa numbers available under the numerical limitations prescribed by law. At the present time, visa numbers in your category are *** available only for persons who have a priority date earlier than Nov. 1979.

On October 1, 1984, decedent applied for and was issued an immigrant visa and alien registration based on his status as the parent of a U.S. citizen. On the application, decedent indicated that his wife and children would not be accompanying or following him, but that he intended to stay in the United States permanently. On January 20, 1985, decedent entered the United States on a permanent resident visa. Decedent was issued an alien registration receipt card ("green card") that identified him as a resident alien entitled to reside permanently and work in the United States. Decedent's wife, his two daughters, and his son Ashiq remained in Pakistan.

While in the United States, decedent resided with Aslam and his family. Aslam lived in a house owned by the family partnership. He added a bedroom and bath to the house for decedent's use. Decedent obtained a Social Security number. Decedent did not obtain a library card or join any social organizations, such as the American Association of Retired Persons. He was often visited by friends and associates who had come to the United States from Pakistan.

For purposes of filing decedent's 1985 tax return, Lucchesi advised Woodmansee that decedent had come to the United States during 1985 to live. Woodmansee prepared a Form 1040 marked "dual status" for decedent for the taxable year 1985, because decedent resided in Pakistan for part of the year and in the United States for the remainder of the year. Aslam filed the Form 1040 for decedent for the 1985 taxable year.

Decedent and Aslam frequently met with Kutz to discuss the division of the remaining assets of the Fazal-Namat Ranch. Although decedent understood a little English, he did not read, write, or speak English. Aslam served as a translator for decedent.

In 1986, decedent thought he had reached an oral agreement with Chrag and Mohammed Ali for the division of the partnership property. During that year, Aslam became ill and was hospitalized for about a month. Aslam was not able to travel to Pakistan because of his poor health. On December 24, 1986, decedent traveled to Pakistan to visit his family and to formalize the agreement with Chrag and Mohammed Ali for the division of the partnership property.

Before leaving for Pakistan, decedent applied for a permit to reenter the United States. A reentry permit shows that the person to whom the permit is issued is returning to the United States from a temporary visit abroad and relieves the person from the necessity of securing a visa from an American Consul before returning to the United States. On January 7, 1987, the Sacramento office of the Immigration and Naturalization Service issued decedent a permit to reenter the United States without a visa (reentry permit); the reentry permit was valid for multiple entries and had an expiration date of January 6, 1989. The following "Important Information" concerning the effect of claiming nonresident alien status for Federal income tax purposes is provided on the last page (page 16) of the reentry permit:

An alien who has actually established residence in the United States after having been admitted as an immigrant or after having adjusted status to that of an immigrant, and who is considering the filing of a nonresident alien tax return or the non-filing of a tax return on the ground that he is a nonresident alien, should consider carefully the consequences under the immigration and naturalization laws if he does so.

If an alien takes such action, he may be regarded as having abandoned his residence in the United States and as having lost his immigrant status under the immigration and naturalization laws. As a consequence, he may be ineligible for a visa or other document for which lawful permanent resident aliens are eligible; he may be inadmissible to the United States if he seeks admission as a returning resident; and he may become ineligible for naturalization on the basis of his original entry or adjustment as an immigrant.

The reentry permit was mailed to decedent's California address. Aslam read the reentry permit to determine the expiration date and then mailed the permit to decedent in Pakistan. Aslam did not read the "Important Information" on the last page of the permit.

Aslam's wife Sarwaree and his eldest daughter Robeena accompanied decedent on his trip to Pakistan. Sarwaree and Robeena purchased round-trip tickets and, after a 5-week visit, returned to the United States. Decedent did not purchase a round-trip ticket because he did not know how long it would take to finalize the partnership agreement.

Decedent's wife lived with Ashiq and his family in Pakistan. When decedent returned to Pakistan, he stayed with Ashiq.

When preparing decedent's return for 1986, Lucchesi informed Woodmansee that decedent had left the United States permanently on December 24, 1986. On the basis of that information, Woodmansee prepared a Form 1040NR for decedent for the 1986 taxable year. On the return, Woodmansee indicated that decedent had left the United States permanently on December 24, 1986. Decedent's 1986 Form 1040NR was filed with the Internal Revenue Service at the Philadelphia Service Center on October 20, 1987.

In Pakistan, decedent found it difficult to work out the agreement with Chrag. During 1987, decedent again thought he had reached an agreement. Kutz drafted an agreement and sent it to Pakistan. Again Chrag refused to sign the agreement.

While decedent was in Pakistan, his health began to fail. He was hospitalized in Pakistan from October 28 through November 10, 1988. Decedent's reentry permit expired January 6, 1989. Following his hospitalization, he was very weak and his health continued to deteriorate. He was hospitalized again from February 9 through February 15, 1989, and December 11 through December 20, 1990.

Aslam visited his father in Pakistan in 1990. At that time decedent was not able to walk and often needed assistance with bathing and eating. Decedent wanted to return to the United States at that time, but his health would not permit him to make the long trip.

Woodmansee prepared decedent's income tax returns on Forms 1040NR for taxable years 1987 through 1990. Lucchesi took the returns to Aslam and mailed them after Aslam signed the returns.

Decedent died in Pakistan on February 25, 1991. In his will, decedent bequeathed $7,000 to his wife and $15,000 to each of his daughters. He bequeathed $2,000 in trust for the benefit of the poor of Pakistan. Decedent left the remainder of his estate (valued at $646,190 on the estate tax return) to be divided equally between his sons, Aslam and Ashiq.

Kutz assisted Aslam with the probate of decedent's estate. In order to prepare an inventory and evaluation of the assets, Kutz requested a copy of decedent's last income tax return. Kutz noticed that a nonresident return had been filed. Since he understood that decedent was a resident, he thought the wrong return had been filed. He called Woodmansee to question the filing of the nonresident return. Kutz followed up the phone call with a letter to Woodmansee after researching the income tax rules pertaining to the filing of returns by resident aliens.

On or about March 25, 1992, an amended Form 1040X for each of the taxable years 1986 through 1990 was filed with the Internal Revenue Service at the Philadelphia Service Center, on the basis of decedent's status as a resident alien during those years.

On the Form 706, United States Estate Tax Return, petitioner indicated that decedent's domicile at the time of death was Butte City, California, and that decedent established the domicile in 1985. Most of decedent's business and property interests were located in the United States. At the time of decedent's death, those interests were valued at approximately $746,000. Decedent also maintained bank accounts in the United States. At the time of his death the value of the deposits in his bank accounts was over $70,000. The only property decedent owned in Pakistan was the 15-acre farm, valued at $15,000 at the time of his death. In computing the Federal estate tax, petitioner claimed a unified credit of $192,800.

Respondent determined that decedent was not a resident of the United States on the date of his death and limited petitioner's unified credit to $13,000.

OPINION

Section 2001 imposes a transfer tax on the taxable estate (determined under section 2053) of every decedent who is a citizen or resident of the United States. Section 2010 permits a credit of $192,800 against the estate tax imposed by section 2001. By contrast, section 2101 imposes a transfer tax on the taxable estate (determined under section 2106) of every decedent who is not a citizen and not a resident of the United States. Section 2102 generally permits a credit of $13,000 against the estate tax imposed by section 2101.

Decedent was a citizen of Pakistan at the time of his death. Therefore, since decedent was not a citizen of the United States, the proper computation of the estate tax liability depends upon whether decedent was a resident of the United States at the time of his death within the meaning of the estate tax provisions of the Internal Revenue Code.

For purposes of the estate tax, a resident is an individual who, at the time of his death, had his domicile in the United States. Sec. 20.0-1(b)(1), Estate Tax Regs. A nonresident is an individual who, at the time of his death, had his domicile outside the United States. Sec. 20.0-1(b)(2), Estate Tax Regs.

The term "residence" or "domicile" as contemplated by the Federal estate tax statutes has never been construed or defined by an all-inclusive or all-exclusive definition. "In fact, it seems that such a definition is impossible. Every case possesses peculiarities different from any other case, and the issue must be decided in the light of the facts peculiar to each case." Bank of New York & Trust Co. v. Commissioner, 21 B.T.A. 197, 203 (1930).

Under ordinary circumstances, the place of birth is one's first domicile. Id. There is no question about decedent's having been domiciled in Pakistan before his coming to the United States in 1971 on a temporary visitor visa.

We start with the fundamental principle that "a domicile once acquired is presumed to continue until it is shown to have been changed." Mitchell v. United States, 88 U.S. (21 Wall.) 350, 353 (1874); Estate of Nienhuys v. Commissioner, 17 T.C. 1149, 1159 (1952). If there is doubt, the presumption is that the domicile has not been changed. Weis v. Commissioner, 30 B.T.A. 478, 487 (1934). Section 20.0-1(b)(1), Estate Tax Regs., provides in part:

A person acquires a domicile in a place by living there, for even a brief period of time, with no definite present intention of later removing therefrom. Residence without the requisite intention to remain indefinitely will not suffice to constitute domicile, nor will intention to change domicile effect such a change unless accompanied by actual removal.

Thus, for decedent to have established a new domicile in the United States, two things are indispensable: (1) Decedent must have lived in the United States, and (2) he must have intended to remain here indefinitely. Both elements must be present, and one without the other is insufficient to establish a new domicile. Mitchell v. United States, supra; Forni v. Commissioner, 22 T.C. 975 (1954); Estate of Nienhuys v.

Commissioner, supra; sec. 20.0- 1(b)(1), Estate Tax Regs.

Decedent lived in the United States from April of 1971 until February of 1974 and from January of 1985 until December of 1986. We must examine the facts to determine whether during either of those periods, decedent intended to remain indefinitely. As the Supreme Court stated in Williamson v. Osenton, 232 U.S. 619, 624 (1914): "The essential fact that raises a change of abode to a change of domicile is the absence of any intention to live elsewhere, or, "the absence of any present intention of not residing permanently or indefinitely in" the new abode." (Citations omitted.)

After careful consideration of the entire record, we conclude that when decedent came to the United States in 1985, he intended to reside here permanently.

Decedent first came to the United States in 1971 on a temporary visitor visa, and he obtained extensions that allowed him to stay in the United States for almost 3 years. He began seeking a permanent resident visa at least as early as 1975 but was informed that he would not be granted a permanent visa until his son Aslam became a naturalized citizen of the United States. In 1984, after Aslam obtained his citizenship, decedent applied for and obtained a permanent resident visa. He entered the United States on that permanent visa on January 20, 1985, and immediately obtained a green card and a Social Security number.

Most of decedent's business and property interests were located in the United States. As early as 1976, decedent maintained a bank account in the United States. He owned substantial farming and business interests located in California that he had inherited from his father in 1958. Decedent gave his house in Pakistan to his son Ashiq, and the only property decedent owned in Pakistan was the 15-acre farm.

Decedent's family had a long history of immigrating to the United States. When decedent was a young child, his father and three uncles immigrated to the United States and established extensive farming and real estate operations. Decedent's eldest son, Aslam, came to the United States in 1958, was granted a permanent resident visa in 1973, and acquired his U.S. citizenship in 1982.

Decedent's second son, Ashiq, also wanted to immigrate to the United States. He applied for a permanent resident visa in 1984, after Aslam obtained his citizenship, but was not able to obtain an immigrant visa at that time because of the limitation on the number of immigration visas available as prescribed by law. He finally was granted permanent immigration visas for his family in 1996, after waiting 12 years.

We do not think that decedent's failure to obtain a library card or driver's license after immigrating to the United States indicates that he did not intend to permanently reside in this country, considering he could not read or write English (or any other language). Nor would we expect an individual who did not speak English to join social organizations such as the American Association of Retired Persons.

Additionally, we do not think the fact that decedent's wife remained in Pakistan shows that decedent did not intend to reside permanently in the United States. From the time decedent was 2 years old until his parents' deaths, his mother resided in Pakistan while his father resided in the United States.

On the basis of the record, we conclude that decedent lived in the United States in 1985 and at that time decedent intended to remain in the United States permanently. Therefore, decedent became domiciled in the United States in 1985.

The fundamental principle that a domicile once acquired is presumed to continue until it is shown to have been changed now applies to decedent's domicile in the United States. To establish that decedent reestablished domicile in Pakistan, it must be shown that he lived in Pakistan and intended to remain there indefinitely. Both elements must be present, and one without the other is insufficient to establish a new domicile.

Decedent lived in Pakistan from December 24, 1986, until the time of his death. Living in Pakistan without the requisite intent to remain there indefinitely, however, will not suffice to constitute domicile. Sec. 20.0-1(b)(1), Estate Tax Regs. A person acquires a domicile in a place by living there "*with no definite present intention of later removing therefrom.*" Sec. 20.0-1(b)(1), Estate Tax Regs. (emphasis added).

Respondent contends that the filing of Forms 1040NR for the taxable years after 1985 on decedent's behalf indicates that decedent intended to abandon his domicile in the United States. We disagree.

Decedent's tax returns were prepared by Woodmansee on the basis of information provided by Lucchesi. When Lucchesi took the returns to Aslam to be signed, he did not read or explain the returns to Aslam. Because of Aslam's poor eyesight, he did not read the returns himself. Aslam signed the returns under a power of attorney, and decedent never saw the returns. We do not think that the filing of the Forms 1040NR

43

on decedent's behalf under these circumstances establishes that decedent intended to abandon his domicile in the United States.

Furthermore, the term "resident" has different meanings in different settings under differing statutes. Forni v. Commissioner, 22 T.C. at 986. An individual's classification as a resident of the United States for purposes of the Federal estate tax is dependent upon his being domiciled in the United States, whereas an individual's classification as a resident for purposes of the Federal income tax is determined by the standards set forth in section 7701(b). [11] Since an individual can have but one domicile, an individual may be a resident of only one country for purposes of the Federal estate tax. An individual, however, may be a resident of more than one country for purposes of the Federal income tax under section 7701(b). Marsh v. Commissioner, 68 T.C. 68, 72 (1977), affd. without published opinion 588 F.2d 1350 (4th Cir. 1978). Since the legal standard for determining residency for estate tax purposes differs substantially from that for determining residency for income tax purposes, we do not think the filing of the Forms 1040NR establishes that decedent did not intend to return to the United States.

Decedent returned to Pakistan in 1986 to visit with his family and to meet with his Pakistani cousins to formalize the agreement to divide the partnership property. Before leaving the United States, decedent applied for a reentry permit. Decedent's actions indicate that when he left the United States, he intended to return as soon as the agreement was finalized. We think he did not purchase a round-trip ticket because he did not know exactly how long it would take to formalize the agreement with Chrag and Mohammed Ali. Decedent had a definite intention of leaving Pakistan and returning to the United States. A change of abode with present intent to return to the former abode upon the contemplated happening of an event in the indefinite future, such as completion of business, recovery of health, termination of employment, or recall by employer, is not a change of residence or domicile. Crespi v. Commissioner, 44 B.T.A. 670, 676 (1941). Therefore, decedent did not acquire a new domicile in Pakistan when he left the United States in December of 1986.

We also do not think that the expiration of the reentry permit indicates that decedent changed his mind and abandoned his intention to return to the United States. The reentry permit expired after decedent's health began to fail and following his first hospitalization in Pakistan. The expiration of the reentry permit meant that decedent would have had to apply for a returning resident visa from the American Consul before returning to the United States. It was not unreasonable for decedent or a family member to wait until decedent's health improved and he was able to travel before applying for a returning resident visa.

A domicile is not changed even by long continued absence if there is any intention of returning, "*even though intention be doubtful*". Weis v. Commissioner, 30 B.T.A. at 487 (emphasis added). Decedent had a definite intention of leaving Pakistan and returning to the United States. Most of decedent's business and property interests were located in the United States. At the time of decedent's death, those interests were valued at approximately $746,000. Decedent also maintained bank accounts in the United States. At the time of his death the value of the deposits in his bank accounts was over $70,000. By contrast, the only property decedent owned in Pakistan was the 15-acre farm, valued at $15,000 at the time of his death. The record shows that decedent wanted to return to the United States, but his poor health prevented him from doing so.

No one, except the individual, knows or can know with absolute certainty whether, in fact, he chooses to abandon his domicile and adopt a new one. "We can only have a belief of varying degrees of certainty, after considering that person's declarations, conduct, character, temperament, etc." Bank of New York & Trust Co. v. Commissioner, 21 B.T.A. at 203. On the basis of the record as a whole, we conclude that decedent never abandoned his domicile in the United States. We hold, therefore, that decedent was a resident of the United States on the date of his death.

To reflect the foregoing and because of concessions by petitioner,

Decision will be entered under Rule 155.

Estate of Paquette,
United States Tax Court Memorandum Decisions, 1983.
46 T.C.M. (CCH) 1400, T.C.M. (P-H) ¶ 83,571.

MEMORANDUM FINDINGS OF FACT AND OPINION

WILES, *Judge:*

Respondent determined a deficiency in decedent's Federal estate tax in the amount of $164,811.68. The sole issue for decision is whether the decedent was a resident of the United States under the estate tax provisions at the time of his death.

FINDINGS OF FACT

Some of the facts have been stipulated and are found accordingly. Edouard H. Paquette (hereinafter decedent) died on January 21, 1975, at the age of 77 in Orlando, Florida. He died testate with a will executed in Canada. The executor of decedent's estate is the Trust General du Canada (sometimes referred to as petitioner), a Canadian corporation, existing and operating under the laws of Canada. The executor filed a nonresident alien estate tax return (Form 706 NA) with the Philadelphia Service Center on May 2, 1976.

Decedent was born in Quebec, Canada, on July 13, 1897, and throughout his entire life and at the time of his death he was a citizen of Canada. He was married in Montreal, Canada. His widow, Marie-Ange Paquette, (hereinafter Mrs. Paquette) is also a Canadian citizen.

Beginning sometime prior to 1950, decedent owned and operated two retail hosiery stores in Montreal. He also owned two houses in Canada, one located at 2600 St. Catherine Road in Montreal (hereinafter referred to as the "city house") and the other, a large house situated on two acres of land, located at 1792 Boulevard Mattawa in Laval (hereinafter referred to as the "country house"). The city house was conveniently located near the decedent's two retail outlets.

Commencing no later than 1950 and up to the year of his death, decedent made yearly trips to Florida. He generally visited Florida in the winter months, from October through April, and then returned to Canada for the summer.

On November 11, 1955, decedent retired and sold his retail hosiery business, and he sold the city house on June 18, 1956. Following the sale of the city house, decedent, while in Florida for the winter, purchased a house in Orlando, Florida (hereinafter sometimes referred to as the Florida house) on March 5, 1957. Decedent furnished his Florida house with the contents of the recently sold city house. Decedent filed a "Declaration of Domicile and Citizenship" with the State of Florida on March 22, 1957, but then filed a "Revocation of Declaration of Domicile and Citizenship" with that state on February 13, 1958.

During the period from 1957 through 1971, decedent and his wife continued to spend the winter months in Florida. They returned to their country house in Canada for the remaining portion of the year, generally from April through October. During 1971, decedent's wife became ill and underwent a throat operation, and she also began to experience difficulty walking that year. After 1971, she no longer accompanied decedent on his trips to Canada because of her inability to move about comfortably. Decedent, however, continued to return to Montreal every summer through 1974.

On September 23, 1971, decedent sold the country house because it was too big and required too much work. Following the sale of the country house, decedent intended to buy a small house or rent an apartment in Montreal, and he discussed his intention with Jacques Bourgeois (hereinafter Mr. Bourgeois), his accountant and financial advisor. During the spring of 1972, decedent developed skin cancer on his left hand. In June of that year, he was hospitalized in Florida for surgery on that hand and he was again hospitalized in Florida the next month for a second operation on the same hand.

In November of 1972, decedent returned to Montreal. While in Canada, he met with his investment portfolio manager at Trust General of Canada, Andre Larouche (hereinafter Mr. Larouche), and at that time he also met with Mr. Bourgeois, and various friends.

During February of 1973, decedent was again hospitalized in Florida for an operation to remove a cancerous tumor on his left lung. After recovery from this operation in May of 1973, he returned to Canada

45

for at least two months. While in Canada, decedent again discussed his intention to buy or rent an apartment in Canada with Mr. Bourgeois. He also met with Mr. Larouche and various friends. During February 1974, decedent was hospitalized in Florida for an operation to remove a cancerous tumor on his right lung. He was discharged from the hospital in March and returned to Canada for the summer of 1974. Decedent was thin and weak; nonetheless, he met with Mr. Bourgeois and reiterated his intention to buy or rent an apartment in Montreal. As usual, he consulted with Mr. Larouche and visited friends.

On July 19, 1974, decedent executed his last will and testament while in Montreal and stated therein that he was a resident of Montreal. Also, in August 1974, he was admitted into a Montreal hospital for the purpose of checking the condition of his lungs. Decedent visited Orlando, Florida, in November of 1974, where he resided until he died on January 21, 1975.

At all times mentioned herein and up until the date of his death, decedent filed all of his income tax returns in Canada; maintained a valid Canadian driver's license; a valid Canadian passport; voted in Canada; and he purchased, registered, and insured his automobile in Canada. Decedent never applied for a Florida driver's license, nor did he apply for naturalization as a citizen of the United States.

In addition to the above contacts which decedent maintained with his native country, the situs of the bulk of decedent's assets were located in Canada and were either deposited in Canadian banks or invested in stocks and bonds of Canadian corporations. His accountant, Mr. Bourgeois and his investment manager, Mr. Larouche, both resided in Canada. Decedent met with Mr. Bourgeois yearly from 1968 through 1974 to discuss his investments and prepare his tax returns. During the period from 1971 through 1975, decedent met with Mr. Larouche twice a year concerning possible changes in his investment portfolio. Decedent actively managed his investments while in Canada. Decedent was a very conservative man, and Mr. Larouche was prohibited from making changes in his portfolio unless he received in person authorization from decedent.

ULTIMATE FINDING OF FACT

Decedent was domiciled in Canada on the date of his death.

OPINION

We must determine whether decedent was a resident of the United States within the meaning of the estate tax statutes at the time of his death. Both parties are in agreement that a "resident" under the applicable estate tax provisions means "domiciliary." Petitioner argues that, while decedent did own a house in Florida and resided there in the winter, he lacked the intent necessary to acquire a new domicile in the United States. Respondent, on the other hand, maintains that decedent established a domicile in Orlando, Florida, during either 1957 or 1971. Alternatively, respondent contends that in the event we find that decedent was domiciled in Canada at the time of his death, the value of decedent's automobile, physically located within the United States at such time, is properly includable in decedent's gross estate.

Section 2001 imposes a transfer tax on the taxable estate of every decedent who is a citizen or resident of the United States. Section 20.0-1(b)(1), Estate Tax Regs., provides in pertinent part that:
A "resident" decedent is a decedent who, at the time of his death, had his domicile in the United States.

A person acquires a domicile in a place by living there, for even a brief period of time, with no definite present intention of later removing therefrom. *Residence without the requisite intention to remain indefinitely will not suffice to constitute domicile*. [Emphasis added.]

Thus, to be a resident for estate tax purposes, decedent must have been domiciled in the United States at the time of his death.

We start with the fundamental principle that a domicile once acquired is presumed to continue until it is shown to have been changed. Estate of Jan Willem Nienhuys v. Commissioner, 17 T.C. 1149, 1159 (1952), citing Mitchell v. United States, 88 U.S. (Wall.) 350 (1874). There is no question about decedent having been domiciled in Canada prior to 1957, the year in which he purchased a home in Orlando, Florida. We must examine the facts to determine whether after 1957, events occured which would overcome that presumption. To establish a new domicile two things are indispensable: first, decedent must have resided in the United States, and second, he must have intended to remain here indefinitely. Both elements must be present, and one without the other is insufficient to establish a new domicile. Mitchell v. United States, supra; F. Giacomo Fara Forni v. Commissioner, 22 T.C. 975 (1954); Estate of Jan Willem Nienhuys v. Commissioner, supra; sec. 20.0-1(b)(1), Estate Tax Regs.

Respondent, in support of his first position that decedent established a domicile in Florida during 1957, relies on the fact that decedent retired and sold his business in Canada in 1955; he sold his city house during 1956; and decedent purchased a home in Orlando, Florida during March 1957. Petitioner, however, argues that the home which decedent purchased in Florida during 1957, was merely a vacation home, for the purpose of continuing his usual practice of spending the winter in Florida's warm climate. For the reason set forth below, we agree with petitioner.

On November 11, 1955, decedent sold his business and retired. As he no longer required a house near his retail stores, he sold the city house during June 1956. On March 5, 1957, decedent, while vacationing in Florida, purchased a house there in Orlando. Respondent, on brief, places substantial weight on the fact that decedent furnished his Florida house with the contents of his recently sold city house. He maintains that this is strong evidence of decedent's intent to acquire a new domicile in Florida during 1957. Upon considering all the circumstances in this case, we disagree with respondent's claim that the movement of furniture from the city house to Florida is strong evidence of decedent's intent to acquire a United States domicile. We find nothing unusual in decedent furnishing his newly purchased home with furniture from his recently sold home. Decedent, after all, still maintained his country home, which was a large fully furnished home in Laval, Canada, to which decedent returned every April for the summer. Furthermore, the duration of decedent's stay in Florida did not increase upon purchase of the Florida house. Their long and consistent practice of spending winter months in Florida and returning to Canada in the summer, continued uninterrupted from 1950 until 1971.

Respondent also points to the "Declaration of Domicile and Citizenship" filed by decedent on March 22, 1957, as additional support for his position. While our determination of decedent's domicile must be based on all of the relevant facts and circumstances, we fail to see how respondent can point to that declaration without giving at least equal weight to decedent's express revocation of that declaration, filed on February 13, 1958, in which decedent stated that he intended to retain his Canadian domicile.

After careful consideration of the entire record, we conclude that decedent was domiciled in Canada prior to 1957, and that his status as such did not change, as respondent has argued, during 1957 when he purchased a home in Orlando, Florida. We now address respondent's alternative position that decedent acquired a United States domicile in 1971 after the sale of his country home.

Respondent maintains that, after the sale of decedent's country house in Canada, Florida was the only place where he owned a home and, therefore, Florida became his domicile. We disagree.

While we agree with respondent that ownership of a home can be some indication of an individual's intent to establish a new domicile, it is merely one of several factors which must be examined to ascertain decedent's intent. In determining decedent's intent, we have evaluated all of the evidence and we are convinced that decedent's failure to own a home in Canada after 1971 was due to his medical problems rather than an intent to change his domicile to the United States. After the sale of his Canadian country house, decedent informed Mr. Bourgois that he intended to purchase or rent a small residence in Montreal to replace that house as soon as he returned to Canada in the spring of 1972. Unfortunately, decedent's health began to decline in 1972 until the date of his death. In 1972 he had two operations on his hand for skin cancer; one in June, the second in July. Notwithstanding his medical problems, decedent returned to Canada in November of that year. While in Canada he visited friends [5] and conducted business. He met with Mr. Larouche and Mr. Bourgois with whom he discussed his investments and reiterated his present intent to locate an apartment in Montreal when his health improved.

Decedent's health, however, continued to decline, and in February 1973, he underwent major surgery to remove a cancerous tumor from his left lung. Obviously weakened from the operation, he returned to Canada in May for two months, during which period he again visited friends and managed his financial affairs, and met with both Mr. Larouche and Mr. Bourgois. Again, he informed Mr. Bourgois that he still intended to find an apartment in Montreal when his health improved. Unfortunately, decedent's health continued to worsen and, during February 1974, he underwent surgery to remove a second cancerous tumor, this time from his right lung. Although in failing health, decedent returned to Canada for the summer of 1974.

Following his usual practice, he met with Mr. Larouche to discuss and manage his investments. He also met with Mr. Bourgois and restated his intent to buy or rent an apartment as soon as he was able to do so. While in Canada, decedent executed his last will and testament in July of 1974, and he stated therein that he was a resident of Montreal.

In addition to his yearly visits to Canada, decedent maintained numerous contacts with his country of citizenship which evidenced his intention to retain his Canadian domicile. Up until the date of his death, he filed income tax returns in Canada, he voted in Canada, and he maintained a valid Canadian driver's license as well as a valid Canadian passport. In addition, decedent's automobile was purchased, registered, and insured in Canada. Moreover, it is not without significance that most of decedent's assets, valued at $556,351.76, were located in Canada. [6] He met with Mr. Larouche and Mr. Bourgois regularly in Canada concerning his investments. In order to keep his assets liquid, decedent's portfolio was divided between deposits in Canadian banks and stocks and bonds of Canadian corporations. Decedent returned yearly to actively manage his investments. Decedent met at least twice a year with Mr. Larouche at which time he personally made the decisions of when and where to invest his money. In fact, Mr. Larouche was prohibited from making changes in decedent's portfolio unless he received in person authorization.

Moreover, we found all of petitioner's witnesses to be most credible and their testimony lends additional support to all of the other facts in the record which indicate that decedent was a Canadian domiciliary at the date of his death. Mrs. Paquette testified that her husband always intended to retain his Canadian domicile. Mr. Bourgois testified that the reason decedent sold his country home in Canada was because it was too large a home for decedent to maintain. [7] This testimony clearly indicates that decedent's sale of his Canadian country home should not be regarded as evidence of his intent to abandon his Canadian domicile and establish a new domicile in the United States.

After careful evaluation of all the evidence, including testimony by those who were well acquainted with decedent, we find that decedent never had any intention to establish a United States domicile. Decedent maintained many contacts with his native country, and followed a 25 year old practice of spending winters in Florida. We find that decedent never intended to remain in the United States indefinitely.

The record supports the presumption of continuance of original domicile and overcomes the presumption of the correctness of respondent's deficiency. For all of the foregoing reasons, we hold that decedent was a nonresident of the United States at the time of his death under the estate tax statutes.

We now turn to respondent's final argument that the value of decedent's automobile, which was located in Florida at the time of his death, should have been included in decedent's gross estate. [8] Respondent raises this argument for the first time on brief, and his doing so, has prejudiced petitioner as he obviously did not address this question at trial. It is well settled law that issues raised for the first time on brief will not be considered by this Court when to do so prevents the opposing party from presenting evidence that he might have if the issue had been timely raised. See Shelby U.S. Distributors v. Commissioner, 71 T.C. 874, 885 (1979); Estate of Horvath v. Commissioner, 59 T.C. 551, 555 (1973). Therefore, we will not pass upon the merits of respondent's untimely argument.

To reflect the foregoing,

Decision will be entered for the petitioner.

Giacomo Fara Forni v. Commissioner,
United States Tax Court, 1954.
22 T.C. 975.

Fisher, Judge:

Respondent determined a deficiency in gift tax for the year 1948 in the amount of $7,200. The issue is whether petitioner was a resident of the United States for gift tax purposes and therefore entitled to a specific exemption of $30,000 within section 1004 (a) (1), Internal Revenue Code.

FINDINGS OF FACT.

Some of the facts were stipulated by the parties. Those facts are found accordingly and incorporated herein.

The petitioner was born on July 12, 1864, at Pettenasco, Province of Novara, Italy, and at all times was and now is a citizen of Italy. In 1889, the petitioner entered the diplomatic service of the Italian Government. While in that service, he was stationed at many places including Pittsburgh, New York, New Orleans, and Philadelphia.

The petitioner married in 1913. His wife, Annina Fabbricotti, had been a citizen of the United States of America prior to her marriage to petitioner. From 1913 until the time of her death Signora Fara Forni was a citizen of Italy.

The petitioner resigned from the diplomatic service in 1925. Thereafter, he went to Paris as special counsellor of the Italian Embassy, and after 2 years he returned to Milan, Italy. After 1927 petitioner was retired, and he engaged in no business or diplomatic activity.

From 1927 to 1934, the petitioner lived part of the time in Milan and part of the time in Luino, Lago Maggiore, Italy. At the end of 1934, the petitioner and his wife, on the advice of a doctor, moved to Cimiez, Nice, France, where they lived for 2 years. At Cimiez, Nice, the petitioner and his wife lived in a hotel, and then rented an apartment, for which he bought the furniture. His wife was ill, and there was a night nurse and a day nurse for her.

In 1936, the doctors advised petitioner to take his wife into the interior of the country, and in that year the petitioner terminated his lease for the apartment in Nice, and he and his wife went to live in Lugano, Switzerland. In Lugano, petitioner rented a villa and furnished it with the furniture which he brought with him from Cimiez.

In 1938 Signora Fara Forni died, and the petitioner took her remains to the United States where they were buried.

Under the will of his deceased wife, the petitioner received the residuary estate, valued at about $415,000. These assets had been held by his wife in an agency account with the United States Trust Company, New York, N. Y. That company, acting as her executor, continued to hold the assets after her death in an estate account. In 1939 the major part of the estate was distributed to the petitioner by transferring the assets, consisting principally of securities, from the estate account to an agency account in the United States Trust Company in the name of the petitioner. On June 12, 1939, the petitioner granted to the United States Trust Company a general power of attorney to do all things necessary in the handling of his financial interests in the United States.

Following the death of Signora Fara Forni, the petitioner returned to Lugano, Switzerland, where he lived until 1946 in a rented apartment.

The President of the United States, by Executive Order No. 8785, dated June 14, 1941, amending Executive Order No. 8389 of April 10, 1940, regulated transactions in foreign exchange and foreign-owned property, and in effect prohibited the transmission of payments by the United States Trust Company to the petitioner, except as thereafter authorized by the Secretary of the Treasury. On October 23, 1941, General License No. 32 was amended to permit remittances of $100 per month. On February 9, 1943, General License No. 32 was amended to permit remittances of $500 per month, but only $100 per month if the payee was within Portugal, Spain, Finland, Sweden, or Switzerland, and was a national of any blocked country other than Portugal, Spain,

Finland, Sweden, or Switzerland. On July 24, 1945, General License No. 32 was amended to permit remittances for living expenses of $1,000 per month, provided that if the payee was within Portugal, Spain, Sweden, Switzerland, or Tangier and was a national of Germany, Italy, Japan, Bulgaria, Hungary, or Rumania, the remittances might not exceed $100 per month.

Between 1940 and 1945, the petitioner's American property in the possession of the United States Trust Company was thus "blocked." The United States Trust Company continued, however, to manage, invest, and reinvest this property, and collect the income therefrom. It attempted to remit money to petitioner, but the Swiss regulations prevented him from converting it into Swiss currency.

On January 10, 1945, the petitioner resumed correspondence with his New York attorneys, Conklin and Bentley, and thereafter letters were frequently exchanged concerning petitioner's financial interests. On May 18, 1945, petitioner wrote to his attorneys from Lugano in part as follows:

The war in Europe is over; how long do you think I ought to keep my domicile in Switzerland? When will be possible to send to my address in Italy those remittances [sic]?

Petitioner was subsequently advised by his attorneys to continue his domicile in Switzerland because funds could not be remitted to him in Italy without a special license from the Treasury Department. The attorneys considered it doubtful whether such a license would be issued.

During August 1945, petitioner wrote that he had decided to continue his domicile in Switzerland and that he hoped the end of the war and the prospect of peace with Italy would allow him "very soon" to change his domicile to Italy and to receive remittances there.

In September 1945, his attorneys wrote petitioner to the effect that the only feasible way for him to receive the income from his property was for him to come to the United States, and they suggested that he initiate inquiries along that line.

The next year, in June 1946, petitioner inquired of his attorneys when it would be possible for him to dispose of his property in view of the accord between the Swiss and United States Governments which affected the blocked property of Swiss residents. He wrote in July 1946, however, that he had been informed by his Swiss attorney that he would incur special taxes and be fined for not having previously "denounced" his American property if he should attempt to obtain its release through the Swiss Government. He stated that he was willing to transfer his residence to France, and he inquired whether he could receive remittances there and whether they would be able then to "retake control of my blocked account in New York (out of the U. S.-Switzerland agreement)." In reply, petitioner's New York attorneys wrote that they had no objection to his transferring his residence to France. They also wrote in part as follows: If you came to the United States as a visitor, the Foreign Funds Control Division would not unblock your account, but if you came to the United States as a permanent resident, an application to free your account could be made with a reasonable chance of success.

Since your family resides abroad, we presume that you would not consider making your home in the United States, and, therefore, we cannot recommend to you that you come to New York in the hope of freeing your account from control, although, of course, we should take great pleasure in your visit.

Thereafter, in October 1946, petitioner went to Paris, France, and he regularly thereafter received monthly remittances of $1,000. He terminated his lease for the apartment in Lugano and sold the household furnishings. Thereafter he lived in hotels when not in Italy.

On November 21, 1946, while visiting Monte Carlo, Principality of Monaco, petitioner wrote to his attorneys in New York in part as follows:

In Nice and in Monte Carlo, where I am now as a tourist, competent people manifested the possibility that in the near future the French Government might be compelled to control or take over our American property or list such property with them in order to tax it. For the moment the thing is only in prospect-just what you mentioned in your letter of August 6th-anyhow another serious reason for me to be uncertain about my doing.

Now I see in the Swiss newspapers notice of a new financial accord with Switzerland. The blocked accounts in the United States will become free (libres) through the certification in conformity to the General License 95-

I should be delighted if you could now remove any control with respect to my money: It would also save me taxes and fine in Switzerland-menaced.

My dear Mr. Butler, it is now with all my aching heart that I apply, with confidence and trust, to the benevolent friendship of Mr. Conklin and of yourself toward me; am 82 years old with a weak heart and other infirmities, tired and exhausted by these years of exile, am longing for my family in Italy. You know that an Italian going to live permanently in Italy, is obliged to remit to the Italian Government all money, bonds, stocks (except real estate) that he may possess abroad. The compensation of course is far below the real value.

I think we spoke already in New York about this problem and you suggested a *donation* in favour of my daughter, but taxes were high and we dismissed the matter.

Now an English lady living here, with an only daughter married in Boston, told me that she was advised to perform in Boston a trust in favour of her grandchildren and reserving to herself the income during her life. Could Mr. Conklin and yourself take in serious consideration my ardent wish and arrange, in accord with the U. S. Trust Company, my belonging in some legal way that would surely prevent the Italian Government from taking hold of my money? I am ready to renounce to my right of using the capital. I would be pleased to satisfy myself with the income during my life and reserving the same usufruct after my death to my daughter-appointing my grandchildren heirs to the estate.

Could this or something else be done with not a great expense?

I would be very grateful to Mr. Conklin and yourself for a kind reply. I hope to go to my home in Milan about the 10th of December and remain there for the holidays so please address me; Via Spiga, 25, Milan (Italy).   Please accept with Mr. Conklin my kindest personal regards. In order to avoid listing his foreign property with the French Government, petitioner remained in Monte Carlo. From there, on November 30, 1946, petitioner wrote to his New York attorneys in part as follows:

The Principality has granted me today other three months of stay: it means until the beginning of March 1947. No declaration of any kind I had to sign-except taking the engagement not to have a remunerative work. In the meantime *I keep by domicile in Switzerland* and I enjoy of a visa allowing me to travel to Italy and to Switzerland as many times as I like, during the next three months, and after that period-another three months may be granted to me, if I ask-and so on.

I want now to inform you that urgent business in Milan calls me back to Italy. There is a *loan of reconstruction* from the Government, which I cannot overlook, besides that we received already notice of a very onerous War Taxation on property and of course I have to provide funds for both operations.

I shall stay in Italy two or three weeks, spend a few days in Lugano in order to confer with my lawyer there, and then come back as soon as possible to Monte Carlo, waiting for your desirable advice. I mean: the unblocking of my account with reference to the recent financial accord-United States and Switzerland-and the possibility of arranging my property in New York in some legal way, which would surely prevent the Italian Government from taking hold of such property-when I should take up again my residence in Italy, *with your previous approval.*

On December 3, 1946, the New York attorneys wrote petitioner that, if he could procure a certification from the Swiss Compensation Office, he would be treated as a Swiss national by the United States and his assets would be unconditionally released. They also wrote that they were doubtful about the outcome of the situation if petitioner should resume his Italian residence before obtaining the Swiss certification. They suggested that petitioner create a trust before taking up residence in Italy in order to protect his American property. Petitioner replied to this letter on December 23, 1946, from his country seat at Pettenasco, Italy, where he was spending a few weeks. He wrote that he would carefully consider the trust suggestion later and that he was planning to confer with his attorney in Lugano concerning the Swiss certification. Thereafter, on January 9, 1947, petitioner wrote from Lugano that he had been advised to return to France and to apply for certification through the French Government in order to avoid the Swiss taxes and fine. He stated that he expected to return to Milan, Italy, at the end of that month and then take up his residence again in the Principality of Monaco.

On March 8, 1947, petitioner wrote that he was back in Monte Carlo and that he had discovered that there would be considerable delay in obtaining certification from France. On June 14, 1947, he wrote that, on the advice of his doctors, he would spend most of the summer in Italy, and that mail should be addressed to him at Via Spiga, 25, Milan, Italy, until further notice. On July 14, 1947, petitioner wrote his attorneys from Pettenasco, Italy, to the effect that he wished to avoid any possibility that the Italian Government might take his American property and compensate him with Italian money or bonds at the low official rate of exchange. Thereafter, in response to his attorneys' advice not to take up a residence or domicile in Italy, petitioner wrote to them from Milan, Italy, on August 18, 1947, in part as follows:

I do not intend to take up a residence or domicile in Italy. I shall endeavor to maintain my residence and domicile either in Switzerland or in Monaco. My preference would go to Lugano, two hours railway train from Milan, while my heart condition do not support the twelve hours journey from Monaco.

In October 1947, pursuant to the advice of his Swiss attorney, petitioner again took up residence in Lugano, Switzerland, where he was then able to convert his remittances into Swiss money. From there, on November 5, 1947, petitioner wrote to his New York attorneys in part as follows: "As I wrote, my old age oblige me to avoid long journey: So I am settled down again in Lugano, near my home and my family in Italy."

On January 28, 1948, petitioner's New York attorneys wrote to him that there was some danger that his property might be seized after June 30, 1948, by the United States Government as part of a policy then being considered to assist foreign countries to obtain dollar balances. They suggested that he reconsider the irrevocable trust plan to protect the property if it becomes unblocked. In reply, petitioner wrote to his attorneys on February 5, 1948, from Lugano in part as follows:

Considering the reasons given to me: the fact already reported to you that I should incur in heavy taxes and penalty for the certification from Switzerland (10-15-20% of the amount to be declared), I resolved to come to New York.

Today I went to Zurich and inquired about the visa on my passport at the American Consulate General. I would have liked a visa as a permanent resident: They informed me that it would take about two months to get it. So I had to make a formal application for a non-immigrant visa (six months in the U. S.). In a couple of weeks I ought to get the visa and be able to come.

The principal reason to come to New York is my firm will to consider now the irrevocable trust plan outlined by you in your letters and which would prevent any government from seizing my property.

Please consider very carefully my situation. If advisable, could you have the State Department cable the Consulate General in Zurich to deliver me a visa as a permanent resident, in order to allow you the possibility of making an application to free my account? If that step is not feasible would you advise me to come by airplane next March the 25th?

In reply to his letter, the attorneys wrote to petitioner that his account would not be unblocked unless he took up residence in the United States as a permanent resident which would require entry under an immigration visa and the spending of about 6 months in the country. On March 17, 1948, they wrote to advise petitioner that unless he obtained certification from the Swiss authorities prior to June 1, 1948, the Office of Alien Property would investigate his account and advise the Swiss Government of his holdings.

By reason of his former rank in the Italian diplomatic service, the Italian Government, as was customary, had issued to petitioner a diplomatic passport which was valid for his entire lifetime. On March 1, 1948, the United States Legation at Bern issued to petitioner a non-immigrant visa under section 3 (2) of the Immigration Act of 1924. The visa stated: "Valid for single journey," and that the purpose was "Personal Visit." On April 8, 1948, petitioner wrote to his attorneys from Lugano. He stated that he hoped to sail on April 21, 1948, and he wrote in part as follows:

Am willing to become a permanent resident and stay long enough to obtain the unblocking of my account.

Once in New York, I am advised to proceed to obtain certification from the Italian Government in my [illegible] of Italian resident and domiciliated abroad since the year 1931.

Petitioner entered the United States at New York on April 27, 1948. The nonimmigrant registration form issued to petitioner by the immigration inspector stated under "Date to Which Admitted," October 25, 1948.

The petitioner went to the Hotel Chesterfield, New York, New York, and stayed at that hotel all the time that he remained in the United States. The Hotel Chesterfield is a "transient hotel." It is the practice of the Hotel Chesterfield to extend special weekly or monthly rates to guests who are staying for longer periods of time. At the time the petitioner registered he did not attempt to arrange for a weekly or monthly rate. On the registration card the petitioner gave his foreign mail address as "25 Via Spiga, Milan, Italy." His luggage consisted of three suitcases. Petitioner admitted that he made no efforts to rent a suitable apartment in New York City, to purchase a dwelling house in the United States, or to find a suitable place of abode, but stated that he began to make inquiries about the possibility of buying property with money which he would have received from Italy.

On April 27, 1948, September 21, 1948, and October 2, 1948, the petitioner owned both his house in Milan, Italy, and his country seat in Pettenasco, Italy. His immediate family then consisted of the following:

1. His daughter who lived in Rome, Italy, with her husband and three children;

2. His brother who lived in petitioner's house in Milan, Italy; and

3. His two sisters who lived in Pettenasco, Italy.

Petitioner had no relatives in the United States and he did not see any relatives of his deceased wife while he was in this country. He did, however, have friends in New York City.

On April 27, 1948, petitioner executed a signature card for the United States Trust Company in which he declared that he was a resident alien, a citizen of Italy, and a resident of New York State for Federal and State income tax purposes.

On April 30, 1948, petitioner executed an application for a Treasury Department license which would unblock his accounts with the trust company. It included the following sworn statement:

That the applicant is and at all times has been a citizen of Italy and has never been a citizen of any other country. That prior to the year 1937 the applicant took up a residence and domicile in Switzerland and was a resident there until May 28, 1947, when he became a resident of and domiciled in Monaco. On April 27, 1948, the applicant came to the U. S. A. to stay for an indefinite period and does not intend to return to Switzerland as a resident or as a person domiciled there, and the applicant has no definite plans for any residence or domicile in the event he should leave the U. S. A.

In a supplemental statement which petitioner subsequently submitted to the Treasury Department, he stated in part as follows:

5. I consider myself a permanent resident of the United States of America.

6. I intend to stay in the United States of America for an indefinite period.***

9. By reason of advanced years, I do not intend to apply for citizenship.

10. By reason of a heart difficulty, Lugano, Switzerland, is no longer a suitable place for me to live, and I felt that the climate in Monaco would be favorable. My property in Italy was greatly damaged during the war, and at the present time I have no income from my property in Italy, nor any income from any source except my property in the United States. I came to the United States to look after my property here, and possibly to arrange for the creation of an *inter vivos* trust of a large part of my property so that a New York trust company may assume the care of the property as trustee, and I may be assured of the income during my life with an appropriate provision for my daughter after my death.

Pursuant to the petitioner's application, the Foreign Funds Control Division of the Treasury Department on September 14, 1948, issued a license authorizing the United States Trust Company to regard his account as property in which no blocked country or national thereof had any interest.

In July and August 1948, the petitioner had a number of discussions with his attorneys regarding the creation of an irrevocable trust. On September 21, 1948, at Greenwich, Connecticut, the petitioner executed an indenture of trust with the United States Trust Company as trustee. Under the terms of this trust he was the income beneficiary for life, with remainder interests in his daughter and her children.

During the summer of 1948, petitioner became ill. He was advised by his physician that he had suffered a thrombosis and that he should stay in bed for at least 15 days in order to avoid the danger of a second stronger attack. Petitioner became frightened. He decided to leave New York and go to Europe in order to be near his sister.

On October 2, 1948, the petitioner departed from the United States aboard the SS *Queen Mary*. He went to Cherbourg and Paris, France, and then to Geneva, Switzerland, where his daughter was residing. In the middle of October 1948, he arrived in Lugano, Switzerland.

From October 1948 to May 1949, the petitioner lived in Lugano in a rented apartment. From May until October 1949, he lived in his country seat in Pettenasco, Italy. He follows the same procedure each year, except for trips to Rome and to Milan, where he has business interests.

On November 2, 1948, the petitioner wrote from Lugano to his attorneys that his permanent address was Via Spiga, 25, Milan, Italy. On November 30, 1948, the petitioner's attorneys wrote to him as follows:

Upon receipt of your letter advising us that your legal residence was Via Spiga, 25, Milan, Italy. We communicated that fact to the United States Trust Company who asked us to have the enclosed income tax status card signed by you and forwarded to them.

Everything seems to be proceeding smoothly here, and we hope that you are feeling well and are comfortably settled.

With further reference to the income tax status card enclosed, we would say that if we are mistaken and you do not consider yourself a resident of Italy, then of course the card should not be signed.

On December 10, 1948, the petitioner wrote from Lugano to his attorneys stating as follows:

In answer to your letter of November 30, I beg to state that I am a citizen of Italy, that my legal domicile in Italy is Pettenasco (Novara) and that I am now a resident of Lugano (Switzerland).

In Milan I own the house in Via Spiga, 25, but it is not my legal residence (*residence*-in the Italian Civil Code-is considered the locality where you stay with your body.)

Being an Italian citizen, I must have a legal domicile in Italy and it is in the village where I was born: Pettenasco (Italy)-and where I am expected to exercise the right of political and administrative vote. My *actual residence*, where I am living now, is Lugano (Switzerland).

I return the card enclosed in your letter, filled in accordance to the Italian laws. Please consider now if it will be of use for the local requirements.

The card which was enclosed was dated November 20, 1948, and originally was filled in as follows: "My legal residence is Via Spiga, 25, Milan, Italy." This was changed by petitioner, however, to read as follows: "My legal domicile is: Pettenasco (Novara), Italy."

The petitioner filed his gift tax return for the calendar year 1948 in the office of the collector of internal revenue for the second district of New York (in connection with his gift in trust dated September 21, 1948) claiming therein a specific exemption of $30,000.

OPINION.

Fisher, *Judge:*

Petitioner was born in 1864 in Pettenasco, Novara, Italy, and he has at all times been a citizen of Italy. He entered the diplomatic service of that country and served at numerous posts throughout the world until his complete retirement in 1927. At all times he owned a house in Milan, Italy, and a country seat in the place of his birth.

He married an American, and, after his retirement from the diplomatic service, he lived with her in Italy, France, and Switzerland. Most of their moves were necessitated by the condition of his wife's health. In 1938, she died in Lugano, Switzerland. After bringing her remains to this country for burial, petitioner returned to Lugano, where he lived until 1946. Lugano is in the southern part of Switzerland near the Italian border and about two hours away from Milan by train. Novara is near Milan in the northern part of Italy.

Under his wife's will, petitioner acquired certain securities and accounts which he permitted to remain in the possession or custody of the United States Trust Company of New York. During World War II, the transfer of funds to petitioner was restricted by Executive Order and his property was blocked. As a resident of Switzerland, petitioner was entitled to receive $100 per month under a general license granted by the Treasury Department. He was unable, however, to convert American money into Swiss currency and such sums were not sent to him by the trust company.

When the war in Europe ended, petitioner went to Paris and then to Monte Carlo, Principality of Monaco, where he regularly received $1,000 per month for his living expenses from the trust company. These payments were the maximum permitted out of blocked accounts under the pertinent general license. In 1947 petitioner returned to live in Lugano after he was advised that he would be able to receive his remittances there and convert them into Swiss currency.

Petitioner desired greatly to return to live in Italy near his relatives. His brother lived in Milan; his two sisters lived in Pettenasco; and his daughter and three grandchildren lived in Rome. Although he frequently traveled into Italy for visits and for business reasons, on the advice of his New York attorneys, petitioner did not return to Italy to live permanently. The attorneys feared that the property would be seized by the United States Government if he became an Italian resident before a treaty of peace with Italy was consummated.

During this period, petitioner was also influenced greatly by his desire to protect his American property from seizure by a European government which would compensate him in local money at a low rate of exchange. Accordingly, he corresponded with his attorneys concerning the possibility of transferring the property irrevocably in trust in order to eliminate this danger. It was necessary, however, that his American property be unblocked before such a trust could be created.

Petitioner was reluctant to apply for the release of his funds through the Swiss Government because a disclosure of this property would subject him to heavy taxes and penalties for having failed to "denounce" his American property during the war. He was afraid to apply through the Italian Government because of the possibility that the funds would be seized by that country pursuant to the terms of a pending treaty of peace with the United States. Petitioner considered applying through the French Government but discovered that action by that Government would be delayed considerably.

In early 1948, petitioner was advised by his New York attorneys that, unless he was able to obtain the release of his funds by the following June 1, the Alien Property Custodian would investigate his account and report its contents to the Swiss Government. They subsequently advised him that, if he came to the United States and stayed long enough to convince the Treasury Department that he was a permanent resident of this country, his account would be unblocked, and that he could then execute the desired irrevocable trust.

Thereafter, petitioner arrived in New York on April 27, 1948. Three days later his application for a license to unblock his account was filed with the Treasury Department. On September 14, 1948, the license was granted, and on September 21, 1948, petitioner executed the trust agreement which irrevocably transferred certain assets to the United States Trust Company as trustee. On October 2, 1948, petitioner sailed for Europe on the *Queen Mary* and has not returned to this country.

The issue in this proceeding is whether petitioner was a resident of the United States at the time of the transfer to the trust company and thus entitled to take a specific exemption of $30,000 in his gift tax return as provided in section 1004 (a) (1) of the Internal Revenue Code.

The term "resident" has different meanings in different settings and under differing statutes. With respect to the issue before us, the word is construed by Regulations 108, section 86.4, which reads, in part, as follows:

A *resident* is one who has his *domicile* in the United States at the time of the gift. All others are nonresidents. A person acquires a domicile in a place by living there for even a brief period of time with no definite present intention of moving therefrom. *Residence without the requisite intention to remain indefinitely will not suffice to constitute domicile*, nor will intention to change domicile effect such change unless accompanied by an actual removal. [Emphasis supplied.]

Counsel for both parties agree that, for the purpose of this case, "residence" and "domicile" are synonymous. The problem thus resolves itself into the question of whether petitioner was domiciled in the United States on September 21, 1948, when the trust agreement was executed.

In *Mitchell* v. *States*, 21 Wall. 350, the Supreme Court said, at page 353: A domicile once acquired is presumed to continue until it is shown to have been changed. Where a change of domicile is alleged the burden of proving it rests upon the person making the allegation. To constitute the new domicile two things are indispensable: First, residence in the new locality; and, second, the intention to remain there. The change cannot be made except *facto et animo*. Both are alike necessary. Either without the other is insufficient. Mere absence from a fixed home, however long continued, cannot work the change. There must be the *animus* to change the prior domicile for another. Until the new one is acquired, the old one remains.   These principles are axiomatic in the law upon the subject.

There is no dispute in the instant case concerning the first factor necessary to constitute a change of domicile, i. e., petitioner did reside in the United States between April 27 and October 2, 1948. The elements of the second factor, the intention to remain, were discussed further by the Supreme Court in *Williamson* v. *Osenton*, 232 U. S. 619 (1914). In that case, the Court, through Mr. Justice Holmes, said, at page 624:

The essential fact that raises a change of abode to a change of domicile is the absence of any intention to live elsewhere, Story on Conflict of Laws, §43-or, as Mr. Dicey puts it in his admirable book, "the absence of any present intention of not residing permanently or indefinitely in" the new abode, Conflict of

Laws, 2d ed. 111.

In the instant case, we hold that petitioner has not established the requisite intention to remain in the United States indefinitely (or permanently) which is a necessary element in the chain of proof if he is to show that he was domiciled in this country. In this connection, we point out the following:

(1) Petitioner owned two houses in northern Italy, one in Milan and the other in Pettenasco. In New York he lived in a transient hotel.

(2) Petitioner's close relatives were living in Italy. In New York, he had no relatives although he did have friends in that city.

(3) After the war, petitioner expressed his great desire to return to his "home" and family in Italy and to end his long "exile." He remained abroad near northern Italy, however, on the advice of his attorneys, in order to avoid the possible seizure of his American property and to receive remittances from the United States for his living expenses. When these reasons for living outside of Italy were eliminated in 1948, petitioner promptly returned to Europe. He thereafter lived part of each year in Milan, Italy, and part in nearby Lugano, Switzerland.

(4) Petitioner's only motive in coming to the United States was to obtain a license to unblock his property and to create a trust which would eliminate the danger of its seizure by a European government. He was willing to remain here long enough to accomplish these purposes. He knew from correspondence and discussions with his attorneys that the period necessary for the accomplishment of his objectives was relatively limited. He had no intention of living in this country permanently. While he testified that he intended to reside in the United States "indefinitely," it appears from his testimony that he was using the word loosely, indicating merely that he did not know precisely how long it would take to get his property unblocked, or to create the contemplated trust.

(5) Petitioner entered this country on a nonimmigrant visa as a visitor under section 3 (2) of the Immigration Act of 1924, as amended. (8 U. S. C. sec. 203 (2) (1946 ed.)). There is evidence that petitioner inquired about obtaining an immigration visa on February 5, 1948, pursuant to the advice of his attorneys, but that he did not apply for one when he was informed that it would take about 2 months.

(6) Petitioner was authorized to remain in the United States until October 25, 1948. The pertinent immigration regulation then in effect (8 C. F. R. sec. 119.12 (1949 ed.)) provided, with respect to extension of stay, that an application must be filed approximately 30 days before the expiration of the period of admission. There is no evidence that petitioner contemplated extending the period of his stay beyond the 6 months which was granted to him when he entered the country. The contemplation of such an application became unnecessary, in fact, because petitioner had completed his business on September 21, and left the country on October 2, 1948. It is to be noted that the license unblocking his account was issued on September 14, 1948, 14 days before it would have been necessary for him to have applied for an extension of his stay.

(7) With respect to his intentions, petitioner deposed as follows:

Yes, I intended to stay there [in the United States] for an indefinite time, as I had sold everything I had in Europe, except in Italy, *but I did not plan to become a permanent resident.* [Emphasis supplied.]

The foregoing facts, and the record as a whole, present convincing reasons for us to conclude affirmatively that petitioner at all times while in this country had, in the words of the regulation, *supra,* "a definite present intention of moving therefrom" when his financial affairs had been settled. His stay in the United States may be termed of indefinite duration only in the sense that the exact date of his return to Europe could not be forecast precisely. It was abundantly clear to him that the period required to straighten out his affairs would be limited and relatively brief. It is not necessary, however, for us to make an affirmative finding to that effect in this case. Respondent determined that petitioner was not a resident of the United States in 1948 within the meaning of section 1004 (a) (1) of the Code, and his determination is presumptively correct. Upon the whole record, we think it is clear that petitioner has failed to overcome this presumption. We add, however, that if it were necessary to make an affirmative finding, we would concur in respondent's determination.

We hold, therefore, that petitioner has failed to establish that he was domiciled in the United States in 1948, and, as a consequence, may not be deemed to have been a United States resident in 1948 within the meaning of section 1004 (a) (1) of the Internal Revenue Code.

Decision will be entered for the respondent.

These cases demonstrate the fact-intensive nature of determining a person's domicile. Domicile should be clearly established prior to undertaking estate planning.

Questions

How may an individual U.S. Income Tax resident prove non-resident status for U.S. Estate and Gift Tax purposes?

What factors should be considered (from an Estate Tax perspective) by the following prospective immigrants to the U.S.?

      a.   High income professionals

      b.   High net-worth retirees

      c.   Business owners anticipating an imminent liquidation event

      d.   Business owners building business value

Why would a perspective high net-worth immigrant intentionally seek U.S. (estate tax) residency?

How may an individual be a U.S. income tax resident but not a U.S. estate tax resident (and vice versa)?

CHAPTER 3
ESTATE AND GIFT TAX IMPOSED ON U.S. CITIZENS AND RESIDENT NON-CITIZENS

"Worldwide Assets"

The U.S. Estate Tax is imposed on the "Gross Estate" of U.S. Citizens and U.S. residents.[34] The Gross Estate of a U.S. person includes "the value at the time of his death of all property, real or personal, tangible or intangible, wherever situated".[35] This phrase, "wherever situated," imposes the Estate and Gift Tax on "worldwide assets." The Estate Tax and the Gift Tax attach to all assets regardless of the location of the U.S. citizen or resident (or his property) at the time of gift or death. Citizens and non-citizen residents are afforded a unified credit against Estate and Gift Tax, which currently "shields" $11,700,000 in assets. No Gift Tax or Estate Tax is actually payable by U.S. citizens and residents until the value of lifetime gifts and bequests exceed the unified credit.

U.S. citizens and residents generally receive a credit for estate tax paid to a foreign country on property subject to the Estate Tax.[36] Note that the credit may be altered by an applicable estate tax treaty. See page 125 below.

---

[34] IRC §2001; Some countries do not impose estate or inheritance taxes while other countries have Estate Taxes which are imposed on relatively small wealth transfers. For example, the maximum rate imposed by the Brazilian version of an Estate Tax (the Brazilian "Imposto sobre Transmissã Causea Mortis e Doação," or ITCMD) is 8%; however, the threshold for the imposition of the tax is substantially lower than in the United States. In Sao Paulo, the tax is imposed on all transfers exceeding 40,000 Brazilian reals (approximately $14,000 U.S. Dollars) and in Mineas Gerais, on all transfers exceeding 20,000 Brazilian Reals.
[35] IRC §2031(a).
[36] IRC §2014.

Completion of Gifts

To complete a gift for Estate and Gift Tax purposes, the transferor must retain no right to change the disposition of the property transferred.[37] If, for example, the transferor retains the right to name new beneficiaries of a donee trust or change the proportionate benefit of trust beneficiaries, such retained powers may cause the gift to be treated as "incomplete."

Gifts generally remain incomplete if the transferor retains the power to alter beneficial interests in the property (as opposed to retaining rights over the manner or time of enjoyment of the property). By reserving the right to alter beneficial interests, the transferor has not truly parted with dominion and control of the transferred property. The Gift Tax does not apply to such incomplete gifts.[38] Incomplete gifts remain in the taxable estate of the donor.

Technically, the Code makes gifts to trusts "incomplete" when the transferor reserves rights to: (1) change beneficial title to trust property (both income and principal), (2) name new trust beneficiaries, or (3) change the interests of beneficiaries as between themselves (except when the change in interest is limited by a fixed or ascertainable standard).

---

[37] Treas. Reg. §25.2511-2(b).
[38] Treas. Reg. §25.2511-2(c).

Berger v. U.S.,
United States District Court for the Western District of Pennsylvania, 1980
487 F. Supp. 49.

Diamond, District Judge:

OPINION

[1] The plaintiffs C. William Berger and Margaret R. Berger, his wife, brought this action to compel the United States government to refund gift taxes and interest paid in the amount of $31,316.08. The Bergers paid the gift tax in connection with a transfer by Mr. Berger of property into two irrevocable trusts for the benefit of Margaret R. Berger and the Bergers' minor children.

In late 1968 and early 1969 Mr. Berger became interested in federal government service. At that time he was high on the list of those considered for a top level Federal Aviation Administration position, and from the press reports which he had read he believed that he had to place all of his *assets* into an irrevocable trust in order to comply with the Nixon administration's policies on public service conflicts of interest. To this end Mr. Berger liquidated all of his property, including even the sale of his private residence, and placed the bulk of these assets into two irrevocable trusts with the Pittsburgh National Bank. During the preparation of the trust instrument, a trust officer with the bank suggested that the trust be made revocable. However, Mr. Berger rejected this advice and insisted that the trust be irrevocable in order to comply with the government's conflict of interest rules as he understood them. Accordingly, on February 26, 1970, the irrevocable trusts in question were created.

By the summer of 1970, the prospects of employment with the FAA evaporated. The taxpayer sought employment with the State Department, but when this too did not materialize he ceased his efforts to obtain public service employment.

On April 12, 1971, the Bergers filed a gift tax return that indicated a total transfer of $180,000.00. Payment for the gift tax due on the transfer was not included, however, and on July 20, 1971, the Bergers filed an amended gift tax return alleging that no taxable transfer had in fact occurred and that therefore no tax was due.

Mr. Berger sought judicial reformation of the trust in the Court of Common Pleas of Allegheny County, Pennsylvania. And on September 15, 1971, he obtained an order reforming the trusts to trusts which would become revocable on instructions from Mr. Berger. However, since the Court of Common Pleas lacked jurisdiction over trusts, the order of reformation of September 15, 1971, was void. Mr. Berger then sought reformation in the proper forum, the Orphans' Court Division of the Court of Common Pleas of Allegheny County, Pennsylvania. That court also ordered reformation of the trust instrument again converting the trusts from irrevocable trusts to trusts that were revocable on instructions of Mr. Berger.

The Internal Revenue Service denied the July 20, 1971, amended tax return on its merits. Plaintiffs then paid under protest a total of $29,241.70 in taxes and interest of $2,074.38, and brought the instant action seeking a refund.

We have before us cross motions of the parties for summary judgment. The government conceded at the pretrial conference that it would not challenge Mr. Berger's contention that he was motivated to transfer his assets into an irrevocable trust by his mistaken belief that an irrevocable trust was the only means to comply with the Nixon administration's conflicts of interest policy. Plaintiffs raise no other issue of fact in relation to the transfer of Mr. Berger's assets into trust. There remains, therefore, only the following determinative question of law for the court:

 Whether or not the taxpayer's revocation under the laws of the state where it was made of a gift
transfer, complete in law when made, but which was the result of taxpayer's unilateral mistake,
can abrogate the federal gift tax which accrued as a result of such a transfer?
Congress has the authority to decide what property interests and transactions shall be subject to tax, but we must look to state law for the definition of various property interests and transactions. Blair v. Commissioner, 300 U.S. 5 [18 AFTR 1132] (1937). To determine a nature of a state created interest, a federal district court

61

need give "proper regard" to state trial court determinations of a taxpayer's property interest, Estate of Bosch, 387 U.S. 456, 464 [19 AFTR 2d 1891] (1967). However, the district court must independently review state law to determine if the state trial court followed the applicable state doctrines. Bosch, supra, at 465. Pennsylvania law permits the revocation of a gratuitous transfer into trust, made as a result of the grantor's unilateral mistake of fact or law. In Re Curry, 390 Pa. 105, 134 A.2d 497 (1957); First National Bank of Sunbury v. Rockefellar, 333 Pa. 553, 5 A.2d 205 (1939). For equity to grant reformation of a deed, the evidence that the grantor's mistake existed at the time of the transfer must be clear, precise, and convincing. Masgai v. Masgai, 460 Pa. 453, 333 A.2d 861 (1975), La Rocca Trust, 411 Pa. 633, 192 A.2d 409 (1963). Thus, Pennsylvania law will revest the grantor with complete ownership provided the difficult burden of proof is met and the grantor acts promptly upon discovery of his mistake to assert his rights. *See generally,* Summary of Pennsylvania Jurisprudence, Gifts Inter Vivos §§681-684 (1962). Here, however, we need not review the state trial court's record to ascertain the soundness of its rulings since the government concedes that but for Mr. Berger's mistaken conception of the conflicts of interest policy he would not have undertaken the transfer. See footnote 1 supra. The question remains as to whether or not the state-recognized right to reform the trust from irrevocable to revocable based on the grantor's unilateral mistake can abrogate the gift tax imposed upon the original transaction. The impact of the state right upon the federal tax scheme is a federal question. Blair, supra, at 11. The federal gift tax accrues to a grantor's transfer of property when the transfer is beyond his dominion and control as to who will be the beneficiaries of the transferred property. Sanford's Estate v. Commissioner, 308 U.S. 39 [23 AFTR 756] (1939).

In the case sub judice, the original deed of trust created an irrevocable transfer. In contrast with Sanford, where the grantor reserved a right to modify the terms of trust, Mr. Berger intentionally, albeit as the result of a mistake, relinquished all his legal rights over the property. He did, however, retain an equitable right under Pennsylvania law to reformation based upon the mistaken conveyance.

Federal courts have entertained suits to abrogate gift taxes based upon a mistake at the time of conveyance which give rise to the tax. Dodge v. United States, 413 F.2d 1239 [24 AFTR 2d 69-5326] (5th Cir. 1969), Margarita Touche, 58 T.C. 565 (1972). In both cases, due to a scrivener's error the deed conveyed more property than the grantor had intended. The courts relieved the taxpayers of a tax liability on the ground that there existed a right to reformation under the applicable state law upon the production of requisite proof to the courts to establish the basis for reformation.

Commissioner v. Allen, 108 F.2d 961 [24 AFTR 118] (3rd Cir. 1939), cert denied, 309 U.S. 680 (1940) set forth this Circuit's position on the effect of a residual right of revocation under state law upon a gift otherwise complete on its face. The Allen court held that until the grantor relinquished the state law right of revocation, the gift was incomplete and immature and thus, not subject to federal gift tax. Allen, supra, at 963.

Congress devised the gift tax system to complement the estate tax structure Sanford, supra, at 44. By recognizing that the present gift into trust was *incomplete* for mistake, there can be no transfer tax, since Mr. Berger remained owner of the property. However, the integrity and efficacy of the federal gift tax system is in no way threatened, since before the taxpayer may obtain ultimate tax relief from his mistake he must perfect a state right to reform, he must present evidence to the state court to meet the requisite standard of proof under its law, must not be guilty of laches under the state law, and must satisfy the federal court that the state court properly applied its law.

Here, as we have stated, the government has conceded that Mr. Berger acted upon a mistake in creating an irrevocable, hence, taxable, trust; Pennsylvania law permits reformation or revocation of such a gift transfer; Mr. Berger had the trust reformed in Pennsylvania Courts in accordance with Pennsylvania law, and therefore, summary judgement will be entered for the taxpayer.

Order of Court

And Now, to-wit, this 25th day of March, 1980, in accordance with the opinion filed this date on the parties' cross motions for summary judgement, It Is Ordered that the plaintiffs' motion for summary judgement be, and the same hereby is, granted, and It Is Further Ordered that the defendant's motion for summary judgement be, and the same hereby is, denied.

Trevor v. Commissioner,
Board of Tax Appeals, 1939.
40 BTA 1241.

Tyson, Judge:

OPINION.

This proceeding involves a deficiency of $37,803.26 in petitioner's gift tax liability for the year 1935. The two issues are (1) whether in creating a trust in 1935, with reservation to herself of the income for life, the petitioner made a gift of certain future interests subject to tax within the meaning of section 501 of the Revenue Act of 1932 as amended by section 511 of the Revenue Act of 1934; and (2) if so, the value of the property involved for gift tax purposes.

The stipulation of facts is incorporated herein by reference, but only such of those facts as are deemed necessary for determination of the issues involved are set out in this opinion.

On August 9, 1935, the petitioner, a resident of New York, New York, made, executed, and delivered a trust agreement with the Royal Trust Co. of Montreal, Canada, as trustee, and transferred to the latter, in trust, certain foreign stocks and securities having a value of $437,795.15 on that date.

The trust agreement directed the trustee to hold, manage, invest, and reinvest the principal of the trust during the "trust term" of 21 years after the death of the last survivor of the settlor, the settlor's brother, and two nephews of the settlor, and to apply the net income of the trust to the use of the settlor during her life, then to the use of her brother during his life, and after the death of the survivor of the settlor and her brother, to the use of the issue of the settlor's brother in a certain manner. The trustee was further directed, upon termination of the "trust term", to pay over the principal thereof to the then living issue of the settlor's brother.

The sixth article of the trust agreement provided:

This trust shall be irrevocable, except that the Settlor reserves to herself the right at any time and from time to time after the expiration of a period of ten (10) years from the date hereof, with the consent in writing of the Trustee, *** to amend or revoke this Agreement and the trust hereby created, either in whole or in part. ***

At the time of such transfer in trust the petitioner was 61 years of age. It is stipulated that, as shown by the actuaries' or combined experience tables of mortality, the life expectancy of a person aged 61 is 13.18 years; that the value of the right to receive $1 in the event that a person aged 61 should die within 10 years is 30.724 cents; and that the value of the unconditional right to receive $1 on the death of a person aged 61 is 61.163 cents.

The respondent determined, and now contends, that the transfer in trust on August 9, 1935, for the benefit of the settlor's brother and others constituted a completed gift *in praesenti,* subject to gift tax; that the value of the property transferred in trust was $437,795.15; and, the settlor having reserved a life interest, that the value of the gift was $267,768.65, representing the present worth of the unconditional right to receive $1 at the death of a person aged 61, that is, $437,795.15 times the factor .61163.

On the first issue petitioner contends (1) that no completed gift *in praesenti,* and thus no taxable gift, was made upon the creation of the trust on August 9, 1935, because under the settlor's reserved power of revocation, after 10 years, the transfer of the future interest was not complete and might never be consummated; and (2) that because the transfer of the future interest was to take effect only at the settlor's death, the value of the trust corpus would be includable in her estate subject to estate taxes, and, the gift tax and estate tax laws being *in pari materia* and mutually exclusive, there can be no gift tax liability on the transfer in question.

By the trust instrument the petitioner, as grantor, reserved to herself a present life interest in the income of the trust and provided that certain future interests in the income and corpus of the trust should go to certain ascertainable persons upon the happening of certain events. That transfer in trust is irrevocable for a period of 10 years, after the lapse of which period, and not until then, the settlor would have the right to revoke or amend the trust with the consent of the trustee. Such trustee is a person not having any adverse interest in the disposition of the trust corpus or the income therefrom. *Reinecke* v. *Smith,* 289 U. S 172, and *Witherbee* v. *Commissioner,* 70 Fed. (2d) 696; certiorari denied, 293 U. S 582.

Contrary to petitioner's first contention, we hold that the principle announced in *Burnet* v. *Guggenheim,* 288 U. S 280, that "a power of revocation accompanying delivery would have made the gift a nullity" is not decisive of the instant case. There the grantor reserved in the instrument creating the trust the unrestricted power of revocation from the date of the instrument and the Court held that it was not until a subsequent cancellation of such power that a completed gift was made. Here, the grantor did not possess any present power of revocation immediately after the transfer in trust was made and could not thereafter have become vested with such power unless she survived the lapse of a 10-year period, a contingency over which she had no control. A power conditioned upon a contingency does not presently exist, *Corning* v. *Commissioner,* 104 Fed. (2d) 329, and *John Edward Rovensky,* 37 B. T. A. 702.

Having held that the grantor's reserved power of revocation after a lapse of 10 years was not a presently existing power, we must next consider whether, under the provisions of the trust instrument, the transfer of the future interests here involved is otherwise embraced within the scope of the gift tax statute. That statute is not aimed at every transfer without consideration, but, instead, embraces only such transfers as have the quality of consummated gifts, *Burnet* v. *Guggenheim, supra;* that is, absolute *inter vivos* transfers *in praesenti* of the donor's title, dominion, and control of the subject matter of the gift to the donee. Cf. *Heiner* v. *Donnan,* 285 U. S 312. Although the two statutes are not always mutually exclusive, the gift tax statute and the estate tax statute are closely related in structure and purposes, are *in pari materia,* and must be construed in conjunction to ascertain the character of transfers intended to be embraced in each statute, respectively. The gift tax statute does not embrace a transfer which is so incomplete as a gift *inter vivos* when made, that the same transfer is, by the estate tax statute, expressly made subject to estate tax because intended to take effect at the death of the transferor. *Sanford's Estate* v. *Commissioner,* 308 U. S. 39; *Rasquin* v. *Humphreys,* 308 U. S. 54; *Burnet* v. *Guggenheim, supra; Hesslein* v. *Hoey,* 91 Fed. (2d) 954, certiorari denied, 302 U. S. 756; *Lorraine Manville Gould Dresselhuys,* 40 B. T. A. 30; *William T. Walker,* 40 B. T. A. 762; *John S. Mack,* 39 B. T. A. 220; and *Harriet W. Rosenau,* 37 B. T. A. 468.

The trust agreement clearly evidences the grantor's intention that the future interests should vest in certain ascertainable persons only in the event of her death either prior to the lapse of a period of 10 years after August 9, 1935, or thereafter, if she died before the power to alter or revoke was exercised. After the execution of the trust agreement the beneficial remainder, as well as the life estate, was left vested in the grantor and the future interests here in question were interests contingent upon the death of the grantor, whether it occurred prior to the lapse of 10 years, or subsequent thereto without a revocation or alteration of the trust. It is apparent that the death of the grantor, within a given time, was the indispensable event which would bring the future interests here involved into being, that the transmission of such interests would be by reason of the grantor's death, and that upon such event the property so transferred would be includable in her estate under the provisions of the estate tax statute, *Klein* v. *United States,* 283 U. S. 231. The fact that here the grantor retained a vested remainder distinguishes the instant case from *Becker* v. *St. Louis Trust Co.,* 296 U. S 48, and *Helvering* v. *St. Louis Trust Co.,* 296 U. S 39, wherein the grantor had merely a possibility of reverter of the remainder and the event of the grantor's death merely changed that possibility into an impossibility.

We conclude that the transfer of future interests here involved was a conditional transfer to take effect only at death of the grantor and, being includable in her estate, upon her death, as a transfer by reason of her death, it was not a completed transfer by gift *in praesenti* on August 9, 1935, within the meaning of section 501 of the Revenue Act of 1932, as amended by section 511 of the 1934 Act. Cf. *Hesslein* v. *Hoey, supra; John S. Mack, supra.* Accordingly, petitioner is not liable for gift tax on any portion of the value of the property she transferred in trust on August 9, 1935, and the respondent erred in his determination of the deficiency in controversy.

In view of the disposition we have made of the first issue herein, it becomes unnecessary to consider the second issue.

Decision will be entered for the petitioner.

Gifts in trust limiting trustee discretion to a fixed or ascertainable standard (for distributions) are considered complete.[39] Trusts so limiting trustee discretion are deemed to eliminate grantor rights to alter beneficial interests in trust assets. This is true even if the grantor is the trustee.[40] An example of a fixed and ascertainable standard for distribution is the condition that distributions must be made for the health, support, education, or maintenance of the permissible beneficiaries. Gifts to a trust requiring support distributions are considered "completed" gifts because the transferor has relinquished sufficient dominion and control over the transferred asset. The exception (to absolute trustee discretion) for support distributions allows the grantor to complete a transfer yet serve as a fiduciary (i.e. trustee) over the transferred assets.[41]

The subsequent relinquishment or termination of a retained power (which prevented completion of the gift) during the donor's lifetime will complete the gift and trigger Gift Tax.[42] In the event a trust (holding incomplete gifts) makes unfettered distributions of income or principal (during the transferor's lifetime), such trust distributions are considered completed taxable gifts by the grantor to the receiving beneficiaries.[43]

---

[39] Estate of Klafter, 32 T.C. M. (CCH) 1088, T.C.M. (P-H) ¶ 73,230 (1973).
[40] Treas. Reg. §25.2511-2(b)-(c), (g).
[41] Treas. Reg. §25.2511-2(c), (g).
[42] Treas. Reg. §25.2511-2(f).
[43] Treas. Reg. §25.2511-2(b).

Burnet v. Guggenheim,
Supreme Court of the United States, 1933.
288 U.S. 280. 53 S. Ct. 369.

Cardozo, Justice:

OPINION

Appeals which confirmed the assessment of a tax by the Commissioner of Internal Revenue. The Board's decision having been reversed by the Circuit Court of Appeals [58 F. (2d) 188], the Commissioner brings certiorari [287 U. S.-, 53 S. Ct. 85, 77 L. Ed. -].
Reversed.

On Writ of Certiorari to the Circuit Court of Appeals for the Second Circuit.

Judge: Mr. Justice CARDOZO delivered the opinion of the Court.

The question to be decided is whether deeds of trust made in 1917, with a reservation to the grantor of a power of revocation, became taxable as gifts under the Revenue Act of 1924 when in 1925 there was a change of the deeds by the cancellation of the power.

On June 28, 1917, the respondent, a resident of New York, executed in New Jersey two deeds of trust, one for the benefit of his son, and one for the benefit of his daughter. The trusts were to continue for ten years, during which period part of the income was to be paid to the beneficiary and part accumulated. At the end of the ten-year period, the principal and the accumulated income were to go to the beneficiary, if living; if not living, then to his or her children; and, if no children survived, then to the settlor in the case of the son's trust, and in the case of the daughter's trust to the trustees of the son's trust as an increment to the fund. The settlor reserved to himself broad powers of control in respect of the trust property and its investment and administration. In particular, there was an unrestricted power to modify, alter, or revoke the trusts except as to income, received or accrued. The power of investment and administration was transferred by the settlor from himself to others in May, 1921. The power to modify, alter, or revoke was eliminated from the deeds, and thereby canceled and surrendered, in July, 1925.

In the meanwhile Congress had passed the Revenue Act of 1924 which included among its provisions a tax upon gifts. "For the calendar year 1924 and each calendar year thereafter a tax is hereby imposed upon the transfer by a resident by gift during such calendar year of any property wherever situated, whether made directly or indirectly," the tax to be assessed in accordance with a schedule of percentages upon the value of the property. 43 Stat. 253, 313, c. 234, §§319, 320, 26 U. S. Code, §§1131, 1132 (26 USCA §§1131 note, 1132 note).

At the date of the cancellation of the power of revocation, the value of the securities constituting the corpus of the two trusts was nearly $13,000,000. Upon this value the Commissioner assessed against the donor a tax of $2,465,681, which the Board of Tax Appeals confirmed with a slight modification due to a mistake in computation. The taxpayer appealed to the Court of Appeals for the Second Circuit, which reversed the decision of the Board and held the gift exempt. 58 F. (2d) 188. The case is here on certiorari, 287 U. S. -, 53 S. Ct. 85, 77 L. Ed.-.

On November 8, 1924, more than eight months before the cancellation of the power of revocation, the Commissioner of Internal Revenue, with the approval of the Secretary of the Treasury, adopted and promulgated the following regulation: "The creation of a trust where the grantor retains the power to revest in himself title to the corpus of the trust, does not constitute a gift subject to tax, but the annual income of the trust which is paid over to the beneficiaries shall be treated as a taxable gift for the year in which so paid. Where the power retained by the grantor to revest in himself title to the corpus is not exercised, a taxable transfer will be treated as taking place in the year in which such power is terminated." Regulations 67, article I.

The substance of this regulation has now been carried forward into the Revenue Act of 1932, which will give the rule for later transfers. Revenue Act of 1932, c. 209, 47 Stat. 169, 245, §501 (c), 26 USCA §1136a (c). [1]

We think the regulation, and the later statute continuing it, are declaratory of the law which Congress meant to establish in 1924.

"Taxation is not so much concerned with the refinements of title as it is with actual command over the property taxed-the actual benefit for which the tax is paid." Corliss v. Bowers, 281 U. S. 376, 378, 50 S. Ct. 336, 74 L. Ed. 916; Cf. Chase National Bank v. United States, 278 U. S. 327, 49 S. Ct. 126, 73 L. Ed. 405, 63 A. L. R. 388; Saltonstall v. Saltonstall, 276 U. S. 260, 48 S. Ct. 225, 72 L. Ed. 565; Tyler v. United States, 281 U. S. 497, 503, 50 S. Ct. 356, 74 L. Ed. 991, 69 A. L. R. 758; Burnet v. Harmel, 287 U. S. -, 53 S. Ct. 74, 77 L. Ed. -; Palmer v. Bender, 287 U. S. -, 53 S. Ct. 225, 77 L. Ed. -. While the powers of revocation stood uncanceled in the deeds, the gifts, from the point of view of substance, were inchoate and imperfect. By concession there would have been no gift in any aspect if the donor had attempted to attain the same result by the mere delivery of the securities into the hands of the donees. A power of revocation accompanying delivery would have made the gift a nullity. Basket v. Hassell, 107 U. S. 602, 2 S. Ct. 415, 27 L. Ed. 500. By the execution of deeds and the creation of trusts, the settlor did indeed succeed in divesting himself of title and transferring it to others (Stone v. Hackett, 12 Gray [Mass.] 227; Van Cott v. Prentice, 104 N. Y. 45, 10 N. E. 257; National Newark & Essex Banking Co. v. Rosahl, 97 N. J. Eq. 74, 128 A. 586; Jones v. Clifton, 101 U. S. 225, 25 L. Ed. 908), but the substance of his dominion was the same as if these forms had been omitted (Corliss v. Bowers, supra). He was free at any moment, with reason or without, to revest title in himself, except as to any income then collected or accrued. As to the principal of the trusts and as to income to accrue thereafter, the gifts were formal and unreal. They acquired substance and reality for the first time in July, 1925, when the deeds became absolute through the cancellation of the power.

The argument for the respondent is that Congress in laying a tax upon transfers by gift made in 1924 or in any year thereafter had in mind the passing of title, not the extinguishment of dominion. In that view the transfer had been made in 1917 when the deeds of trust were executed. The argument for the government is that what was done in 1917 was preliminary and tentative, and that not till 1925 was there a transfer in the sense that must have been present in the mind of Congress when laying a burden upon gifts. Petitioner and respondent are at one in the view that from the extinguishment of the power there came about a change of legal rights and a shifting of economic benefits which Congress was at liberty, under the Constitution, to tax as a transfer effected at that time. Chase National Bank v. United States, supra; Saltonstall v. Saltonstall, supra; Tyler v. United States, supra; Corliss v. Bowers, supra. The question is not one of legislative power. It is one of legislative intention.

With the controversy thus narrowed, doubt is narrowed too. Congress did not mean that the tax should be paid twice, or partly at one time and partly at another. If a revocable deed of trust is a present transfer by gift, there is not another transfer when the power is extinguished. If there is not a present transfer upon the delivery of the revocable deed, then there is such a transfer upon the extinguishment of the power. There must be a choice, and a consistent choice, between the one date and the other. To arrive at a decision, we have therefore to put to ourselves the question. Which choice is it the more likely that Congress would have made? Let us suppose a revocable transfer made on June 3, 1924, the day after the adoption of the Revenue Act of that year. Let us suppose a power of revocation still uncanceled, or extinguished years afterwards, say in 1931. Did Congress have in view the present payment of a tax upon the full value of the subject-matter of this imperfect and inchoate gift? The statute provides that, upon a transfer by gift, the tax upon the value shall be paid by the donor, 43 Stat. 316, c. 234, §324, and shall constitute a lien upon the property transferred, 43 Stat. c. 234, §§324, 315 (26 USCA §1136 note, and §1115 and note). By the act now in force, the personal liability for payment extends to the donee. Act of June 6, 1932, c. 209, §510, 47 Stat. 249 (26 USCA §1136j). A statute will be construed in such a way as to avoid unnecessary hardship when its meaning is uncertain. Hawaii v. Mankichi, 190 U. S. 197, 214, 23 S. Ct. 787, 47 L. Ed. 1016; Sorrells v. United States, 287 U. S. -, 53 S. Ct. 210, 77 L. Ed. -. Hardship there plainly is in exacting the immediate payment of a tax upon the value of the principal when nothing has been done to give assurance that any part of the principal will ever go to the donee. The statute is not aimed at every transfer of the legal title without consideration. Such a transfer there would be if the trustees were to hold for the use of the grantor. It is aimed at transfers of the title that have the quality of a gift, and a gift is not consummate until put beyond recall.

The respondent invokes the rule that in the construction of a taxing act doubt is to be resolved in favor of the taxpayer. United States v. Merriam, 263 U. S. 179, 44 S. Ct. 69, 68 L. Ed. 240, 29 A. L. R. 1547; Gould v. Gould, 245 U. S. 151, 38 S. Ct. 53, 62 L. Ed. 211. There are many facets to such a maxim. One must view them all, if one would apply it wisely. The construction that is liberal to one taxpayer may be illiberal to others. One must strike a balance of advantage. It happens that the taxpayer before us made his deeds in 1917, before a transfer by gift was subject to a tax. We shall alleviate his burden if we say that the gift was then complete. On the other hand, we shall be heightening the burdens of taxpayers who made deeds of gift after the act of 1924. In making them, they had the assurance of a treasury regulation that the tax would not be laid, while the power of revocation was uncanceled, except upon the income paid from year to year. They had good reason to suppose that the tax upon the principal would not be due until the power was extinguished or until the principal was paid. If we disappoint their expectations, we shall be illiberal to them.

The tax upon gifts is closely related both in structure and in purpose to the tax upon those transfers that take effect at death. What is paid upon the one is in certain circumstances a credit to be applied in reduction of what will be due upon the other, 43 Stat. 315, §322, 26 U. S. C. §1134 (26 USCA §1134 and note). The gift tax is part 2 of title 3 of the Revenue Act of 1924 (see 26 USCA §1131 note et seq.); the estate tax is part 1 of the same title (see 26 USCA §1091 et seq.). The two statutes are plainly in pari materia. There has been a steady widening of the concept of a transfer for the purpose of taxation under the provisions of part 1. Tyler v. United States, supra; Chase National Bank v. United States, supra; Saltonstall v. Saltonstall, supra; cf. Bullen v. Wisconsin, 240 U. S. 625, 36 S. Ct. 473, 60 L. Ed. 830. There is little likelihood that the lawmakers meant to narrow the concept, and to revert to a construction that would exalt the form above the substance, in fixing the scope of a transfer for the purposes of part 2. We do not ignore differences in precision of definition between the one part and the other. They cannot obscure identities more fundamental and important.

The tax upon estates, as it stood in 1924, was the outcome of a long process of evolution; it had been refined and perfected by decisions and amendments almost without number. The tax on gifts was something new. Even so, the concept of a transfer, so painfully developed in respect of taxes on estates, was not flung aside and scouted in laying this new burden upon transfers during life. Congress was aware that what was of the essence of a transfer had come to be identified more nearly with a change of economic benefits than with technicalities of title. The word had gained a new color, the result, no doubt in part, of repeated changes of the statutes, but a new color none the less. Cf. Towne v. Eisner, 245 U. S. 418, 425, 38 S. Ct. 158, 62 L. Ed. 372, L. R. A. 1918D, 254; Int. Stevedoring Co. v. Haverty, 272 U. S. 50, 47 S. Ct. 19, 71 L. Ed. 157; Gooch v. Oregon Short Line Co., 258 U. S. 22, 24, 42 S. Ct. 192, 66 L. Ed. 443; Hawks v. Hamill, 287 U. S. - , 53 S. Ct. 240, 77 L. Ed.

The respondent finds comfort in the provisions of section 302 (d) of the Revenue Act of 1924 (26 USCA §1094 note), governing taxes on estates.[2] He asks why such a provision should have been placed in part 1 and nothing equivalent inserted in part 2, if powers for purposes of the one tax were to be treated in the same way as powers for the purposes of the other. Section 302 (d) of the act of 1924 is in part a re-enactment of a section of the Revenue Acts of 1918 and 1921, though it has been changed in particulars. 40 Stat. 1097, c. 18, §402 (c); 42 Stat. 227, c. 136, §402 (c). Cf. Reinecke v. Northern Trust Co., 278 U. S. 339, 49 S. Ct. 123, 73 L. Ed. 410, 66 A. L. R. 397. It is an outcome of that process of development which has given us a rule for almost every imaginable contingency in the assessment of a tax under the provisions of part 1. No doubt the draftsman of the statute would have done well if he had been equally explicit in the drafting of part 2. This is not to say that meaning has been lost because extraordinary foresight would have served to make it clearer. Here as so often there is a choice between uncertainties. We must be content to choose the lesser. To lay the tax at once, while the deed is subject to the power, is to lay it on a gift that may never become consummate in any real or beneficial sense. To lay it later on is to unite benefit with burden. We think the voice of Congress has ordained that this be done.

Precedents are cited as opposed to our conclusion. We find none of them decisive.

United States v. Field, 255 U. S. 257, 41 S. Ct. 256, 65 L. Ed. 617, 18 A. L. R. 1461, holds that under the Revenue Act of 1916 (39 Stat. 777, c. 463), the subject of a power created by another is not a part of the estate of the decedent to whom the power was committed. It does not hold that a revocable conveyance inter vivos is a perfected transfer by gift that will justify the immediate imposition of a tax upon the value. There was no such question in the case.

Jones v. Clifton, 101 U. S. 225, 25 L. Ed. 908, holds that a power of revocation in a deed of conveyance from a husband to his wife does not avail without more to invalidate the transaction as one in fraud of creditors. A transfer within the meaning of a taxing act may or may not be one within the statute of Elizabeth.

We are referred to cases in the state courts, from Pennsylvania and New Jersey. In re Dolan's Estate, 279 Pa. 582, 124 A. 176, 49 A. L. R. 858; In re Hall's Estate, 99 N. J. Law, 1, 125 A. 246. In neither did the court decide that a conveyance inter vivos was taxable as a present gift when the conveyance was subject to revocation at the pleasure of the grantor. No such statute was involved. In each the ruling was that upon the death of the grantor the subject of the conveyance was not taxable as part of his estate, and hence not taxable at all. The ruling might have been different if a choice had been necessary between taxing the conveyance, or its subject, while the power was outstanding, and taxing it later on. New channels of thought cut themselves under the drive of a dilemma.

A decision of the Court of Claims, Means v. United States, 39 F.(2d) 748, 69 Ct. Cl. 539, upholds the contention of the government that within the meaning of the act of Congress the termination by a settlor of the power to revoke a trust is a transfer of the property and as such subject to taxation.

The argument for the respondent, if pressed to the limit of its logic, would carry him even farther than he has claimed the right to go. If his position is sound that a power to revoke does not postpone for the purpose of taxation the consummation of the gift, then the income of these trusts is exempt from the tax as fully as the principal. What passed to the beneficiaries was the same in either case, an interest inchoate and contingent till rendered absolute and consummate through receipt or accrual before the act of revocation. Congress did not mean that recurring installments of the income, payable under a revocable conveyance which had been made by a settlor before the passage of this statute, should be exempt, when collected, from the burden of the tax.

The judgment is Reversed.

The CHIEF JUSTICE took no part in the consideration or decision of this case.

Mr. Justice SUTHERLAND and Mr. Justice BUTLER are of opinion that the termination of the donor's power of revocation was not a transfer by gift of any property within the meaning of the statute, and that the judgment of the Circuit Court of Appeals should be affirmed.

Estate and Gift Tax Consequences of Completed Gifts

If a U.S. person creates a trust benefitting someone else, parts with dominion and control over transferred property (leaving him with no power to change its disposition), the Gift Tax will apply to such transfer. The Settlor may use his unified credit to offset the Gift Tax otherwise due. See page 3. In 2021, the unified credit provides a $11,700,000 Gift Tax exemption. To the extent that the value of assets transferred to an individual beneficiary or to an irrevocable trust (foreign or domestic) exceeds $11,700,000, a 40% tax (Gift Tax or GST, or both, as the case may be) is imposed on the Settlor.

Transfers Between U.S. Citizen Spouses

U.S. citizens may delay the imposition of either the Gift Tax or the Estate Tax on transfers between citizen spouses. If both spouses are citizens of the United States, either spouse may transfer assets to the other spouse and receive a tax deduction for the entire value of the property transferred.[44]

Such transfers may be accomplished during life or at death and either by outright gift or through gifts in trust (for the benefit of the other spouse).

The first spouse to die may leave his or her entire estate to the surviving U.S. citizen spouse without triggering the Estate Tax (payable on the death of the second spouse).[45] Thus, any Estate Tax owed by the first spouse to die may be delayed (by devising the deceased's estate to the surviving spouse). This concept is known as the "unlimited" marital deduction.

---

[44] IRC §2523(a) and (i); §2056(a).

[45] IRC §2056(a). Under this code section, a deduction is allowed for "*any interest in property which passes or has passed from the decedent to his surviving spouse*" (emphasis added).

A U.S. citizen or resident may also "port" his or her individual exclusion amount (currently $11,700,000[46]) to the surviving spouse. Any exclusion amount not used by the first spouse to die (by lifetime and testamentary non-spousal gifts) may be transferred (or "ported") to the qualifying surviving spouse.[47] The total amount of property excluded from the Estate Tax ($11,700,000 times two, or $23,400,000) may therefore be "pooled" by U.S. spouses (and applied against the taxable estate of the second spouse to die).

Certain limitations are, however, imposed on the marital deduction for property transferred to a non-U.S. citizen spouse (even if the recipient spouse is a U.S. resident). The restrictions are discussed in the following sections.

---

[46] IRC §2010(c)(3)(A), (B).
[47] IRC §2010(c)(4).

Questions

Why would a wealthy U.S. couple use the entire unified credit of the first spouse to die (upon the death of such spouse) instead of "porting" the remaining credit of the deceased to the survivor?

CHAPTER 4
TESTAMENTARY TRANSFERS TO NON-CITIZEN SPOUSES

<u>Marital Deduction for Bequests</u>

The unlimited marital deduction (sheltering spousal bequests by a U.S. citizen or resident) is restricted for transfers to a surviving non-citizen spouse. A surviving non-citizen spouse may not generally receive a bequest (from a citizen or resident deceased spouse) tax-free.[48] The restriction is intended to limit the risk of the surviving non-citizen spouse (even if a U.S. resident) leaving the U.S. with the decedent's taxable estate. A shift in domicile by the surviving (non-citizen) spouse could allow for avoidance of Estate Tax, as the survivor (with the estate assets) could permanently leave the U.S. and elude Estate Tax on "worldwide" assets. Titling (during marriage) marital assets (especially assets not located in the U.S.) in the name of the non-citizen spouse should be considered if the intention is for the survivor to leave the U.S. A NRNC surviving spouse is subject to Estate Tax only on U.S. situs assets.

---

[48] IRC §2056(d)(1).

Private Letter Ruling 9017015, IRC Sec(s). 2056

Date: January 25, 1990

Dear

This letter responds to your authorized representative's letter dated September 18, 1989, requesting a ruling on the qualification of the reformed trust in Decedent's estate for a martial deduction under section 2056(d) of the Internal Revenue Code.

The Decedent died testate on Date 1 survived by his spouse, A, and his son, B. Both the Decedent and A at all pertinent times were permanent resident aliens. The Decedent provided for A in Article Fourth of his Will as follows: "I give, devise and bequeath one-half (1/2) of my residuary estate to my wife, [A], if she survives me, or if she predeceases me to my son, [B]."

On Date 2, the executor of the estate petitioned the local court to reform the Decedent's Will to create a testamentary trust qualifying as a for the marital deduction under section 2056(d) of the Code. The court granted the reformation by Order dated Date 3.

Article Fourth of the Decedent's Will, as reformed, provides that one half of the Decedent's residuary estate shall be placed in trust for A. All income is to be paid at least quarterly to or for the use of A. Principal may be paid to or for the use of A in such sums as the Trustees deem advisable or as A requests in writing. On A's death, all accrued and unpaid income and all remaining principal is to be paid to A's estate. The executor is authorized to elect to have property in the trust qualify for the martial deduction pursuant to section 2056A of the Code. Furthermore, no individual who is not a United States citizen and no corporation that is not a United States domestic corporation shall act as trustee of the trust. The trustees, when necessary to maintain the trusts qualification under section 2056A, have the power to amend the trust.

Section 2001 of the Code imposes a tax on the transfer of the taxable estate of every decedent who is a citizen or resident of the United States.

Section 2056(a) of the Code provides that for purposes of the tax imposed by section 2001, the value of the taxable estate is to be determined except as limited by subsection (b), by deductions from such value any interest in property which passes or has passed from the decedent to his surviving spouse but only to the extent that such property is included in determining the value of the gross estate.

For purposes of the tax imposed by section 2001 of the Code, for decedents dying after November 10, 1988, section 2056(d)(1) as added to the Code by the Technical and Miscellaneous Revenue Act of 1988 (TAMRA), disallows the federal estate tax marital deduction under section 2056(a) where the surviving spouse is not a United States citizen.

Section 2056(d)(2)(A) of the Code provides an exception to the disallowance for property passing to a noncitizen surviving spouse in a QDT. Section 2056(d)(2)(B), amended by section 7815(d)(4) of Public Law 101-239, 103 Stat. 2106, provides that if any property passes from the decedent to the surviving spouse of the decedent, for purposes of subparagraph (A), such property shall be treated as passing to such spouse in a QDT if (i) such property is transferred to such a trust before the date on which the return of the tax imposed by this chapter is made, or (ii) such property is irrevocably assigned to such a trusts under an irrevocable assignment made on or before such date which is enforceable under local law.

Section 2056(d)(4)(A) of the Code, added by section 7815(d)(8) of Pub. L. 101-239 provides time for reforming a trust to meet QDT requirements. The new section states that, in the case of any property with respect to which a deduction would be allowable under subsection (a) but for this subsection, the determination of whether a trust is a qualified domestic trust shall be made (i) as of the date on which the return of the tax imposed by this chapter is made, or (ii) if a judicial proceeding is commenced on or before the due date (determined with regard to extensions) for filing such return to change such trust into a trust which is a qualified domestic trust, as of the time when the changes pursuant to such proceeding are made.

Under Section 2056A(a) of the Code, as amended by section 7815(d)(7)(A) of Pub. L. 101-239, a QDT is defined as any trust if --

(1) the trust instrument requires that at least 1 trustee of the trust be an individual citizen of the United States or a domestic corporation and that no distribution form the trust may be made without the approval

of such a trustee,

(2) The surviving spouse of the decedent is entitled to all the income from the property in such trust, payable annually or at more frequent intervals,

(3) the trust meets such requirements as the Secretary may by regulations prescribe to ensure the collection of any tax imposed by sub section 2056A(b), and

(4) an election is made by the executor of the decedent with respect to such trust.

Under section 2056A(b) of the Code, an estate tax is imposed on any distribution before the date of death of the surviving spouse from a QDT other than a distribution of income as required by section 2056A(a)(2). In addition, a tax is imposed on the value of the property remaining in a QDT on the date of death of the surviving spouse. The estate tax is also imposed if the trust ceases to meet the requirements of a QDT at any time or if the trust ceases to meet the requirements for the collection of tax that may be prescribed by the Secretary in regulations. The amount of the tax is the additional federal estate tax that would have been imposed had the property subject to the tax been included in the estate of the first spouse to die.

In the present case, but for the sub section 2056(d) of the Code, the estate would have been permitted a marital deduction under section 2056(a) for the outright bequest of one-half of the Decedent's estate to A. However, non-marital deduction is permitted for property passing to resident aliens spouses unless the property is, by the time of the filing of the estate tax return, either in the form of a QDT or has been irrevocably transferred to a trust that is good for local law purposes. Here, a judicial proceeding was commenced prior to the due date of the estate tax return and the property was irrevocably transferred to a trust valid under state law before the due date of the return (with regard to extensions.) Pursuant to the Date 3 Order, one-half of the Decedent's residuary estate was transferred to a trust for the sole benefit of A. A will receive all the income at least quarterly and can demand principal payments at any time. In addition, the remainder of the trust, including accrued but undistributed income and principal will be distributed to A's estate to A's death. Finally, the trust provides that all of the trustees of the Trust must be either United States citizens or Domestic Corporations. Consequently, as of the due date of the estate tax return, the bequest to A meets the requirements of section 2056(d)(2) and 2056A(a) and is a qualified domestic trust. Accordingly, if a proper election is made, the estate will be eligible for a marital deduction under section 2056. However, principal distributions, if any, will be taxed in accordance with section 2056A(b). Except as specifically provided herein, no opinion is expressed as to the consequences of this transaction under any other provision of the Code.

This ruling is directed only to the taxpayer who requested it. Section 6110(j)(3) of the Code provides that is may not be used or cited as precedent. Temporary or final regulations pertaining to one or more of the issues addressed in this ruling have not yet been adopted. Therefore, this ruling will be modified or revoked by adoption of temporary or final regulations to the extent the regulations are inconsistent with any conclusion in the ruling. See section 17.07 of Rev. Proc. 90-1, 1990-1 I.R. 8. However, when the criteria in section 17.07 of Rev. Proc. 90-1 are satisfied, a ruling is not revoked or modified retroactively except in rare or unusual circumstances.

In accordance with the power of attorney on file with this office, a copy of this letter is being sent to the attorney.

Sincerely,

Assistant Chief Counsel
(Passthroughs and Special
Industries)
By: Lee A. Dunn
Senior Technician Reviewer

Qualified Domestic Trusts

Any U.S. citizen or resident may defer Estate Tax on testamentary transfers to a non-citizen spouse through a special trust. The grantor spouse must leave his or her estate to a "qualified domestic trust" ("QDOT"),[49] as a condition to receiving the marital deduction. The fiduciary of the estate must make the QDOT election on the deceased spouse's Estate Tax return. In the absence of an Estate Tax treaty, only through the QDOT may Estate Tax (on assets held by a U.S. citizen or resident spouse) be deferred until the death of a surviving non-citizen spouse.

Transfers to QDOTs thus qualify for the marital deduction. Distributions from a QDOT of trust principal are subject to the Estate Tax. To qualify for the marital deduction, the deceased's property must pass either (i) directly to a QDOT before filing the deceased's estate tax return,[50] or (ii) from the NRNC recipient spouse (to the QDOT) within nine months of the decedent's death.

Restrictions limit who may act as a QDOT trustee. Trustee distributions are also restricted, to ensure payment of U.S. income tax[51] (with certain exclusions for QDOTs with minimal assets and for QDOTs holding the personal residence of the non-citizen spouse).

If the surviving non-citizen spouse becomes a U.S. citizen before the deceased's Estate Tax return is filed, direct bequests to the survivor will qualify for the marital deduction. If the surviving spouse later becomes a U.S. citizen, all QDOT assets may then be distributed directly to the survivor (free of tax, through the marital deduction).

---

[49] IRC §2056(d)(2)(A); §2056A.
[50] §2056(d).
[51] Treas. reg. §20.2056A-2.

To qualify for the marital deduction, the QDOT must (i) be executed under U.S. law,[52] (ii) have at least one trustee that is a U.S. citizen or U.S. corporation, and (iii) not allow for distributions unless the trustee has the right to withhold tax on transfers from the trust to the surviving (non-citizen) spouse.[53] The executor of the first spouse to die must elect to treat the trust as a QDOT and pass property directly to the QDOT.[54] Certain other mandatory trustee powers must be included to secure U.S. tax compliance.

Any distributions of principal from the QDOT to the surviving noncitizen spouse are subject to the Estate Tax at the time of distribution. Any principal remaining upon the death of the non-citizen spouse will also be subject to Estate Tax (as part of the estate of the first spouse to die). Distributions of income are not subject to the Estate Tax.[55]

Treasury regulations permit a modified "portability" election to be made (to allow a surviving non-citizen spouse to utilize the deceased's unused Estate Tax exemption).[56] Estates of NRNC spouses may not, however, elect portability.[57]

The modified portability credit (applied through the QDOT) delays imposition of Estate Tax until the death of the second (non-citizen) spouse. Upon the death of the non-citizen spouse, the first spouse's unused Estate Tax exemption is applied. The determination of the amount of exemption (left by the first spouse to die) involves a series of valuation procedures. The formula is influenced by the appreciation or depreciation of assets in the QDOT.

---

[52] Treas. Reg. §20-2056A-2(a).
[53] IRC §2056A(a)(1)(B).
[54] IRC §2056A(a)(3).
[55] IRC §2056A(b)(3)(A).
[56] Treas. Reg. §20.2010-2(a)(5).
[57] *Id.*

Rules of administration exempt the QDOT from "foreign trust" status (and the associated onerous reporting requirements).[58]

---

[58] IRC §7701(a)(30), IRC §7701(a)(31).

Private Letter Ruling 201421006

Date: 5/23/2014

Dear [Redacted Text]:

This letter responds to your authorized representative's letter dated August 15, 2013, and other correspondence requesting an extension of time under §301.9100-3 of the Procedure and Administration Regulations to satisfy the requirements for a qualified domestic trust under section 2056A of the Internal Revenue Code.

Decedent, a United States citizen, died on Date 1, survived by Spouse, who is not a United States citizen. Spouse is a resident and a citizen of Country. At his death, Decedent created a trust (Trust) to be held for the benefit of Spouse during her life. Trust is administered under the laws of State.

Trust provides that Trust shall at all times have at least one acting U.S. Trustee that is either an individual who is a United States citizen or a qualified domestic corporation. To the extent an effective election is required to be made to qualify Trust for the estate tax marital deduction, the trustee is directed to amend or reform the terms of Trust as may be required to comply with federal estate tax statutes and regulations relating to the allowance of a marital deduction for property passing to a spouse who is not a United States citizen.

The executor of Decedent's estate timely filed the estate tax return Form 706 (United States Estate and Generation-skipping Transfer Tax Return) on Date 2. The return, on Schedule M, includes the executor's election to treat Trust as a qualified domestic trust (QDOT) within the meaning of §2056A.

Executor now seeks an extension of time to amend Trust to provide that Trust shall at all times have at least one acting U.S. Trustee that is a bank as defined in §581, as required by §20.2056A-2(d)(1)(i)(A) of the Estate Tax Regulations for the Bank Trustee security alternative. Trust will further provide that no distribution of principal shall be made from Trust without the approval of the corporate trustee that is then serving as the U.S. Trustee.

Section 2001(a) imposes a tax on the transfer of the taxable estate of every decedent who is a citizen or resident of the United States.

Section 2056(a) provides that, for purposes of the tax imposed by §2001, the value of the taxable estate is determined by deducting from the value of the gross estate an amount equal to the value of any interest in property that passes or has passed from the decedent to the surviving spouse.

Section 2056(d)(1)(A) provides that if the surviving spouse is not a citizen of the United States, no deduction shall be allowed under §2056(a). Under §2056(d)(2)(A), §2056(d)(1)(A) will not apply to any property passing to the surviving spouse in a qualified domestic trust.

Under §2056A, in order for a trust to qualify as a QDOT: (1) the trust instrument must require that at least one trustee of the trust be an individual citizen of the United States or domestic corporation and that no distribution other than a distribution of income may be made from the trust unless a trustee who is an individual citizen of the United States or a domestic corporation has the right to withhold from the distribution the additional estate tax imposed by §2056A(b)(1) on the distribution; (2) the trust must meet the requirements that are prescribed under Treasury regulations to ensure the collection of the tax imposed by §2056A(b); and (3) the executor must make the election prescribed by §2056A(d) to treat the trust as QDOT.

Section 20.2056A-2(d)(1)(i) provides, in part, that if the fair market value of the assets passing to the QDOT exceeds $2 million as of the date of the decedent's death, the trust instrument must meet the requirements of either paragraph (d)(1)(i)(A), (B), or (C) of §20.2056A-2 at all times during the term of the QDOT.

Section 20.2056A-2(d)(1)(i)(A) provides, in part, that the trust instrument must provide that whenever the Bank Trustee security alternative is used for the QDOT, at least one U.S. Trustee must be a bank as defined in §581.

Section 301.9100-1(c) provides, in part, that the Commissioner has discretion to grant a reasonable extension of time under the rules set forth in §§301.9100-2 and 301.9100-3 to make a regulatory election, or a statutory election (but no more than six months except in the case of a taxpayer who is abroad), under all

81

subtitles of the Internal Revenue Code except in subtitles E, G, H, and I.

Section 301.9100-2 provides automatic extensions of time for making certain elections. Section 301.9100-3 provides extensions of time for making elections that do not meet the requirements of §301.9100-2.

Section 301.9100-3 sets forth the standards that the Commissioner uses to determine whether to grant an extension of time to make an election whose due date is prescribed by a regulation (and not expressly provided by statute). These standards indicate that the Commissioner should grant relief when the taxpayer provides evidence proving to the satisfaction of the Commissioner that the taxpayer acted reasonably and in good faith, and that granting relief will not prejudice the interests of the government. Based on the facts submitted and the representations made, we conclude that the requirements of §301.9100-3 have been satisfied. Therefore, the executor is granted an extension of time until 120 days after the date of this letter to: (i) amend Trust to meet the requirements of §20.2056A-2(d)(i)(A), and (ii) file with the Internal Revenue Service a supplemental Form 706 with a copy of the amended Trust. The supplemental Form 706 should be filed with the Internal Revenue Service Center, Cincinnati OH 45999. A copy of this letter should also be attached to the return.

In accordance with the Power of Attorney on file with this office, a copy of this letter is being sent to your authorized representative.

The ruling contained in this letter is based upon information and representations submitted by the taxpayer and accompanied by a penalty of perjury statement executed by an appropriate party. While this office has not verified any of the material submitted in support of the request for ruling, it is subject to verification on examination.

Sincerely yours,
Lorraine E. Gardner
Senior Counsel, Branch 4
(Passthroughs & Special Industries)

Questions

Under what circumstances (from a U.S. Estate Tax perspective) should a non-U.S. citizen spouse consider becoming a U.S. citizen?

Under what circumstances should the non-U.S. citizen spouse remain a non-citizen?

When should a non-resident spouse (of a U.S. citizen or resident) avoid U.S. residency?

What was the policy basis for the QDOT?

CHAPTER 5
LIFETIME GIFTS TO CITIZEN
AND NON-CITIZEN SPOUSES

Only citizens enjoy an unlimited deduction (i.e., no tax imposed) for lifetime spousal gifts.[59] Similar to the restriction on tax-free testamentary gifts to non-citizen spouses, tax-free lifetime gifts are also limited. If the spouse receiving a lifetime gift is not a U.S. citizen, the gifting spouse may only deduct $149,000 in tax-free spousal gifts during any calendar year.[60]

The limitation on lifetime gifts applies even if both spouses are domiciled in the U.S. at the time of the gift. The domicile of the donor and donee is irrelevant. Annual lifetime gifts to non-citizen spouses are thus taxed on value exceeding $149,000 (adjusted annually for inflation). Interestingly, the limitation on gifts to non-citizen spouses does not limit tax-free gifts by a non-citizen spouse to a U.S. citizen spouse.

A NRNC considering U.S. residency should generally make any intended large spousal gifts of foreign property and U.S. intangible property (free of Estate and Gift Tax) before moving to the U.S. Once domiciled in the U.S., the grantor becomes subject to the Gift Tax on all assets held worldwide (along with the $149,000 limited deduction on spousal gifts to a non-citizen spouse).

To avoid Gift Tax on spousal gifts to a foreign spouse, a U.S. spouse may: (i) make gifts through shared title, as tenants by the entireties (if available) or joint tenancy with rights of survivorship; (ii) apply (to the extent available) his or her remaining Estate and

---

[59] IRC §2523(i).
[60] IRC §2523(i)(2). The deduction was initially set at $100,000 in 1989, indexed for inflation.

Gift Tax exclusion (against the value of gifts exceeding the limitation on gifts to a non-citizen spouse); or (iii) defer the spousal gift until death. Unfortunately, joint titling will only defer transfer tax until the death of the donor spouse, when Estate Tax is due on all jointly titled U.S. situs assets (unless contributed to a QDOT).[61] Deferral of the gift until death will potentially avoid Estate Tax entirely through either (i) testamentary transfers to a QDOT trust (explained on page 28 above) or (ii) applying the grantor's Estate Tax Credit (to the extent sufficient to cover the value of the gift).[62]

---

[61] IRC §2040(a); *see also* Treas. Reg. §20.2056A-8.
[62] *Id.*

Questions

What is the policy reasoning for imposing Gift Tax on gifts to non-citizen spouses (above the current (limited) deduction)?

CHAPTER 6
ESTATE TAX IMPOSED ON
NON-RESIDENT NON-CITIZENS

Property "Situated in the United States"

The Estate Tax imposed on NRNCs[63] is limited to property owned "which at the time of the NRNC's death is situated in the United States."[64] The U.S. taxable estate of a NRNC also includes U.S. assets held in a foreign or U.S. trust generally controlled by or accessible to the NRNC.[65] The NRNC receives a tax credit (against the Estate Tax) for any tax paid to a foreign jurisdiction arising on death and imposed on the value of the decedent's assets.[66]

To avoid the Estate Tax, the NRNC should avoid owning or controlling assets "situated" in the United States. To determine where an asset is "situated," one must first look to the U.S. Treasury Regulations which deem certain assets U.S. "situs" property.[67] Assets deemed located in the U.S. include U.S. real estate, stock in U.S. corporations and certain tangible personal property.[68] Determining the "situs" of other assets is a more factual inquiry.[69] Factors include the owner's rights to the asset and the connections between the asset and a given country.

---

[63] IRC §2101.
[64] IRC §2103.
[65] *See* Treas. Reg §20.2104-1(a).
[66] Rev. Rul. 82-82, 1982-1 C.B. 127; *see also* IRC §2014.
[67] *Id.*
[68] IRC §2104; Treas. Reg. §§20.2104-1, 20.2105-1 (with respect to property not deemed located within the U.S.).
[69] *Id.*

Estate of Fabbricotti Fara Forni v. Commissioner,
Board of Tax Appeals, 1942.
47 BTA 76.

Van Fossan, Judge:

OPINION

The respondent determined a deficiency of $8,459.70 in the estate tax of the estate of Annina Fabbricotti Fara Forni. The petitioner claims an overpayment of $9,434.71.

The petition raised several issues, all of which have been settled except the question whether or not a fund of $41,020.48, held by the United States Trust Co., constituted "moneys deposited" within the meaning of that phrase as found in section 303 (e) of the Revenue Act of 1926, as amended by section 403 (d) of the Revenue Act of 1934.

The facts were stipulated and as so stipulated we adopt them as our findings of fact. In so far as they are material to the issue they are substantially as follows:

Annina Fabbricotti Fara Forni, the decedent, died on June 29, 1938. On November 22, 1938, the petitioner, United States Trust Co., of New York, hereinafter referred to as the trust company, was duly appointed as executor of the last will and testament of the decedent and duly qualified as such executor. On August 31, 1939, the executor filed with the collector of internal revenue for the second district of New York a Federal estate tax return, wherein the executor elected that the value of the gross estate should be determined as of the date of distribution, May 22, 1939, in accordance with subdivision (j) of section 811 of the Internal Revenue Code.
On the return under schedule C, "Mortgages, Notes and Cash", the executor, among other items, reported the following as part of the decedent's gross estate:

	Subsequent valuation date	Value under option	Value at date of death
Cash in Custodian Account at United States Trust Company of New York___	5/22/39	$41,020.48	$41,020.48

On or about November 29, 1939, the executor sent to the collector of internal revenue for the second district of New York a letter reading as follows:

November 28, 1939.
Collector of Internal Revenue,
    Second District of New York,
        Custom House, New York, N. Y.
            In re: Annina Fabbricotti Fara
Forni Estate

Sir: Referring to the estate tax return on Form 706 filed by this Company as executor of the estate of Annina Fabbricotti Fara Forni, who died June 29, 1938, a resident of Lugano, Switzerland, and an Italian citizen, which return was filed in your office on August 31, 1939, we would say that upon further examination we find that Item 18 in Schedule C reading as follows:

	Subsequent Valuation	Value at Date	Option of Death
Cash in Custodian Account at United States Trust Company of New York_____	5/22/39	$41,020.48	$41,020.48
Should read as follows: "Cash on deposit with United States Trust Company of New York in checking account___		$0.00	0.00"

The decedent was not engaged in business within the United States at the time of her death and was a non-resident, and hence the moneys so deposited are specifically excluded from gross estate under subdivision e of section 303 of the Revenue Act of 1934.

This change will result in reducing Item 1 of Schedule R to $501,470.72 and correspondingly Item 12 to $473,895.99, with a corresponding reducing in tax.
We would also request that the appropriate adjustment in tax be had upon the audit of the return.
Yours very truly,
United States Trust Company of New York
By As Executor of the Estate of
    Annina Fabbricotti Fara Forni.

At the time of her death the decedent was a citizen of the Kingdom of Italy and resided at Lugano, Switzerland, and was a non-citizen (*sic*) not a resident of the United States, and was not engaged in business in the United States of America.

The trust company was duly incorporated by the Legislature of the State of New York on April 12, 1853. At all times material hereto, the Banking Law of the State of New York provided that:

Every trust company incorporated by a special law shall possess the powers of trust companies incorporated under this chapter and shall be subject to such provisions of this chapter as are not inconsistent with the special laws relating to such specially chartered company.

During all the years material hereto, the trust company conducted a general banking and trust business in the city of New York. It did not have any savings department or savings accounts. The greater part of the trust company's business consisted of acting as agent, custodian, executor, administrator, guardian, trustee, and committee and in other fiduciary capacities. The draft accounts which it maintained for customers who were not in one way or another related to its business as agent, custodian, executor, etc., above referred to, were few in number, but the balances carried in such accounts were large in amount.

On or about May 15, 1902, the decedent, then known as Annina F. Kingsley, delivered to the trust company certain securities and mortgages owned by her and the sum of $10,000 in cash or check, under an agreement no copy of which can be found at the present time.

Thereupon the trust company opened on its books two accounts in the name of the decedent, one referred to as a "Property Account" and the other bearing no title, but which after November 1924 was termed "Agency Account." These accounts were thereafter continuously maintained by the trust company and were in existence at the time of her death. The latter account will be referred to as "Agency Account."

In the property account in the name of the decedent the trust company included and listed the securities in the possession of the trust company which the decedent from time to time owned, but the property account did not include any cash. The property account referred to above was contained in a ledger known as a "Property Ledger", which contained accounts for all personal property for which the trust company acted as agent, custodian, executor, administrator, guardian, trustee, or committee, or in other fiduciary capacities, under written instruments or otherwise. No cash was ever entered in the property ledger. Where acting as agent, custodian, or fiduciary, any cash transactions, including receipts and disbursements of either income or corpus, were entered in a separate account for each trust, estate, etc., or person, which included only cash. With respect to decedent and any trust, estate, or property for whom the trust company acted, the company kept no separate account in its banking department as distinguished from the accounts hereinabove described.

The trust company credited to the decedent the sum of $10,000 in the agency account and thereafter credited to the decedent in the agency account all sums of money from time to time received by the trust company from the decedent or for her account, whether by way of principal or income, including, among other things, cash, proceeds of the sale of investments, and other property, interest, dividends, and other sums of money.

During all the years material hereto the trust company collected the income on the securities and investments included in the property account. The percentage commission which the trust company charged for collecting income for the decedent's account was substantially the same as was charged for collecting the income for any other account where the corpus or principal was in an amount substantially similar to the amount of securities held for the decedent or where the amount of income was comparable.

About the year 1924 the trust company became trustee of a trust created under the will of decedent's former husband, H. S. Kingsley, under the terms of which the decedent was entitled to the income for life on certain trust corpus. Accounts for such trust were kept by the trust company and the income from the trust for the benefit of decedent was regularly credited to her agency account.

It was the general practice of the trust company to advise the decedent concerning suitable investments and, upon instructions from her, to make investments. The purchase price of securities was charged to the agency account. There were also charged to that account expenses in connection with the foreclosure of mortgages, income taxes, purchases of foreign exchange, collection commissions, and other items. Collections of income and proceeds of sales of securities were credited to the agency account.

The decedent filed signature cards with the trust company on February 24, 1906, and again on November 30, 1931. It is not known whether the words "Agency Account" written by the trust company on the signature card of February 24, 1906, were placed thereon before or after the filing thereof with the trust company.

From time to time after the opening of the account the decedent drew drafts or checks upon the trust company to the number of at least 569, which were duly paid by the trust company on presentation and charged against the agency account.

The items credited to the agency account consisted principally of interest, dividends, the sale of stock rights, amounts received from the executors of the H. S. Kingsley estate, amounts deposited, the sale of securities, and other similar entries. The items debited to the account consisted largely of drafts, commissions on income account, purchases of stocks and bonds, income tax payments, amounts cabled abroad, and minor charges relating to real estate.

At all times material to this issue the trust company maintained in its own name an account with the Bank of the Manhattan Co., in which account the trust company deposited all sums of money which it received from all sources, including, among other things, agency accounts, draft accounts, trust accounts, income from loans, investments, and other property owned by the trust company, income from investments and other property held by it as executor, administrator, guardian, trustee, or other fiduciary capacity, income from investments and other property held by the trust company as custodian or agent, proceeds of loans made by the trust company in the regular course of business, proceeds from the sale of investments and other property owned by the trust company, or held by it as executor, administrator, guardian, trustee, or other fiduciary capacity, or held by the trust company as custodian or agent, and commissions for services rendered by the trust company; and from which account the trust company from time to time withdrew and paid all sums of money required in connection with its business, including among other things, salaries of officers and employees, operating expenses, corporation taxes, real estate and other taxes, dividends to stockholders of the trust company, interest, loans made in the regular course of its business, purchase price of investments and other property purchased by the trust company, or acquired by it as executor, administrator, guardian, trustee, or other fiduciary, or held by the trust company as custodian or agent, and moneys remitted to or for the account of customers, beneficiaries, distributees, and others.

The trust company was not a member of the New York Clearing House Association, and all checks or drafts which it received from all sources were cleared by the Bank of the Manhattan Co. through the said account.

All sums of money received by the trust company and credited to the accounts maintained with it, including the decedent's agency account, were deposited by the trust company in the account maintained by it in the name of the trust company with the Bank of the Manhattan Co., and all sums of money charged against the accounts maintained with the trust company, including the decedent's agency account, were paid by the trust company's check drawn on its account with the Bank of the Manhattan Co., except items covered by the trust company's debit slips or other office or bookkeeping memoranda. Between May 15, 1902, and June 16, 1933, the trust company credited to the agency account of the decedent interest on daily balances at rates varying from one-fourth percent to 3 percent.

On December 10, 1907, the decedent wrote to the trust company a letter reading as follows:

43 Fifth Avenue.
Henry E. Ahern, Esq.
Secretary

Dear Sir: I find my account ending with a balance on November 15th ($7,793.37) seven thousand seven hundred and ninety-three dollars and thirty seven cents, quite correct and please accept my thanks. I am once more in this country and shall be at 43 Fifth Ave. for some months. Will you please let me know what interest the U. S. is paying on deposits and how much commissions I am being charged, and oblige
Yours sincerely,
Annina F. Kingsley

Tuesday, December Tenth/07

and on December 11, 1907, the trust company replied as follows:

December 11th, 1907.

Mrs. Annina F. Kingsley,
43 Fifth Avenue, New York.

Dear Madam: Replying to your favor of 10th instant, we beg to say that we are paying 2% interest on your deposit with us, and charging 2% commission on the income collected.
Yours very truly,

Henry E. Ahern

Secretary.

In each of the published statements of the trust company from 1902 to June 30, 1938, the item designated as "Deposits" included the balance standing to the credit of the decedent in the agency account in various sums ranging from $2,203.03 to $41,020.48. The item of "Deposits" included the amount of cash shown as a credit balance in all the accounts maintained with the trust company, whether the trust company was acting as a fiduciary or otherwise.

In each of the published statements the item designated as "Interest on Deposits" included accrued interest on all of the accounts on which the trust company was paying interest. In none of the published statements was there included the securities of the decedent held and listed in the property account, nor was there included in the statements any property (other than cash) for which the petitioner was acting as fiduciary or in any other capacity. The cash represented by the credits or balance in any of the trust company's accounts where the trust company was acting as fiduciary or otherwise was never kept separate from other funds or earmarked in any way.

Since January 1, 1934, all cash accounts maintained with the trust company have been insured by the Federal Deposit Insurance Corporation to the extent provided by statute, and since that date the trust company has paid to the Federal Deposit Insurance Corporation insurance premiums at the rates fixed by statute. In determining the sums of money upon which such insurance premiums were computed and paid to the Federal Deposit Insurance Corporation under the Federal Deposit Insurance Act, there were included the balances to the credit of the decedent in the agency account, and the balances in all cash accounts maintained with the trust company, whether it was acting in a fiduciary capacity or otherwise.

In 1932, 1933, and 1934 the trust company charged certain sums of money representing Federal taxes upon checks or drafts drawn against the accounts on its books, including the account of the decedent, and paid the amount of such taxes to the collector of internal revenue for the second district of New York.

It was further stipulated that the use in the stipulation of the word "agency" or of any name or language as descriptive of petitioner's account or status, whether or not in juxtaposition with different names, language, or description, is not to be taken as any admission on the part of respondent that decedent's account is not a trust account or other fiduciary account or that the trust company was not acting in a fiduciary or trust capacity with respect to the decedent's cash which it held.

The statute [1] specifically excludes from the gross estate of a nonresident, not a citizen of the United States and not engaged in business in the United States at the time of his death, all moneys deposited by him with any person carrying on a banking business. It has been stipulated that at the time of her death decedent was a nonresident, was not a citizen of the United States, and was not engaged in business in the United States. It is also agreed that the trust company conducted both a general banking and a trust business. The sole issue before us, therefore, is whether the fund of $41,020.48, held by the trust company, represented "moneys deposited" in a banking institution.

In the absence of any specific agreement governing the dealings between the decedent and the trust company at their inception in 1902, we have only the stipulation of facts and the exhibits from which we may discover the real status of the agency account at the date of the decedent's death. If that account reflects "moneys deposited", the balance therein is not taxable.

The agency account, extending from May 21, 1902, to July 1, 1938, is entered on 86 large ledger sheets, each containing approximately 50 credit items and perhaps from 10 to 20 debit items. Balances were usually struck in May and November of each year. In that account the credits consist chiefly of interest, dividends, cash deposits, and distributions from the Kingsley estate. Occasional credit entries represent the sale of investments and infrequent minor receipts. The debits are principally drafts or checks, 569 or more in number, proceeds from sales of securities, commissions, and expenses incidental to specific transactions.

From a careful consideration of the evidence before us, we are of the opinion that the agency account was predominantly a checking account characterized by the use which patrons of a bank customarily make of such bank accounts. Though there are some facts which tend in the opposite direction, the evidence clearly preponderates to the conclusion stated.

The word "deposit" as found in the statute refers to the generally accepted use of that term in banking parlance.

The term "deposit" has a well accepted meaning in the banking business and has been defined as the act of placing or lodging money in the custody of a bank or banker for safety or convenience to be withdrawn at the will of the depositor or under rules and regulations agreed on. [9 Corpus Juris Secundum, sec. 267, p. 544.]
See Black's Law Dictionary, p. 559.

A general deposit *** is the payment of money into the bank to be repaid on demand, in whole or in part, as called for in any current money and has been defined as a deposit generally to the credit of a depositor to be drawn upon by him in the usual course of banking business. [9 Corpus Juris Secundum, sec. 273.]

A special deposit is a delivery of property, securities or even money to the bank for the purpose of having the same safely kept and the identical thing deposited returned to the depositor, or one for some specific purpose.
*** A special deposit becomes such by specific directions or agreement or through circumstances sufficient to create a trust. [9 Corpus Juris Secundum, sec. 274.]

See also Gimbel Brothers., Inc. v. White, 256 App. Div. 439, 441; 10 N. Y. Supp. 2d. 666, and Marine Bank of Chicago v. Fulton County Bank, 2 Wall. 252, 256.

There is no indication in the record that any deposits or credits were hedged in by any special or limiting restrictions which caused them to be termed "special deposits."

We do not deem it necessary to inquire into the original or immediate source of the credits or into the basis of the debits. The face of the account shows that the amounts noted were received and paid and that the corresponding entries were made in the usual course of business. The balance in the account was constantly maintained subject to the decedent's withdrawal, at her will. If it can be said that the trust company served in a fiduciary capacity with reference to some items, it must also be said that after it had discharged that function it placed the monetary results thereof in the decedent's bank account and made it subject to her demand. It ceased to have fiduciary control over such deposits and, on the contrary, affirmatively transferred the right to and disposition of the deposits to the decedent.

The trust company's treatment of the decedent's agency account, its inclusion of the balances as "deposits" in its reports and statements, and its payment of interest on balances are wholly consistent with this view. Also consistent are its acts in insuring the account and in paying a Federal tax on the checks or drafts which it honored against the account. The facts in the case at bar bring the sum to the decedent's credit on the trust company's books at the date of her death clearly within the definition and concept of the statutory phrase "moneys deposited" and hence the amount in controversy is excluded from the taxable estate under the provisions of section 303 (e), as amended.

The facts in this case make unnecessary a study to determine whether there was legal or legislative justification for respondent's action in interpreting the statute narrowly as appears in G. C. M. 22419, C. B. 1940-2, p. 288. Assuming the correctness of respondent's interpretation, the facts here present entitle petitioner to the exclusion asked.

Decision will be entered under Rule 50.

Rate of Estate Tax and Credit

The rate of Estate Tax imposed on NRNCs is identical to that imposed on U.S. citizens and U.S. residents.[70] The Estate Tax credit for NRNCs is significantly lower than the credit allowed U.S. citizens and residents.[71] NRNCs are allowed only a $13,000 credit against the Estate Tax[72] (which shields $60,000 of U.S. situs property).[73] The credit may not be applied against taxable gifts.

Marital bequests are not taxable but (as discussed at page 115 above) non-citizen spouses must receive testamentary gifts through a QDOT trust. The estate of a NRNC may not elect portability of any unused Estate Tax credit to the surviving spouse.[74]

---

[70] IRC §2101(b)(1).
[71] IRC §2102(b)(1). Unlike the applicable exclusion amount afforded to U.S. citizens and residents, the amount for NRNCs is not indexed for inflation.
[72] *Id.*
[73] *Id.*
[74] Treas. Reg. §20.2010-2(a)(5).

Questions

Why would a NRNC hold U.S. situs assets individually?

How may Estate Tax be avoided on such assets without incurring gift tax?

May U.S. real estate held individually be removed from the Estate Tax net?

How may U.S. assets be converted from tangible to intangible property?

CHAPTER 7
GIFT TAX IMPOSED ON NON-RESIDENT NON-CITIZENS

NRNCs are subject to U.S. Gift Tax on transfers of U.S. assets. Intangible assets are, however, excluded.[75] A non-resident non-citizen may therefore make unlimited gifts of U.S. stocks and bonds free of Gift Tax.

Although neither Congress nor the IRS has defined "intangible property," case law allows for certain generalizations. Assets whose value is derived from contract law or a cause of action similar to contract law are considered intangible property.[76] Such assets include annuities, shares of stock, membership interests and other entity ownership rights.[77] Life insurance policies[78] also qualify as intangible property.[79]

Interestingly, if U.S. securities (or other intangible U.S. assets) are not given away during life, they become subject to Estate Tax upon the NRNC owner's death. To minimize Estate Tax (ultimately payable on death), NRNCs should therefore make lifetime transfers of U.S. intangible property. Note that gifts of currency within the U.S. are taxed as gifts of tangible property.[80] Such taxable gifts include (i) cash gifts, (ii) deposits on account at a U.S. bank transferred to another U.S. bank (by check or wire transfer), and (iii) deposits

---

[75] IRC §2501(a)(2).
[76] Pilgrim's Pride Corp. v. Comm'r, 141 TC 533 (2013); Burnett v. Wells, 289 U.S. 670 (1933).
[77] *See* PLR 9347014, where the IRS ruled that a gift by a Canadian resident-citizen of stock owned in a Canadian corporation was not subject to the Gift Tax.
[78] *Id.*
[79] Citizens Bank of Maryland v. Strumpf, 516 U.S. 16 (1995); IT&S of Iowa, Inc. v. Comm'r, 97 T.C. 496 (1991); PLR 8210055, PLR 773706. Note the distinction between bank deposits (intangible) with physical dollar bills which are held in a safe deposit box (tangible).
[80] *See* GCM 36860 (Nov. 24, 1976).

with a domestic branch of a foreign bank, if such branch is engaged in the commercial banking business.[81]

NRNC gifts of tangible U.S. property are taxed to the extent of value exceeding $15,000 (per donee per year).[82] Smaller gifts fall within the annual Gift Tax exclusion. Unlike gifts made by U.S. residents or citizens, Gift Tax incurred by NRNCs may not be offset against the Estate Tax credit.[83]

There are also significant restrictions on tax-free lifetime gifts to non-citizen spouses. The most significant is the absence of the "unlimited" lifetime marital deduction (discussed at page 115 above).

Generation-Skipping Transfer (GST) Tax[84] also potentially applies to transfers made by a NRNC. A NRNC transferor is subject to GST tax for any transfer of assets subject to Estate or Gift Tax which skips the next generation.[85] NRNC transferors are afforded a GST exemption of $1,000,000.[86]

---

[81] Treas. Reg. §20.2105-1 (tangible property located outside the U.S. is considered situated outside of the U.S. and not subject to tax).
[82] IRC §2503(b)(1).
[83] IRC §2505.
[84] IRC §2601.
[85] *Id.*; *see also* Treas. Reg §26.2663-2
[86] Treas. Reg. §26.2663-2(a).

Questions

Are gifts of bank deposits by NRNCs subject to U.S. gift tax?

Are transfers of paper cash subject to U.S. gift tax (i.e., is cash a tangible asset)? Why?

CHAPTER 8
UNIQUE ASSET CONSIDERATIONS FOR NON-RESIDENT NON-CITIZENS

Transfers of Intangible Property

As noted above, U.S. Gift Tax does not apply to lifetime transfers of "intangible property" by NRNCs.[87] The rule allows for avoidance of the Estate Tax through lifetime gifts of U.S. intangible property (otherwise subject to Estate Tax upon the death of the NRNC).[88] NRNCs may therefore reduce their taxable estate by making lifetime transfers of U.S. intangibles.

Note that certain U.S. intangible assets are excluded from Estate Tax (even if owned by the NRNC at death). These exclusions (discussed below) are integral to U.S. Estate Tax planning for NRNCs.

---

[87] IRC §2501(a)(2).

[88] Treas. Reg. §20.2105-1(e), Treas. Reg. §20.2104-1(a)(4) includes in the estate of a NRNC "intangible personal property the written evidence of which is not treated as being the property itself, if it is not issued by or enforceable against a resident of the United States or a domestic corporation or governmental unit." Thus, if the intangible personal property is enforceable against or issued by a U.S. resident, domestic corporation, or governmental unit, it will be treated as located within the U.S. and brought within the NRNC's gross estate under the "situs" rule.

Bank Deposits

Cash deposits by NRNCs in U.S. banks are not subject to Estate Tax, provided that the deposits are "not effectively connected with the conduct of a trade or business in the United States."[89] Deposits connected with a U.S. trade or business (owned by a NRNC) are excluded from Estate Tax if held in foreign branches of domestic banks.[90] Deposits owned by a NRNC at a U.S. branch of a foreign bank are, however, subject to Estate Tax, "whether or not the decedent was engaged in business in the United States at the time of his death."[91] To qualify as a bank "deposit," the account must be maintained "on behalf of, or 'for' the decedent,"[92] meaning that the decedent must have had a direct and enforceable claim on the specific account.[93]

The concept of having a direct and enforceable claim is addressed in the case of *Estate of Ogarrio v. Commissioner.*[94] The decedent, a non-resident Mexican citizen, was owed money by a brokerage house (from a stock sale). The brokerage house put the sale proceeds into a general account, from which the broker could pay a variety of obligations (not solely the broker's obligation to disburse proceeds to the decedent). The decedent's estate argued that the "cash account" constituted an excluded "deposit" (not subject to Estate Tax).

---

[89] IRC §§ 871(i); 2105(b)(1), by cross reference, excludes amounts not effectively connected with the conduct of a trade or business within the United States, provided such amounts are deposited with entities which are (A) engaged in the banking business, (B) are chartered as savings and loans institutions or similar associations or (C) are held by an insurance company with an agreement to pay interest on those deposits.

[90] IRC §2105(b)(2).

[91] Treas. Reg. §20.2104-1(a)(8).

[92] Estate of Ogarrio v. Comm'r, 40 T.C. 242, 248 (1963).

[93] *Id.*

[94] *Id.*

The Tax Court ruled that the brokerage house was not a bank, concluding that the "cash account" was not a deposit account but rather a general liability of the brokerage to the decedent.[95] The decedent had only a general claim against the debtor for non-payment (rather than an enforceable claim against a specific account).[96] To establish an exempt bank account, the decedent must own or control the account (i.e., have the right to unfettered demand of funds held in the account).

This position is supported by the case of *Estate of Gade v. Commissioner*,[97] which expanded the meaning of "deposit" from conventional savings and checking accounts to custodial accounts. The decedent in *Gade* opened an account with a trust company and executed an agreement, which made the trust company both the agent and custodian of the account. The court concluded that, although the trust company managed the funds, the decedent's directives (in the agency agreement) qualified the account as a "deposit."

Note that a "deposit" is distinct from U.S. paper currency on hand in a physical location. Money is generally treated as a tangible asset (if transferred by a NRNC in the U.S.), subject to Gift Tax (and Estate Tax on death).[98] Gifts of paper currency by a NRNC should therefore be made outside the U.S.

---

[95] *Id.* at 246.
[96] *Id.* at 247.
[97] Gade v. Comm'r, 10 T.C. 585 (1948).
[98] *See* Rev. Rul. 55-143 (holding that the cash in the safe-deposit box on the date of decedent's death were not "moneys deposited" with a person carrying on the banking business within the meaning of section 863(b) of the IRC of 1939, and were thus includible in the decedent's gross estate situated in the U.S.).

U.S. Bonds

U.S. government and corporate bonds considered so-called "portfolio debt" are exempt from Estate Tax.[99] Although the definition of portfolio debt is somewhat ambiguous, bonds issued by the U.S. government and publicly traded U.S. entities are generally excluded from the taxable estate of a NRNC owner/lender. Debt owed by NRNCs is considered a non-U.S. situs asset.

Life Insurance

Life insurance proceeds received by the estate of a NRNC (insured by such policy) are not subject to Estate Tax.[100] The Internal Revenue Code explicitly states that life insurance proceeds (paid on a policy insuring the life of a NRNC) "shall not be deemed property within the United States."[101] Proceeds are therefore not included in the estate of the NRNC owner/insured. This makes life insurance a very attractive asset.

The life insurance exclusion does not apply to the cash surrender value of insurance. Life insurance policies are treated as U.S. situs property if issued by a U.S. insurer. If a NRNC owns a U.S. situs policy on the life of another person (even a family member), the value of the policy forms part of the owner's taxable U.S. estate.

Estate tax on the value of life insurance held by a NRNC (insuring other people) may be avoided by purchasing the insurance from insurers outside the U.S. This avoids

---

[99] IRC §2105(b).
[100] IRC §2105(a).
[101] Id.

ownership of a taxable U.S. situs asset at death. Alternatively, direct ownership of U.S. life insurance on another person may be avoided by holding the policy in a foreign entity.

If life insurance is owned by (and benefits) a foreign corporation, neither the cash value nor the payment of proceeds to the owner (upon the death of the insured) creates a taxable event.

This is the case because life insurance proceeds are not subject to income tax[102] and the foreign entity (owning valuable life insurance) has no taxable estate. Please see page 109 below for a discussion on the use of foreign corporations.

---

[102] IRC §101(a)(1).

<u>Questions</u>

What policies led to the legislation exempting NRNAs from U.S. Estate and Gift Tax on certain assets?

Why does planning (to avoid Estate and Gift Tax) by NRNAs often exclude utilization of such exemptions?

CHAPTER 9
SHIFTING ASSETS FROM U.S. SITUS

Foreign Corporations

Although lifetime gifts of U.S. intangibles by NRNCs are exempt from Gift Tax, all U.S. situs assets (both tangible and intangible, unless exempt) trigger the Estate Tax upon the death of a NRNC owner. Those same assets held in a foreign corporation are, however, excluded from Estate Tax.[103]

The foreign corporation is used to break the Estate and Gift Tax ownership connection of U.S. situs assets to the foreign individual or trust. Shares in a foreign corporation held by a NRNC are considered situated outside the U.S. and subject to neither Gift Tax nor Estate Tax.[104]

Treasury Regulations indicate that the "situs" of an entity is determined by looking at the place where the entity is created or organized.[105] The regulations further state that this test applies "irrespective of the location of the (ownership) certificates."[106] Shares of stock owned by a decedent in a U.S. entity are thus subject to Estate Tax.[107] Conversely, ownership by a NRNC in a foreign corporate entity (if properly organized) is not subject to Estate Tax.[108] The income tax aspects of using an entity taxable as a corporation or partnership should also be carefully considered.

---

[103] IRC §2104(a).
[104] Treas. Reg. §20.2105-1(f).
[105] §301.7701-5(a).
[106] Treas. Reg. §20.2104-1(a)(5); §20.2105-1(f) (shares of stock issued by a foreign corporation are not U.S. situs assets).
[107] Id.
[108] This conclusion is reached because IRC §2104(a) states that shares of stock are treated as having a US "situs" "only if issued by a domestic corporation."

Estate of Garvan,
Board of Tax Appeals, 1932.
25 BTA 612.

Goodrich, Judge:

OPINION

This proceeding is for the redetermination of a deficiency in estate tax of $9,661.04. Petitioner also challenges the validity of the original assessment of estate tax in the amount of $71,914.58, which it has heretofore paid under protest.

The following stipulation was filed:

(1) It is hereby stipulated by and between the parties in the above-entitled action that the following facts are admitted and need not be proved.
(2) The petitioner is the First National Bank of Boston as Administrator of the Estate of Sir John Joseph Garvan. The legal residence of the decedent, Sir John Joseph Garvan, at the time of his death and at the time he made the transfers set forth in paragraph 4 infra was Sydney, New South Wales, Australia. The decedent at the time of his death and at the time he made these transfers was not engaged in any business in the United States. His death occurred on July 18, 1927, and on May 24, 1928, the First National Bank of Boston, a corporation duly organized under the laws of the United States and having a usual place of business in Boston, Massachusetts, was appointed administrator of said Estate with the will annexed by the Probate Court of Suffolk County, Massachusetts.
(3) The gross estate of the decedent within the United States if as a matter of law said property may be included in determining gross estate situated within the United States (not including certain property which he transferred prior to his death, a list of which is set forth in Schedule B infra, and the value of which the Commissioner of Internal Revenue included in the gross estate of the decedent within the United States) consisted of the following securities at the values shown in the last column.

Schedule A	Fair Market Value at Date of Death
Item	
1. 2,300 shs. Swift International _____	$51,750.00
2. 4,102 " Swift & Company _____	480,959.50
3. 798 " Libby, McNeil & Libby _____	6,783.00
4. 933 " National Leather Co _____ _	2,915.63
5. $57,000--Dominion of Canada 5s 1952 _	59,850.00
Interest on above _____	609.58

6. $38,000--Dominion of Canada 5 1/2s 1934 __ 39,282.50
  Interest on above _____ 447.03
7. $50,000--Province of Ontario 6s 1943 ___ 55,625.00
  Interest on above _____ _ 1,025.00
8. $33,000--Province of Ontario 5s 1948 __ 33,825.00
  Interest on above _____ 426.25

    Total _____ 733,498.49

At the time of the decedent's death the securities set out in said Schedule A were held by the said bank; they were not at that time and never had been hypothecated or pledged as security for any debt or obligation nor were they employed in whole or in part in any business carried on in the United States; they were held by said bank solely for the purpose of collection of the income therefrom for the account of the decedent.

(4) On or about October 26, 1926, the decedent transferred by gift outright to his brothers and sisters four identical lots of personal property, the value of all of which the Commissioner of Internal Revenue included in the gross estate of the decedent within the United States under the provisions of the Revenue Act of 1926 for purposes of the Federal Estate Tax. The detailed items contained in each of the four lots are as follows:

Schedule B.	Fair Market Value at Date of Death
Item	
1. 970 shs. Swift & Company __ __ _	$113,732.50
2. 600 " Swift International _____ _	13,500.00
3. 190 " Libby, McNeil & Libby _____	1,615.00
4. 230 " National Leather Co _____	718.75
5. $15,000--Dominion of Canada 5s 1952 _____	15,750.00
Interest on above _____	160.42
6. $2,500--Dominion of Canada 5 1/2s 1934 _____	2,584.38
Interest on above ____ _____	29.41
7. $12,000--Province of Ontario 6s 1943 _____	13,350.00
Interest on above _____	244.00
8. $8,000--Province of Ontario 5s 1948 _____	8,200.00
Interest on above _____	102.22
Total _____	$169,986.68

At the time of said transfer on or about October 26, 1926, the securities set out in Schedule B were held by said bank; from the time of said transfer to the date of death of the decedent they were held by the National City Bank of New York; they were not at any time either before or after said transfer hypothecated or pledged as security for any debt or obligation nor were they employed in whole or in part in any business carried on in the United States; they were held by said banks solely for the purpose of collection of the income therefrom for the account of the decedent prior to said transfer and thereafter for the account of the transferees.

(5) The Commissioner of Internal Revenue has determined the value of the gross estate within the United States to be $1,413,445.21, the details being as follows: 4 times $169,986.68 (total of Schedule B) equals ___ $679,946.72
Total   of   Schedule   A   above   _____   733,498.49

     Grand   total   _____ $1,413,445.21

(6) These four transfers were gifts and were made without an adequate and full consideration in money or money's worth. The petitioner does not admit that these transfers were made in contemplation of death.

(7) All of the bonds included in Schedule A supra were physically present in the United States at the time of the decedent's death. All of the bonds included in Schedule B supra were physically present in the United States at the time the transfers were made. All the certificates of the shares of stock in Schedule A were physically present in the United States at the time of the descendant's death. All the certificates of the shares of stock included in Schedule B were physically present in the United States at the time the transfers were made.

(8) Compania Swift Internacional (Swift International) is a corporation organized under the laws of the Argentine Republic.

(9) There was no property of the decedent in the United States at the time of his death, other than as listed in Schedules A and B herein.

(10) None of the bonds included in Schedule A or in Schedule B was secured by any interest in real estate situate within the United States.

(11) The value of the decedent's gross estate situated outside of the United States was $765,314.49. The amount of the gross deductions from the decedent's estate (Item 4, Schedule M, Federal Estate Tax Return) was $29,999.53.

(12) Either party may introduce further evidence on any of the matters in issue in this case which is not inconsistent with the facts herein stipulated.

Later an additional stipulation was filed presenting a table of the mortality statistics contained in the 29th annual report of the Bureau of the Census, the relevancy and materiality of which is denied by respondent, and showing that a tax of $71,914.58 disclosed by petitioner's estate-tax return filed on May 17, 1928, was paid under protest on the same date.

It is further agreed upon the record that Swift International owned no property within the United States; that Swift & Company, Libby, McNeil & Libby, and National Leather Company are domestic corporations; and that Dominion of Canada bonds and bonds of the Province of Ontario are bonds of a foreign government, not secured by property within the United States.

Petitioner's allegations of error amount to a contention that, because decedent was a nonresident alien, his estate cannot be subjected to an estate tax by the United States. Specifically, it alleges that respondent erred in including in the estate for purposes of taxation:

(1) shares of stock of a foreign corporation, and bonds of foreign governments;

(2) shares of stocks of domestic corporations;

(3) property transferred by decedent by gift, after the effective date of the Revenue Act of 1926 and within two years prior to his death.

Petitioner also alleges that respondent failed to allow as deductions in determining the net estate subject to tax, miscellaneous administration expenses. Such expenses should be allowed on the basis of gross deductions of $29,999.53 in determining the net estate subject to tax in accordance with the stipulation entered into between the petitioner and the respondent.

The provisions of the Revenue Act of 1926 pertinent to the issues here read in part as follows:

Sec. 301. (a) *** a tax *** is hereby imposed upon the transfer of the net estate of every decedent dying after the enactment of this Act, whether a resident or nonresident of the United States. ***

Sec. 302. The value of the gross estate of the decedent shall be determined by including the value at the time of his death of all property, real or personal, tangible or intangible, wherever situated-

(a) To the extent of the interest therein of the decedent at the time of his death;

(c) To the extent of any interest therein of which the decedent has at any time made a transfer, by trust or otherwise, in contemplation of or intended to take effect in possession or enjoyment at or after his death, except in case of a bona fide sale for an adequate and full consideration in money or money's worth. Where within two years prior to his death but after the enactment of this Act and without such a consideration the decedent has made a transfer or transfers, by trust or otherwise, of any of his property, or an interest therein, not admitted or shown to have been made in contemplation of or intended to take effect in possession or enjoyment at or after his death, and the value or aggregate value, at the time of such death, of the property or interest so transferred to any one person is in excess of $5,000, then, to the extent of such excess, such transfer or transfers shall be deemed and held to have been made in contemplation of death within the meaning of this title. Any transfer of a material part of his property in the nature of a final disposition or distribution thereof, made by the decedent within two years prior to his death but prior to the enactment of this Act, without such consideration, shall, unless shown to the contrary, be deemed to have been made in contemplation of death within the meaning of this title;

Sec. 303. (d) For the purposes of this title, stock in a domestic corporation owned and held by a nonresident decedent shall be deemed property within the United States, and any property of which the decedent has made a transfer, by trust or otherwise, within the meaning of subdivision (c) or (d) of section 302, shall be deemed to be situated in the United States, if so situated either at the time of the transfer, or at the time of the decedent's death.

We have previously held that bonds of a foreign government and shares of stock of a foreign corporation owned by the estate of a nonresident decedent, the paper evidences of which were held in this country for certain restricted purposes, as in the case now at bar, may not be included in determining the value of decedent's estate situated in the United States. *Ernest Brooks et al.,* 22 B. T. A. 71. That case arose under the Revenue Act of 1924, the pertinent provisions of which are not materially different from those of the 1926 Act above quoted. Following that decision, we reverse respondent's action in including in decedent's estate the bonds of foreign governments and the shares of stock of a foreign corporation. See also *Shenton* v. *United States,* 53 Fed. (2d) 249.

But, as pointed out in the *Brooks* case, in determining the net estate of a nonresident decedent, section 303 (d) provides that stock of a domestic corporation shall be deemed property within the United States. There is no ambiguity in this statutory provision and it is conceded that the taxability of the shares of stocks of domestic corporations here involved depends squarely upon it. Petitioner urges that such stock was situated outside the United States and, under the rule *mobilia sequuntur personam,* had a situs at the domicile of the owner and contends that so much of section 303 (d) of the Revenue Act of 1926 as operates to tax stock in domestic corporations owned by a nonresident decedent is in conflict with the due process clause of the Fifth Amendment and unconstitutional.

In support of this contention our attention is called to certain recent cases in which the Supreme Court has applied the rule *mobilia sequuntur personam* in fixing the situs of intangible property at the domicile of the owner for the purpose of taxation. *Farmers' Loan & Trust Co.* v. *Minnesota,* 280 U. S., 204; *Baldwin* v. *Missouri,* 281 U. S. 586; *Beidler* v. *South Carolina,* 282 U. S. 1; *Rhode Island Hospital Trust Co.* v. *Doughton,* 270 U. S. 69; *First National Bank of Boston* v. *State of Maine,* 284 U. S. 312. All of these cases arose under the Fourteenth Amendment and, we believe, are not controlling where the power of Congress to tax is considered. These decisions indicate that the underlying reason for the application of the rule to intangibles, as between the States, is to prevent the injustice of double taxation, but this does not apply necessarily, nor has it been held to apply, where the Federal Government imposes a tax. Generally, both the Federal and State Government may tax the same object or the same transfer at the same time, and the taxation by the one is not a limitation upon the taxation by the other. See *Frick* v. *Pennsylvania,* 268 U. S. 473.

The Fourteenth Amendment is a limitation on the power of the States to tax, but the Fifth Amendment under which the issue here arises is not a limitation upon the taxing power of the Federal Government: *McCray* v. *United States,* 195 U. S. 27; *Billings* v. *United States,* 232 U. S. 261; *Flint* v. *Stone Tracy Co.,* 220 U. S. 107; *Brushaber* v. *Union Pacific Railroad Co.,* 240 U. S. 1, *unless* the exercise of the taxing power is so unreasonable and arbitrary as to amount to a confiscation rather than a tax. *Brushaber* v. *Union Pacific Railroad Co., supra; Nichols* v. *Coolidge,* 274 U. S. 531; *Blodgett* v. *Holden,* 275 U. S. 142; 276 U. S. 594; *Untermyer* v. *Anderson,* 276 U. S. 440. For this Board, the clear and definite statutory instruction is stronger authority than the urged analogy and possible application to this case, arising under the Fifth Amendment, of the recent decisions of the Supreme Court invoking and applying the *mobilia* doctrine to cases arising under the Fourteenth Amendment. Here, Congress has expressed a clear intention to tax and if that intention is not consistent with the rule *mobilia sequuntur personam,* we must assume that Congress intended to repeal the rule in so far as it is in conflict. Cf. *In re Whiting's Estate,*

44 N. E. 715.

Petitioner has failed to indubitably demonstrate to us that this statute infringes the constitutional guarantees which he invokes; that the tax here imposed is so arbitrary or unreasonable as to cause us to disregard or reject the explicit provision of the statute under which it is laid. As said by Judge L. Hand in *Cohan* v. *Commissioner,* 39 Fed. (2d) 540, at page 545:

limitations like the Fifth Amendment are not like sailing rules or traffic ordinances; they do not circumscribe the actions of Congress by metes and bounds. *** So it does not seem to us that the situation here calls for so heroic a remedy as to declare the statute unconstitutional, nor indeed, for the lesser one of wringing the words out of their natural meaning. *** while colloquial language is a fumbling means of expression, there are limits to its elasticity; to deny the application of these words to the case at bar seems to us to pass the point of rupture.

Respondent is sustained in including in decedent's estate, for purposes of taxation, the shares of stock in domestic corporations.

We come now to consider petitioner's third issue, in support of which it is urged that section 302 (c) is unconstitutional in so far as it raises a conclusive presumption that gifts made within two years prior to decedent's death were made in contemplation of death. We have so held in *American Security & Trust Co. et al.,* 24 B. T. A. 334. But, as pointed out in that case, section 302 (c) contains two provisions, the first being set out in the first sentence of that section and demanding proof to overcome the presumption of its applicability in any case wherein the Commissioner has made a determination thereunder. It requires that the value of decedent's interest in property which he has *at any time* transferred, except by a bona fide sale, in contemplation of death, or intended to take effect in possession or enjoyment at or after his death, shall be included in the estate for purposes of taxation. Where, acting under authority of that provision, the Commissioner determines that decedent has made such a transfer of an interest in property and includes the value of such interest in decedent's estate, that determination is prima facie correct and the burden of proving it incorrect rests upon the challenger. *Wickwire* v. *Reinecke,* 275 U. S. 101.

In this case respondent has included in decedent's estate the total value of the properties, consisting of shares of stock of domestic and foreign corporations and bonds of foreign governments, which were included in the four transfers made by decedent in October, 1926. Petitioner "does not admit that the transfers were made in contemplation of death." Such a denial, if it be a denial, is not the proof required to rebut respondent's determination, which we must take to be prima facie correct, nor does it serve to shift from petitioner to respondent the burden of proof of the facts relative to the transfers. Nowhere in this record is it indicated that respondent, in so including the property transferred, is relying solely upon the conclusive presumption raised by section 302 (c). On the contrary, the fact that respondent has included in this estate the total value of the properties transferred without deducting therefrom the exemption of $5,000 on each transfer allowed by the second provision of this section, indicates that he has determined as a fact that these transfers were made in contemplation of death.

Nor does it appear upon this record that petitioner was in possession of evidence proving that the transfers in fact were not made in contemplation of death. Petitioner having failed in the proof of facts essential to his contention, we sustain respondent's action in including in decedent's estate the shares of stocks of the domestic corporations embraced by the four transfers. We except, however, the transferred shares of stocks of foreign corporations and the bonds of foreign governments for the reason that, under our decision in the *Brooks* case, *supra,* such stocks and bonds were not situated in the United States, either at the time of the transfer or at the time of decedent's death, as provided in section 303 (d). Consequently, they should not be included in decedent's estate.

Reviewed by the Board.

Judgment will be entered under Rule 50.

A foreign trust formed by a NRNC to invest in U.S. situs assets should make investments through a foreign holding company, to avoid any potential exposure to the Estate Tax on trust assets.[109] Using separate foreign companies to hold different trust assets also segregates corporate liabilities. The holding company must carefully comply with applicable corporate formalities and be treated (for legal, financial and operational purposes) as separate and distinct from its owner(s).

U.S. property transferred by a NRNC to a foreign trust during his or her life remains subject to Estate Tax if the grantor retained at his death the power "to alter, amend, revoke, or terminate" the rights of a trust beneficiary.[110] If the NRNC grantor may revoke or deplete a foreign trust which owns U.S. situs property, the IRS will include in the NRNC's estate any trust assets in the United States.[111] U.S. assets contributed to a foreign trust by a NRNC grantor (with control over the trust) may therefore become subject to Estate Tax upon the grantor's death.

The NRNC grantor of a foreign revocable trust holding U.S. situs property must therefore move trust assets into a foreign holding company (itself owned by the trust) before death. The foreign corporation will generally break the Estate Tax connection to the NRNC. The NRNC grantor may otherwise reduce the risk of incurring Estate Tax by relinquishing control of (and benefit from) the trust. However, if he or she dies within three years after relinquishing such rights, the Estate Tax will not be avoided.[112]

---

[109] See §2104(a).
[110] §2104(b).
[111] §2104(b); *See* Rev. Rul. 55-163, 1955-1 C.B. 674 (situs of equitable interest in conventional private trusts is determined by reference to underlying assets).
[112] IRC §2104(b).

Foreign trust assets may subject a NRNC grantor to Estate Tax even if trust assets are foreign-situs (on the date of the grantor's death).[113] If U.S. property was initially in the trust but was later sold and replaced with foreign assets, such assets may be deemed U.S. if the transfer occurred within three years of the NRNC's death.[114]

Interestingly, transferring U.S. stock in an existing corporation to a foreign holding company may cause a foreign holding company to be treated as a U.S. corporation for tax purposes.[115] Until 2017, the 35% U.S. corporate tax rate was one of the highest on earth and applied to worldwide corporate income. Shifting ownership abroad typically reduced net income tax.

The legislative intent of Code §7874(b) is to block the shift of ownership to a low-income tax jurisdiction. Deemed U.S. corporation status (of a foreign holding company) applies if: (i) the U.S. corporation becomes a subsidiary of a foreign corporation or otherwise transfers substantially all its assets to a foreign corporation; (ii) the former shareholders of the U.S. corporation hold at least 80% of the foreign corporation's stock; and (iii) the foreign corporation does not have substantial business activities in the foreign country of incorporation.[116]

Three common corporate "inversions" (or corporate "expatriations") are as follows. One type is through "substantial activity" or business presence, where a U.S. corporation operating in a foreign country creates a foreign subsidiary. The U.S.

---

[113] IRC §2104.

[114] IRC §2104(b) ("any property of which the decedent has made a transfer, by trust or otherwise, within the meaning of sections 2035 to 2038, inclusive, shall be deemed to be situated in the United States, if so situated either at the time of the transfer or at the time of the decedent's death.").

[115] IRC §7874(b).

[116] *See* H.R. Conf. Rep. No. 108-755, at 560–61 (2004).

shareholder(s) then exchange the U.S. (holding) stock for stock in the subsidiary. The exchange "inverts" the structure, creating foreign ownership of the U.S. entity. This is also called a "naked" inversion and does not result in a change of ultimate control of either corporation.

The second is where a U.S. corporation merges with a foreign corporation. The foreign corporation survives, shifting control and operations outside the U.S.

The third inversion is where a U.S. corporation acquires a smaller foreign corporation (to expatriate corporate residence to the foreign jurisdiction). The U.S. corporation retains control of the newly formed company.

Since 2014, Treasury regulations broaden the regulatory net.[117] Anti-inversion regulations provide that if at least 80% ownership of the new foreign corporation is retained, the offshore entity will be deemed a U.S. corporation and reap no tax benefits from the reorganization. Furthermore, the anti-inversion regulations provide that if the U.S. shareholders retain less than 80% but at least 60% of the new corporation, then the new corporation is not deemed a U.S. corporation, but is prohibited from using U.S. tax credits or net operating losses to offset gains from asset transfers to the new corporation. Also, anti-inversion regulations make it harder for U.S. corporations merging or acquiring a foreign corporation to avoid 80% control (by prohibiting certain techniques prior to the merger, such as inflating the size of the foreign entity, shrinking the U.S. corporation, or inverting only a portion of the U.S. entity).

---

[117] *See* IRS. Notice 2014-52.

Real Property

Real property has tax situs in the jurisdiction in which it is located. Consequently, U.S. real estate (a tangible asset) is included in the taxable estate of a NRNC.[118]

If real estate is instead owned by a foreign corporation (itself owned by the NRNC), the property is excluded from Gift Tax and Estate Tax. The NRNC acquiring U.S. real estate should do so through a foreign corporation. If U.S. real estate is initially purchased directly by the NRNC, the subsequent transfer of the property to an offshore corporation could have tax consequences. Appreciated U.S. real estate held by a NRNC may trigger taxable gain upon transfer to a foreign corporation.[119]

Partnerships

Unlike the rules regarding corporate stock, the tax situs rules for foreign entities taxed as partnerships are ambiguous. The limited case law suggests that a factual examination of the partnership's assets and business activities is necessary to determine the situs of the partnership.[120] The IRS will not rule on exactly how to determine the situs of foreign partnership interests in the hands of a NRNC.[121] Situs may be based on such factors as where the partnership does business or holds assets or where the equity holder resides.

IRS rulings suggest that the taxable estate of an NRNC will include his pro-rata share of U.S. assets held by a foreign partnership if either (i) the country of formation does not recognize the partnership as a legal entity or (ii) the partnership dissolves upon the

---

[118] Treas. Reg. §20.2104-1(a)(1).
[119] IRC §897(j).
[120] *See* Blodgett v. Silberman, 277 U.S. 1 (1928).
[121] Rev. Proc. 2015-7.

death of a partner.[122] In either case, the partnership entity is disregarded and its U.S. assets are deemed owned by the partners (and situated in the United States).[123] A U.S. federal appeals court confirmed that dissolution of a foreign entity upon the death of one of its owners causes its U.S. assets to be included in the NRNC owner's estate.[124]

If the country where the partnership was organized recognizes the partnership as a legal entity (which survives the death of a partner), then equity in the partnership will likely be recognized by the IRS. Situs of equity in the partnership must then be determined.

One court ruled that if equity in a foreign partnership is intangible property, situs is the domicile of the decedent.[125] Treaties (if applicable) typically follow the same logic.

One IRS position is that equity has situs at the business location of the partnership. In any case, the situs of an IRS recognized partnership seems unrelated to the location of partnership property.[126]

If the entity is recognized by the IRS, avoidance of U.S. situs can therefore likely be accomplished by, for example, either, avoiding U.S. operations or holding equity in a foreign corporation. Foreign situs will keep the value of partnership equity outside the U.S. estate of the NRNC partner.

---

[122] *C.f.* Sanchez v. Bowers, 70 F. 2d 715 (2d. Cir. 1934) (reasoning that where the marriage partnership entity in Cuba dissolved upon the death of the husband, it substantially changed the entity such that it would necessarily terminate upon liquidation, and the dissolution of the entity was enough basis to levy an excise tax upon the decedent's share of assets).
[123] Sanchez v. Bowers, 70 F. 2d 715 (2d Cir.1934).
[124] *Id.*
[125] *See* Blodgett v. Silberman, 277 U.S. 1 (1928).
[126] Revenue Ruling 55-701., 1955-2 C.B. 836.

The Limited Liability Company

The clarity of U.S. law establishing the country of organization as situs of "corporate" stock, makes foreign limited liability companies ("LLCs") an attractive option. The LLC is generally more protective of owner equity than the corporation. Although LLC membership interests are not identical to corporate stock, Treasury Regulations treat foreign LLCs as corporations for tax purposes (unless the LLC elects otherwise), if all members have limited liability.[127] If any of the members do not have limited liability, the LLC is treated as a tax partnership.[128] Establishing limited liability is typically not difficult.

If a foreign LLC is treated as a corporation for tax purposes, ownership interests in the LLC are not U.S. situs property and may be transferred tax-free by NRNCs (during life or at death).[129] One planning technique (discussed on page 203) is to own U.S. real estate (or a U.S. real estate holding company) through a foreign LLC (itself owned by the NRNC or a foreign entity). Such structure moves the situs of ultimate ownership offshore (avoiding Estate and Gift Tax). In the case of appreciated real estate (and other U.S. assets subject to U.S. tax on gains from sale), no tax is payable on appreciation until the property itself is sold (irrespective of any transfer of the foreign entity owner).

---

[127] Treas. Reg. §301.7701-3(b)(2)(i)(B). Technically, this section classifies an entity as an "association," but Treas. Reg. §301.7701-2(b)(2) makes clear that this designation is akin to being a corporation.
[128] Treas. Reg. §301.7701-3(b)(2)(i)(A).
[129] *Pierre v. Comm'r*, 133 T.C. 24 (2009) (holding that although a single-member LLC is disregarded for *income tax* purposes, the entity must be respected for *Gift Tax* purposes when determining whether the assets gifted were the LLC's assets or ownership in the LLC itself).

Questions

What is typically the most efficient means for an NRNC to avoid all Estate and Gift tax on otherwise taxable U.S. situs assets?

When should an NRNC hold assets through an offshore partnership?

- Corporation?
- LLC?
- Individually?

Are uncertificated LLC membership interests subject to U.S. Gift Tax?

CHAPTER 10
TREATIES

Double Taxation

People living, investing or doing business in more than one country face exposure to "double" estate and gift tax. This is true because different countries may impose estate or gift tax on the same asset. Two (or more) countries may claim (i) tax situs over the same property or (ii) domicile over the same person (owning taxable property). If two or more countries impose transfer tax on a particular asset or class of assets, tax planning is required.

The U.S. imposes Estate and Gift Tax on its citizens <u>and residents</u>, assessed on the value of assets held anywhere on earth.[130] See page 59 above. Most other countries tax only persons living within their borders.[131] U.S. citizens living abroad are taxed worldwide by the U.S. and (potentially) by the country of domicile. Non-citizens living in the U.S. similarly face potential double Estate and Gift Tax, by the U.S. and their home country. Double taxation of U.S. citizens and residents may arise in a variety of scenarios, including the following:

- o The U.S. imposes tax on the basis of U.S. citizenship and another country taxes on the basis of a different domicile or residence (for example, U.S. citizens residing outside the U.S.);

---

[130] IRC §§2001; 2501.

[131] For example, a U.S. citizen with assets in the U.S. and Cuba is subject to U.S. Estate and Gift Tax on all assets (both in Cuba and the U.S.). A Cuban national (living in Cuba) with assets in Cuba and the U.S. subjects only assets in Cuba to Cuban estate and gift tax (leaving the IRS to tax the U.S. situs assets).

- o The reverse, where a foreign nation taxes all assets of a deceased foreign national (based on citizenship) and the U.S. taxes all such assets based on the deceased's U.S. domicile at death;

- o The U.S. and the other country both impose tax on the basis of citizenship when the decedent has dual citizenship;

- o The U.S. taxes based on the situs of assets (within the U.S.) and the other country taxes the assets on the basis of domicile or relationship of the decedent to the foreign nation;

- o The foreign country imposes tax on the basis of the situs of assets (in that country) and the U.S. taxes the same assets based on the U.S. domicile or citizenship of the decedent;

- o Two decedents may be taxed on the same asset if one country taxes the (resident or citizen) owner and another taxes the (resident or citizen) beneficiary (of the same asset).

Foreign Estate Tax Credit

In the absence of a treaty, the Code may provide a U.S. Estate Tax credit, to the extent of estate tax (or any similar succession tax) paid to a foreign country on property also taxed by the U.S.[132] There is no similar U.S. tax credit for gift tax paid abroad. Gift tax treaties, do, however, provide for the credit. See page 128.

---

[132] IRC §2014(a).

If an estate tax treaty applies, double tax may be avoided by utilizing the foreign tax credit available either under the treaty or under the Code. If a treaty position is taken on a U.S. tax return, Form 8833, *Treaty-Based Return Position Disclosure Under Section 6114, or 7701(b)*, may be required.[133]

Treaties Generally

U.S. Estate and Gift Tax treaties are intended to prevent double taxation by the U.S. and another country (of the same property).

Treaties generally eliminate double taxation for both (i) NRNC decedents dying with U.S. assets[134] and (ii) U.S. citizens and residents with foreign assets.

As noted, U.S. citizens or residents are generally credited (against U.S. Estate and Gift Tax) for estate or gift tax paid abroad. Foreign nationals with U.S. property are generally credited by their home country for U.S. Estate and Gift Tax incurred. The benefit of statutory tax credits may, however, be more limited than the tax savings offered by a treaty.

Estate tax treaties determine: (a) domicile of the individual taxpayer; (b) tax situs of certain assets; (c) property taxable by the country not of domicile or citizenship; (d) available exemptions, deductions, and credits; (e) how foreign tax credits are applied; (f)

---

[133] §6114 and §6712; Reg. §301.6114-1.
[134] IRC §2102(b)(3)(A) governs the unified credit available to NRNCs under treaties and was amended by the Small Business Job Protection Act of 1996, P.L., 104-188, §1704(f)(1), effective Aug. 20, 1996.

rights of estates to negotiate tax problems with treaty partners; and (g) financial information exchanged by treaty nations.[135]

Domicile treaties assign dual residents a single nation of residence (typically the country with closer ties to the individual). Additionally, to benefit from situs-type estate tax treaties, a decedent must have a personal affiliation, such as domicile or citizenship, with at least one treaty country.

Although one country may tax a lifetime gift, a different (non-treaty) country may impose estate tax on the same asset. Only by treaty may the gift tax be credited against the later death tax. Only a few treaties resolve the issue.[136] For example, Article 11(5) of the U.S.-Germany Treaty provides: "In order to avoid double taxation, each contracting state shall …take into account in an appropriate way… any tax imposed by the other Contracting State upon a prior gift of property made by the decedent, if such property is included in the estate subject to taxation by the first-mentioned State… ."[137]

As of July 2020, the U.S. has in force the following treaties governing the Estate Tax, Gift Tax or both.

Estate and Gift Tax Treaties:

>Australia

>Austria

>Denmark

---

[135] *See, e.g.*, U.S.-Australia Treaty.

[136] All U.S. domicile-type treaties (except the treaty with the Netherlands) apply to gifts and estates, but generally, fail to credit gift tax paid against estate tax. Situs-type treaties (assigning tax situs to different classes of property), similarly, make no reference to adjustment of estate tax for tax paid on lifetime gifts, with the exception of the U.S.-Japan situs treaty.

[137] U.S.-Germany Estate and Gift Tax Treaty art. 11(5).

France

Germany

Japan

United Kingdom

Estate Tax Treaties:[138]

Finland

Greece

Ireland

Italy

Netherlands

South Africa

Switzerland[139]

Estate and gift tax treaties avoid double taxation pursuant to either a situs or domicile format. The country of applicable situs or domicile is afforded the right to impose estate or gift tax on the individual. Situs treaties establish assets as inside the borders of (and taxable by) only one treaty partner. Domicile treaties deem the relevant person as

---

[138] Since 1972, Canada has no estate tax and instead imposes an income tax on capital gains from a deemed disposition of property at death. Therefore, the U.S. and Canada do not have an Estate Tax Treaty, but rather handle functional "death tax" matters under the 2007 Protocol Amending the Convention Between the United States of America and Canada with Respect to Taxes on Income and Capital, Sept. 21, 2007 (hereinafter "2007 U.S.-Canada Protocol").

[139] Canada imposes no gift tax, yet lifetime dispositions of appreciated property will generate a capital gains tax. See 2007 U.S.-Canada Protocol: *See also* Dept. of the Treasury Technical Explanation of the Protocol done at Chelsea on Sept. 21, 2007 Amending the Convention between the United States of America and Canada with respect to Taxes on Income and on Capital done at Washington on Sept. 26, 1980, July 10, 2008, (hereinafter "Treasury Technical explanation of U.S.-Canada Protocol on Income and on Capital").

domiciled in (and taxed by) only one treaty country. In general, treaties established prior to 1970 are situs-based. Later treaties are generally domicile-based. The fifteen existing U.S. estate tax treaties (broken-down by type) are as follows:

Situs	Domicile
Australia	Austria
Finland	Canada
Greece	Denmark
Ireland	France
Italy	Germany
Japan	Netherlands
South Africa	Switzerland
	United Kingdom

The IRS requires notice of a treaty-based tax position.[140] Taxpayers seeking treaty benefits must file Form 8833, Treaty-Based Return Position Disclosure, under §6114 or 7701(b). Dual-resident taxpayers also use this form for treaty-based return position disclosure, required by Treasury Regulations §§301.7701(b)-7.

Situs Treaties

Situs treaties allow citizens and residents of a treaty country to avoid double taxation on particular classes of property. Treaty benefits only apply to domiciliaries or citizens of either treaty partner.

---

[140] IRC §6114.

130

Situs treaties establish the situs of assets and assign taxing authority (over such assets) to the situs country. Planning should make clear which country has situs to assets (pursuant to the treaty). Once situs is clear, the country with situs may impose estate tax (and the other country provides a credit for such tax against any estate tax it would otherwise impose). This avoids double taxation.

The following example may be helpful in understanding how double taxation occurs, based on differing definitions of situs. Consider an NRNC with stock in a U.S. corporation, certificates for which are held in a non-treaty country. U.S. tax law places situs in the U.S. (the country of incorporation). The foreign country where the share certificates are located may also impose estate tax on the value of the shares. The NRNC would receive no U.S. tax credit for the foreign tax imposed on the shares because the U.S. does not recognize the foreign tax situs of the shares. The stock would therefore be subject to double estate tax upon the death of the owner.

Situs treaties (limiting situs to a single country) eliminate the imposition of estate tax by two countries on the same property. The situs treaty permits only one country to tax a particular asset based on an agreed situs. If agreed situs is (for example) the location of stock certificates, the U.S. would credit the NRNC against U.S. Estate Tax for the amount of foreign estate tax paid on the shares to the situs country.[141]

One additional complexity is that the treaty country without situs (over a particular asset) may still tax the asset based on the "personal affiliation" of the decedent, beneficiary,

---

[141] *See e.g.*, Convention Between the United States of America and Japan for the Avoidance of Double Taxation and the Prevention of Fiscal Evasion with Respect to Taxes on Estates, Inheritances, Gifts, Apr. 1, 1955, U.S.-Japan, T.I.A.S. (hereinafter "U.S.-Japan Estate and Gift Tax Treaty").

grantor or grantee (to the non-situs country). Thus, one country may tax an estate asset based on situs (established by treaty) and the other may tax the same asset based on the owner's affiliation to that country. The personal affiliation (triggering double taxation) is typically domicile, residence or citizenship. Double taxation of the particular asset (based on personal affiliation) may be reduced by a treaty requirement that the affiliated country (without situs) credit (against its estate tax) the affiliated individual for the tax imposed by the situs country.[142] Without such particular treaty language, the country of domicile or "affiliation" could deny any tax credit against estate tax imposed by the affiliated country.[143]

The following is an example of how a situs treaty may eliminate double taxation based on personal affiliation. An Argentine citizen domiciled in Miami with real estate in Australia is subject (upon his death) to Australian estate tax on such real estate. The U.S. also imposes estate tax on the real estate (and all other property of the Argentine) based on his U.S. domicile. Pursuant to the U.S./Australia treaty, the U.S. will credit the Argentine's U.S. Estate Tax (dollar-for-dollar tax) by the amount of (situs-based) estate tax imposed by Australia.

Note that Argentina imposes estate tax on the worldwide assets of its citizens. In light of the absence of a treaty between Argentina and Australia, Argentina may not offer a credit against estate tax paid in Australia.

---

[142] *Id.*, (explaining in Article V., that where either State taxes on personal affiliation such as nationality or domicile, such State will allow a credit for tax imposed by the other with respect to property situated at the time of the transfer in such other State).
[143] Generally, situs-type treaties are limited to death or estate taxes, with the exception of Japan, which has a situs treaty with the U.S. with respect to gift taxes. *See id.* at 6.

Our Argentine national could return permanently to Argentina but retain ownership of stock in a U.S. corporation. The stock is deemed by the United States to have a situs in the United States. If the stock certificates are held in Japan, the asset is deemed by Japan to have a situs in Japan. Although the treaty between the United States and Japan specifies that the situs of corporate stock is the location of stock certificates, the treaty does not apply. The situs treaty requires the decedent to have a relationship (domicile/residence/citizen) with either treaty country (i.e., Japan or U.S.).

The application of a tax credit is therefore conditioned on the decedent being a citizen or domiciliary of either the United States or Japan.[144] The U.S., Japan and Argentina may therefore all impose estate tax on the shares (with potentially no means of relief from double (or triple) taxation). The foreign tax credit available under Internal Revenue Code (§2014 for Estate Tax paid abroad) is also not available, because the United States deems the stock to have a U.S. situs (making a credit for situs-based tax paid abroad unavailable).

Situs-type treaties primarily apply to the Estate Tax. The U.S./Japan (situs) treaty is the only situs treaty also covering gift tax.[145] The U.S. does not otherwise credit U.S. domiciliaries for gift tax paid abroad (against U.S. Gift Tax paid to the IRS on the same gifts).

---

[144] Convention between the United States of America and Japan for the Avoidance of Double Taxation and the Prevention of Fiscal Evasion with Respect to Taxes on Estates, Inheritances, and Gift, Apr. 16, 1954, T.I.A.S. (hereinafter "U.S.-Japan Estate and Gift Tax Treaty") (explaining in Article V(1) that the country of domicile or other personal affiliation will grant an estate the tax credit, leaving the situs country to collect estate tax).
[145] U.S.-Japan Estate and Gift Tax Treaty art. I(1)(a)(b).

The double taxation of gifts by resident aliens (RAs) and NRNCs is an open exposure. Also, certain assets, such as bank accounts, are not covered by several existing situs treaties.[146] Moreover, the situs of certain assets, such as rights to real estate and equity in hybrid business entities (like LLCs), may (depending on the treaty) be unclear.

---

[146] Treaties with Australia, Japan (U.S.-Japan Estate and Gift Tax Treaty art. III(1)(c)), and Greece (U.S.-Greece Estate Tax Treaty art. IV(2)(j)) provide for the situs of bank accounts (as located in the country of domicile or residence of the decedent) and define bank accounts and the rights associated with them, whereas other situs treaties do not so provide.

CONVENTION BETWEEN THE UNITED STATES OF AMERICA AND JAPAN FOR THE AVOIDANCE OF DOUBLE TAXATION AND THE PREVENTION OF FISCAL EVASION WITH RESPECT TO TAXES ON ESTATES, INHERITANCES AND GIFT.

The Government of the United States of America and the Government of Japan, desiring to conclude a Convention for the avoidance of double taxation and the prevention of fiscal evasion with respect to taxes on estates, inheritances, and gifts, have appointed for that purpose as their respective Plenipotentiaries:

The Government of the United States of America: Mr. Walter Bedell Smith, Acting Secretary of State of the United States of America, and

The Government of Japan: Mr. Sadao Iguchi, Ambassador Extraordinary and Plenipotentiary of Japan to the United States of America, who, having communicated to one another their respective full powers, found in good and due form, have agreed upon the following Articles:

ARTICLE I

(1) The taxes referred to in the present Convention are:
(a) In the case of the United States of America: The Federal estate and gift taxes.

(b) In the case of Japan: The inheritance tax (including the gift tax).

(2) The present Convention shall also apply to any other tax on estates, inheritances or gifts which has a character substantially similar to those referred to in paragraph (1) of this Article and which may be imposed by either contracting State after the date of signature of the present Convention.

ARTICLE II

(1) As used in the present Convention:
(a) The term "United States" means the United States of America, and when used in a geographical sense means the States, the Territories of Alaska and Hawaii, and the District of Columbia.

(b) The term "Japan", when used in a geographical sense, means all the territory in which the laws relating to the tax referred to in paragraph (1)(b) of Article I are enforced.

(c) The term "tax" means those taxes referred to in paragraph (1)(a) or (b) of Article I , as the context requires.

(d) The term "competent authorities" means, in the case of the United States, the Commissioner of Internal Revenue as authorized by the Secretary of the Treasury; and, in the case of Japan, the Minister of Finance or his authorized representative.

(2) In the application of the provisions of the present Convention by either contracting State any term not otherwise defined shall, unless the context otherwise requires, have the meaning which such term has under the laws of such State relating to the tax.

(3) For the purposes of the present Convention, each contracting State may determine in accordance with its laws whether a decedent at the time of his death or a beneficiary of a decedent's estate at the time of such decedent's death, or a donor at the time of the gift or a beneficiary of a gift at the time of the gift, was domiciled therein or a national thereof.

ARTICLE III

(1) If a decedent at the time of his death or a donor at the time of the gift was a national of or domiciled in the United States, or if a beneficiary of a decedent's estate at the time of such decedent's death or a beneficiary of a gift at the time of the gift was domiciled in Japan, the situs at the time of the transfer of any of the following property or property rights shall, for the purpose of the imposition of the tax and for the purpose of the credit authorized by Article V , be determined exclusively in accordance with the following rules:
(a) Immovable property or rights therein (not including any property for which specific provision is otherwise made in this Article) shall be deemed to be situated at the place where the land involved is located.

(b) Tangible movable property (including currency and any other form of money recognized as legal tender in the place of issue and excepting such property for which specific provision is otherwise made in this Article) shall be deemed to be situated at the place where such property is physically located, or, if in transitu, at the place of destination.

(c) Debts (including bonds, promissory notes, bills of exchange, bank deposits and insurance, except bonds or other negotiable instruments in bearer form and such debts for which specific provision is otherwise made in this Article) shall be deemed to be situated at the place where the debtor resides.

(d) Shares or stock in a corporation shall be deemed to be situated at the place under the laws of which such corporation was created or organized.

(e) Ships and aircraft shall be deemed to be situated at the place where they are registered.

(f) Goodwill as a trade, business or professional asset shall be deemed to be situated at the place where the trade, business or profession to which it pertains is carried on

(g) Patents, trade-marks, utility models and designs shall be deemed to be situated at the place where they are registered (or used in case they are not registered).

(h) Copyrights, franchises, rights to artistic and scientific works and rights or licenses to use any copyrighted material, artistic and scientific works, patents, trade-marks, utility models or designs shall be deemed to be situated at the place where they are exercisable.

(i) Mining or quarrying rights or mining leases shall be deemed to be situated at the place of such mining or quarrying.

(j) Fishing rights shall be deemed to be situated in the country in whose government's jurisdiction such rights are exercisable.

(k) Any property for which provision is not hereinbefore made shall be deemed to be situated in accordance with the laws of the contracting State imposing the tax solely by reason of the situs of property within such State, but if neither of the contracting States imposes the tax solely by reason of the situs of property therein, then any such property shall be deemed to be situated in accordance with the laws of each contracting State.

(2) The application of the provisions of paragraph (1) of this Article shall be limited to the particular property, and any portion thereof, which without such provisions would be subjected to the taxes of both contracting States or would be so subjected except for a specific exemption.

ARTICLE IV

Where one of the contracting States imposes the tax solely by reason of the situs of property within such State, in the case of a decedent who at the time of his death, or of a donor who at the time of the gift, was a national of or domiciled in the United States, or in the case of a beneficiary of a decedent's estate who at the time of such decedent's death, or a beneficiary of a gift who at the time of the gift, was domiciled in Japan, the contracting State so imposing the tax:

(a) shall allow a specific exemption which would be applicable under its laws if the decedent, donor, or beneficiary, as the case may be, had been a national of or domiciled in such State, in an amount not less than the proportion thereof which (A) the value of the property, situated according to Article III in such State and subjected to the taxes of both contracting States or which would be so subjected except for a specific exemption, bears to (B) the value of the total property which would be subjected to the tax of such State if such decedent, donor, or beneficiary had been a national of or domiciled in such State; and

(b) shall (except for the purpose of subparagraph (a) of this paragraph and for the purpose of any other proportional allowance otherwise provided) take no account of property situated according to Article III outside such State in determining the amount of the tax.

ARTICLE V

(1) Where either contracting State imposes the tax by reason of the nationality thereof or the domicile therein of a decedent or a donor or a beneficiary of a decedent's estate or of a gift, such State shall allow against its tax (computed without application of this Article) a credit for the tax imposed by the other contracting State with respect to property situated at the time of the transfer in such other State and included for the taxes of both States (but the amount of the credit shall not exceed that portion of the tax imposed by the crediting State which is attributable to such property). The provisions of this paragraph shall not apply with respect to any property referred to in paragraph (2) of this Article.

(2) Where each contracting State imposes the tax by reason of the nationality thereof or the domicile therein of a decedent or a donor or a beneficiary, with respect to any property situated at the time of the transfer outside both contracting States (or deemed by each contracting State to be situated in its territory, or deemed by one contracting State to be situated in either contracting State and deemed by the other contracting State to be situated outside both contracting States or deemed by each contracting State to be situated in the other contracting State), each contracting State shall allow against its tax (computed without application of this Article) a credit for a part of the tax imposed by the other contracting State attributable to such property. The total of the credits authorized by this paragraph shall be equal to the amount of the tax imposed with respect to such property by the contracting State imposing the smaller amount of the tax with respect to such property, and shall be divided between both contracting States in proportion to the amount of the tax imposed by each contracting State with respect to such property.

(3) The credit authorized by this Article, if applicable, shall be in lieu of any credit for the same tax authorized by the laws of the crediting State, the credit applicable for the particular tax being either credit authorized by this Article or credit authorized by such laws, whichever is the greater. For the purposes of this Article, the amount of the tax of each contracting State attributable to any designated property shall be ascertained after taking into account any applicable diminution or credit against its tax with respect to such property (other than any credit under paragraph (1) or (2) of this Article), provided, however, in case another credit for the tax of any other foreign State is allowable with respect to the same property pursuant to any other Convention between the crediting State under the present Convention and such other foreign State, or pursuant to the laws of the crediting State, the total of such credits shall not exceed the amount of tax of the crediting State attributable to such property computed before allowance of such credits.

(4) Credit against the tax of one of the contracting States for the tax of the other contracting State shall be allowed under this Article only where both such taxes have been simultaneously imposed at the time of a decedent's death or at the time of a gift.

(5) No credit resulting from the application of this Article shall be allowed after more than five years from the due date of the tax against which credit would otherwise be

allowed, unless claim therefor was filed within such five-year period. Any refund resulting from the application of this Article shall be made without payment of interest on the amount so refunded, unless otherwise specifically authorized by the crediting State.

(6) Credit against the tax of one of the contracting States shall not be finally allowed for the tax of the other contracting State until the latter tax (reduced by credit authorized under this Article, if any) has been paid.

ARTICLE VI

(1) The competent authorities of both contracting States shall exchange such information available under the respective tax laws of both contracting States as is necessary for carrying out the provisions of the present Convention or for the prevention of fraud or for the administration of statutory provisions against tax avoidance in relation to the tax. Any information so exchanged shall be treated as secret and shall not be disclosed to any person other than those, including a court, concerned with the assessment and collection of the tax or the determination of appeals in relation thereto. No information shall be exchanged which would disclose any trade, business, industrial or professional secret or any trade process.

(2) Each of the contracting States may collect the tax imposed by the other contracting State (as though such tax were the tax of the former State) as will ensure that the credit or any other benefit granted under the present Convention by such other State shall not be enjoyed by persons not entitled to such benefits.

ARTICLE VII

Where a representative of the estate of a decedent or a beneficiary of such estate or a donor or a beneficiary of a gift shows proof that the action of the tax authorities of either contracting State has resulted, or will result, in double taxation contrary to the provisions of the present Convention, such representative, donor or beneficiary shall be entitled to present the facts to the competent authorities of the contracting State of which the decedent was a national at the time of his death or of which the donor or beneficiary is a national, or if the decedent was not a national of either of the contracting States at the time of his death or if the donor or the beneficiary is not a national of either of the contracting States, to the competent authorities of the contracting State in which the decedent was domiciled or resident at the time of his death or in which the donor or beneficiary is domiciled or resident. Should the claim be deemed worthy of consideration, the competent authorities of such State to which the facts are so presented shall undertake to come to an agreement with the competent authorities of the other contracting State with a view to equitable avoidance of the double taxation in question.

ARTICLE VIII

(1) The provisions of the present Convention shall not be construed to deny or affect in any manner the right of diplomatic and consular officers to other or additional exemptions now enjoyed or which may hereafter be granted to such officers.

(2) The provisions of the present Convention shall not be construed so as to increase the tax imposed by either contracting State.

(3) Should any difficulty or doubt arise as to the interpretation or application of the present Convention, or its relationship to Conventions between one of the contracting States and any other State, the competent authorities of the contracting States may settle the question by mutual agreement; it being understood, however, that this provision shall not be construed to preclude the contracting States from settling by negotiation any dispute arising under the present Convention.

(4) The competent authorities of both contracting States may prescribe regulations necessary to interpret and carry out the provisions of the present Convention and may communicate with each other directly for the purpose of giving effect to the provisions of the present Convention.

ARTICLE IX

(1) The present Convention shall be ratified and the instruments of ratification shall be exchanged at Tokyo as soon as possible.

(2) The present Convention shall enter into force on the date of exchange of instruments of ratification and shall be applicable to estates or inheritances in the case of persons who die on or after the date of such exchange and to gifts made on or after that date.

(3) Either of the contracting States may terminate the present Convention at any time after a period of five years shall have expired from the date on which the Convention enters into force, by giving to the other contracting State notice of termination, provided that such notice is given on or before the 30th day of June and, in such event, the present Convention shall cease to be effective for the taxable years beginning on or after the first day of January of the calendar year next following that in which such notice is given.

In witness whereof, the undersigned Plenipotentiaries have signed the present Convention.

Done at Washington, in duplicate, in the English and Japanese languages, each text having equal authenticity, this sixteenth day of April, 1954.

For the United States of America:
  Walter Bedell Smith

For Japan:
  S. Iguchi

Domicile Treaties

Double taxation often arises from investment or residency in foreign countries. Domicile-based Estate and Gift Tax treaties generally resolve the issue of double taxation by permitting the country of domicile to tax the entire estate of the deceased (on a worldwide basis).

The non-domicile country may only tax certain classes of assets.[147] For example, under the U.S.-Austria Estate and Gift Tax Treaty art. 5, the non-domiciliary country may tax only real estate or property associated with a fixed place of business (in that country).[148]

The key is to clearly establish "fiscal domicile" in a single country (assigned tax jurisdiction). The "fiscal domicile" is typically where the individual has a "closer connection" to the governing country.[149] To qualify for the benefits of a domicile-based estate/gift tax treaty, the decedent/grantor must be domiciled in a treaty nation at the time of the applicable death or gift. If the nation competing with the U.S. for domicile is not party to a treaty with the U.S., double taxation is a concern.

For example, if a French citizen and resident gifts U.S. tangible property to a child in France, the Code taxes the transfer. However, the U.S.-France Treaty assigns exclusive

---

[147] *See, e.g.*, Convention Between the Government of the United States of America and the Republic of Austria for the Avoidance of Double Taxation and the Prevention of Fiscal Evasion with respect to Taxes on Estates, Inheritances, Gifts, and Generation-Skipping Transfers, July 1, 1983, U.S.-Austria, T.I.A.S. (hereinafter "U.S.-Austria Estate and Gift Tax Treaty") (explaining in Article 5 that the contracting state in which the real property is located gets to tax that property).
[148] *Id.*
[149] *See, e.g.*, Convention between the United States of America and the French Republic for the Avoidance of Double Taxation and the Prevention of Fiscal Evasion with respect to Taxes on Estates, Inheritances, and Gifts, Nov. 24, 1978, U.S.-France, T.I.A.S. (hereinafter "U.S.-France Estate and Gift Tax Treaty") (explaining in Art 4(2)(b) that if a decedent was permanently domiciled in both contracting states or neither, then his domicile is deemed to be in the state wherein his personal relations were closest, also referred to as the "center of vital interests.").

taxing jurisdiction to France.[150] Interestingly, if France does not impose tax on the transfer, the IRS may not impose tax (even though U.S. property was gifted).

The nation of citizenship may also claim tax authority.[151] The definition of domicile (establishing the treaty partner with taxing authority) may differ, even among treaty partners. The U.S. Treasury model tax treaty establishes domicile under the domestic law of each treaty nation.[152] To avoid being considered a dual domiciliary, the model treaty contains a tie-breaking provision, establishing a single domicile country.

A credit is necessary (to avoid double taxation) if (for example) the U.S. taxes based on citizenship and the other treaty country taxes based of domicile. Under domicile treaties, if one treaty country (i.e., the U.S.) taxes assets of its citizens worldwide, it will credit (against its tax) the tax imposed by the country of domicile.[153]

The definition of domicile may differ among countries. Certain domicile treaties establish a single definition of "fiscal domicile" (to avoid more than one nation claiming estate or gift tax domicile over the same person).[154] Where the U.S. and a foreign nation

---

[150] U.S.-France Estate and Gift Tax Treaty art. 7(1) (except to the extent taxed by the other treaty country under the "permanent establishment rules," the situs state may tax such property, and if the property is in transit, it is taxed at the destination).

[151] *See, e.g.,* Convention Between the Government of the United States of America and the Government of the Kingdom of Denmark for the Avoidance of Double Taxation and the Prevention of Fiscal Evasion with Respect to Taxes on Estates, Inheritances, and Gifts and Certain Other Transfers, Nov. 7, 1984, U.S.-Denmark, T.I.A.S. (hereinafter "U.S.-Denmark Estate and Gift Tax Treaty") (references in Article 4(3) to citizenship as the determinative personal affiliation for discerning fiscal domicile); *see also* U.S.-Austria Estate and Gift Tax Treaty art. 4(3).

[152] *See* United States Model Income Tax Convention, Feb. 17, 2016, IRS, www.irs.gov.

[153] IRC §2014.

[154] *See, e.g.,* Convention Between the United States of America and the Federal Republic of Germany for the Avoidance of Double Taxation with Respect to Taxes on Estates, Inheritances, and Gifts, Dec. 3, 1980, U.S.-Germany, T.I.A.S. (hereinafter "U.S.-Germany Estate and Gift Tax Treaty") (Article 4(1)(a)-(b) defines fiscal domicile as either a domicile or habitual abode); U.S.-France Estate and Gift Tax Treaty art. 4(2)(a)-(e) (each country's domestic laws determine definition of fiscal domicile and if that determination is insufficient to discern taxing authority, the countries apply a hierarchy of personal affiliations to determine which one has domicile).

claim domicile (and estate tax) over one person, treaties with Austria, Denmark, France, Netherlands, United Kingdom and Germany establish a single domicile.[155]

If Australia, Finland, Greece, Ireland, Japan, South Africa, or Switzerland dispute domicile with the U.S., the treaties leave the determination of domicile to the laws of the treaty partners (which may not coincide).[156] If two treaty countries claim fiscal domicile, the following factors typically apply to determine proper domicile:

o   where the person maintained a "permanent home";

o   the country with the closest personal relation (center of vital interests);

o   the "habitual abode"; and

o   the country of citizenship.

If neither treaty nation can clearly establish these personal affiliations, the countries must work out an agreement on fiscal domicile.[157] Although domicile treaties afford exclusive taxing authority to the country of fiscal domicile, certain assets (with a strong connection to one situs) may be excluded.

Real estate, business property (at a permanent establishment) and a fixed foreign base for performance of personal services, may be taxed by the situs nation.[158] In such

---

[155] *See* U.S.-Denmark Estate and Gift Tax Treaty art. 4(1)(a)-(b); U.S.-Germany Estate and Gift Tax Treaty art. 4(1)-(2); U.S.-Austria Estate and Gift Tax Treaty art. 4(1)-(2); U.S.-France Estate and Gift Tax Treaty art. 4(1)-(2); U.S.-U.K. Estate and Gift Tax Treaty art. 4(1)(a)-(b); and U.S.-Netherlands Estate Tax Treaty art. 4(1)-(2).

[156] *See, e.g.,* Article III of the Convention between the Government of the United States of America and the Government of the Union of South Africa with Respect to Taxes on the Estates of Deceased Persons, Apr. 10, 1947, U.S.-South Africa, T.I.A.S. (hereinafter "U.S.-South Africa Estate Tax Treaty"); and U.S.-Japan Estate and Gift Tax Treaty art. II.

[157] *See, e.g.,* U.S.-Germany Estate and Gift Tax Treaty art. 11(5) (where fiscal domicile changes over time and each country's test still results in double taxation, each treaty country can form agreements as to certain credits or refunds).

[158] *See* U.S.-Austria Treaty art. 5(1) (real property can be taxed by the situs country); *id.* art. 6(1) (business property can be taxed by the situs country).

case, the domicile country will allow a credit for tax by the situs treaty partner. All other assets are taxable exclusively by the domicile country. An Estate or Gift Tax credit (by the domicile country for tax paid in the situs country) is therefore only necessary to avoid double taxation on certain classes of property (as all other property may only be taxed by the domicile country).

The exceptions to domicile-based taxation (permitting the taxation of certain assets situated in the non-domicile country by the country of situs) can (as with situs treaties) raise the issue of differing definitions of asset situs. Where situs is disputed, double taxation is possible.

Consider a U.S. resident (non-citizen) who owns a business enterprise in a domicile treaty country. The treaty partner (where the business is operated) may claim that the business is a "permanent establishment" (inside the treaty partner). The treaty will allow the nation of business establishment to tax the business assets, even if it is not the fiscal domicile of the decedent. The typical problem is that the U.S. may deem the business assets as U.S. situs (owned by the resident non-citizen), even if the assets are not in the U.S. In such case, the U.S. provides no credit for tax paid abroad. A treaty may resolve the issue but often fails to provide a clear answer.[159] The problem is not that a permanent business establishment (exception to domicile-based taxation) exists, but that the treaty countries disagree as to its situs.

---

[159] *See* U.S.-Austria Estate and Gift Tax Treaty art. 7(2) (which lacks a clear definition of whether a property right is real property or business property; the treaty says that the law of the non-domiciliary treaty country will govern instead of providing a clear answer).

CONVENTION BETWEEN THE GOVERNMENT OF THE UNITED STATES OF AMERICA AND THE GOVERNMENT OF THE UNITED KINGDOM OF GREAT BRITAIN AND NORTHERN IRELAND FOR THE AVOIDANCE OF DOUBLE TAXATION AND THE PREVENTION OF FISCAL EVASION WITH RESPECT TO TAXES ON ESTATES OF DECEASED PERSONS AND ON GIFTS

The Government of the United States of America and the Government of the United Kingdom of Great Britain and Northern Ireland:
Desiring to conclude a new Convention for the avoidance of double taxation and the prevention of fiscal evasion with respect to taxes on estates of deceased persons and on gifts:

Have agreed as follows:

ARTICLE 1 SCOPE
This Convention shall apply to any person who is within the scope of a tax which is the subject of this Convention.

ARTICLE 2 TAXES COVERED
(1) The existing taxes to which this Convention shall apply are:
(a) in the United States: the Federal gift tax and the Federal estate tax, including the tax on generation-skipping transfers; and

(b) in the United Kingdom: the capital transfer tax.

(2) This Convention shall also apply to any identical or substantially similar taxes which are imposed by a Contracting State after the date of signature of the Convention in addition to, or in place of, the existing taxes. The competent authorities of the Contracting States shall notify each other of any changes which have been made in their respective taxation laws.

ARTICLE 3 GENERAL DEFINITIONS
(1) In this Convention:
(a) the term "United States" means the United States of America, but does not include Puerto Rico, the Virgin Islands, Guam or any other United States possession or territory;

(b) the term "United Kingdom" means Great Britain and Northern Ireland;

(c) the term "enterprise" means an industrial or commercial undertaking;

(d) the term "competent authority" means:
(i) in the United States: the Secretary of the Treasury or his delegate, and

(ii) in the United Kingdom: the Commissioners of Inland Revenue or their authorized representative;

(e) the term "nationals" means:
(i) in relation to the United States, United States citizens, and

(ii) in relation to the United Kingdom, any citizen of the United Kingdom and Colonies, or any British subject not possessing that citizenship or the citizenship of any other Commonwealth country or territory, provided in either case he had the right of abode in the United Kingdom at the time of the death or transfer;

(f) the term "tax" means:
(i) the Federal gift tax or the Federal estate tax, including the tax on generation-skipping transfers, imposed in the United States, or

(ii) the capital transfer tax imposed in the United Kingdom, or

(iii) any other tax imposed by a Contracting State to which this Convention applies by virtue of the provisions of paragraph (2) of Article 2 , as the context requires; and

(g) the term "Contracting State" means the United States or the United Kingdom as the context requires.

(2) As regards the application of the Convention by a Contracting State, any term not otherwise defined shall, unless the context otherwise requires and subject to the provisions of Article 11 (Mutual Agreement Procedure), have the meaning which it has under the laws of that Contracting State relating to the taxes which are the subject of the Convention.

ARTICLE 4 FISCAL DOMICILE
(1) For the purposes of this Convention an individual was domiciled:
(a) in the United States: if he was a resident (domiciliary) thereof or if he was a national thereof and had been a resident (domiciliary) thereof at any time during the preceding three years; and

(b) in the United Kingdom: if he was domiciled in the United Kingdom in accordance with the law of the United Kingdom or is treated as so domiciled for the purposes of a tax which is the subject of this Convention.

(2) Where by reason of the provisions of paragraph (1) an individual was at any time domiciled in both Contracting States, and
(a) was a national of the United Kingdom but not of the United States, and

(b) had not been resident in the United States for Federal income tax purposes in seven or more of the ten taxable years ending with the year in which that time falls,
he shall be deemed to be domiciled in the United Kingdom at that time.

(3) Where by reason of the provisions of paragraph (1) an individual was at any time domiciled in both Contracting States, and
(a) was a national of the United States but not of the United Kingdom, and

(b) had not been resident in the United Kingdom in seven or more of the ten income tax years of assessment ending with the year in which that time falls,
he shall be deemed to be domiciled in the United States at that time. For the purposes of this paragraph, the question of whether a person was so resident shall be determined as for income tax purposes but without regard to any dwelling-house available to him in the United Kingdom for his use.

(4) Where by reason of the provisions of paragraph (1) an individual was domiciled in both Contracting States, then, subject to the provisions of paragraphs (2) and (3), his status shall be determined as follows:
(a) the individual shall be deemed to be domiciled in the Contracting State in which he had a permanent home available to him. If he had a permanent home available to him in both Contracting States, or in neither Contracting State, he shall be deemed to be domiciled in the Contracting State with which his personal and economic relations were closest (centre of vital interests);

(b) if the Contracting State in which the individual's centre of vital interests was located cannot be determined, he shall be deemed to be domiciled in the Contracting State in which he had an habitual abode;

(c) if the individual had an habitual abode in both Contracting States or in neither of them, he shall be deemed to be domiciled in the Contracting State of which he was a national; and

(d) if the individual was a national of both Contracting States or of neither of them, the competent authorities of the Contracting States shall settle the question by mutual agreement.

(5) An individual who was a resident (domiciliary) of a possession of the United States and who became a citizen of the United States solely by reason of his
(a) being a citizen of such possession, or

(b) birth or residence within such possession, shall be considered as neither domiciled in nor a national of the United States for the purposes of this Convention.

ARTICLE 5 TAXING RIGHTS
(1)
(a) Subject to the provisions of Articles 6 (Immovable Property (Real Property)) and 7 (Business Property of a Permanent Establishment and Assets Pertaining to a Fixed Base Used for the Performance of Independent Personal Services) and the following paragraphs of this Article, if the decedent or transferor was domiciled in one of the Contracting States

at the time of the death or transfer, property shall not be taxable in the other State.

(b) Sub-paragraph (*a*) shall not apply if at the time of the death or transfer the decedent or transferor was a national of that other State.

(2) Subject to the provisions of the said Articles 6 and 7 , if at the time of the death or transfer the decedent or transferor was domiciled in neither Contracting State and was a national of one Contracting State (but not of both), property which is taxable in the Contracting State of which he was a national shall not be taxable in the other Contracting State.

(3) Paragraphs (1) and (2) shall not apply in the United States to property held in a generation-skipping trust or trust equivalent on the occasion of a generation-skipping transfer; but, subject to the provisions of the said Articles 6 and 7 , tax shall not be imposed in the United States on such property if at the time when the transfer was made the deemed transferor was domiciled in the United Kingdom and was not a national of the United States.

(4) Paragraphs (1) and (2) shall not apply in the United Kingdom to property comprised in a settlement; but, subject to the provisions of the said Articles 6 and 7 , tax shall not be imposed in the United Kingdom on such property if at the time when the settlement was made the settlor was domiciled in the United States and was not a national of the United Kingdom.

(5) If by reason of the preceding paragraphs of this Article any property would be taxable only in one Contracting State and tax, though chargeable, is not paid (otherwise than as a result of a specific exemption, deduction, exclusion, credit or allowance) in that State, tax may be imposed by reference to that property in the other Contracting State notwithstanding those paragraphs.

(6) If at the time of the death or transfer the decedent or transferor was domiciled in neither Contracting State and each State would regard any property as situated in its territory and in consequence tax would be imposed in both States, the competent authorities of the Contracting States shall determine the situs of the property by mutual agreement.

ARTICLE 6 IMMOVABLE PROPERTY (REAL PROPERTY)
(1) Immovable property (real property) may be taxed in the Contracting State in which such property is situated.

(2) The term "immovable property" shall be defined in accordance with the law of the Contracting State in which the property in question is situated, provided always that debts secured by mortgage or otherwise shall not be regarded as immovable property. The term shall in any case include property accessory to immovable property, livestock and equipment used in agriculture and forestry, rights to which the provisions of general law respecting landed property apply, usufruct of immovable property and rights to variable or

fixed payments as consideration for the working of, or the right to work, mineral deposits, sources and other natural resources; ships, boats, and aircraft shall not be regarded as immovable property.

(3) The provisions of paragraphs (1) and (2) shall also apply to immovable property of an enterprise and to immovable property used for the performance of independent personal services.

ARTICLE 7 Business Property of a Permanent Establishment and Assets Pertaining to a Fixed Base Used for the Performance of Independent Personal Services
(1) Except for assets referred to in Article 6 (Immovable Property (Real Property)) assets forming part of the business property of a permanent establishment of an enterprise may be taxed in the Contracting State in which the permanent establishment is situated.

(2)
(a) For the purposes of this Convention, the term "permanent establishment" means a fixed place of business through which the business of an enterprise is wholly or partly carried on.

(b) The term "permanent establishment" includes especially:
(i) a branch;

(ii) an office;

(iii) a factory;

(iv) a workshop; and

(v) a mine, an oil or gas well, a quarry, or any other place of extraction of natural resources.

(c) A building site or construction or installation project constitutes a permanent establishment only if it lasts for more than twelve months.

(d) Notwithstanding the preceding provisions of this paragraph, the term "permanent establishment" shall be deemed not to include:
(i) the use of facilities solely for the purpose of storage, display, or delivery of goods or merchandise belonging to the enterprise;

(ii) the maintenance of a stock of goods or merchandise belonging to the enterprise solely for the purpose of storage, display or delivery;

(iii) the maintenance of a stock of goods or merchandise belonging to the enterprise solely for the purpose of processing by another enterprise;

(iv) the maintenance of a fixed place of business solely for the purpose of purchasing goods or merchandise, or of collecting information, for the enterprise;

(v) the maintenance of a fixed place of business solely for the purpose of carrying on, for the enterprise, any other activity of a preparatory or auxiliary character; or

(vi) the maintenance of a fixed place of business solely for any combination of activities mentioned in paragraphs (i)-(v) of this sub-paragraph.

(e) Notwithstanding the provisions of sub-paragraphs *(a)* and *(b)* where a person-other than an agent of an independent status to whom sub-paragraph *(f)* applies-is acting on behalf of an enterprise and has, and habitually exercises, in a Contracting State an authority to conclude contracts in the name of the enterprise, that enterprise shall be deemed to have a permanent establishment in that State in respect of any activities which that person undertakes for the enterprise, unless the activities of such person are limited to those mentioned in sub-paragraph *(d)* which, if exercised through a fixed place of business, would not make this fixed place of business a permanent establishment under the provisions of that sub-paragraph.

(f) An enterprise shall not be deemed to have a permanent establishment in a Contracting State merely because it carries on business in that State through a broker, general commission agent or any other agent of an independent status, provided that such persons are acting in the ordinary course of their business.

(g) The fact that a company which is a resident of a Contracting State controls or is controlled by a company which is a resident of the other Contracting State or which carries on business in that other State (whether through a permanent establishment or otherwise) shall not of itself constitute either company a permanent establishment of the other.

(3) Except for assets described in Article 6 (Immovable Property (Real Property)), assets pertaining to a fixed base used for the performance of independent personal services may be taxed in the Contracting State in which the fixed base is situated.

ARTICLE 8 DEDUCTIONS, EXEMPTIONS ETC
(1) In determining the amount on which tax is to be computed, permitted deductions shall be allowed in accordance with the law in force in the Contracting State in which tax is imposed.

(2) Property which passes to the spouse from a decedent or transferor who was domiciled in or a national of the United Kingdom and which may be taxed in the United States shall qualify for a marital deduction there to the extent that a marital deduction would have been allowable if the decedent or transferor had been domiciled in the United States and if the gross estate of the decedent had been limited to property which may be taxed in the United States or the transfers of the transferor had been limited to transfers of property which may be so taxed.

(3) Property which passes to the spouse from a decedent or transferor who was domiciled

in or a national of the United States and which may be taxed in the United Kingdom shall, where

(a) the transferor's spouse was not domiciled in the United Kingdom but the transfer would have been wholly exempt had the spouse been so domiciled, and

(b) a greater exemption for transfers between spouses would not have been given under the law of the United Kingdom apart from this Convention, be exempt from tax in the United Kingdom to the extent of 50 per cent of the value transferred, calculated as a value on which no tax is payable and after taking account of all exemptions except those for transfers between spouses.

(4)
(a) Property which on the death of a decedent domiciled in the United Kingdom became comprised in a settlement shall, if the personal representatives and the trustees of every settlement in which the decedent had an interest in possession immediately before death so elect and subject to sub-paragraph (*b*), be exempt from tax in the United Kingdom to the extent of 50 per cent of the value transferred (calculated as in paragraph (3)) on the death of the decedent if:
(i) under the settlement, the spouse of the decedent was entitled to an immediate interest in possession,

(ii) the spouse was domiciled in or a national of the United States,

(iii) the transfer would have been wholly exempt had the spouse been domiciled in the United Kingdom, and

(iv) a greater exemption for transfers between spouses would not have been given under the law of the United Kingdom apart from this Convention.

(b) Where the spouse of the decedent becomes absolutely and indefeasibly entitled to any of the settled property at any time after the decedent's death, the election shall, as regards that property, be deemed never to have been made and tax shall be payable as if on the death such property had been given to the spouse absolutely and indefeasibly.

(5) Where property may be taxed in the United States on the death of a United Kingdom national who was neither domiciled in nor a national of the United States and a claim is made under this paragraph, the tax imposed in the United States shall be limited to the amount of tax which would have been imposed had the decedent become domiciled in the United States immediately before his death, on the property which would in that event have been taxable.

ARTICLE 9 CREDITS
(1) Where under this Convention the United States may impose tax with respect to any property other than property which the United States is entitled to tax in accordance with Article 6 (Immovable Property (Real Property)) or 7 (Business Property of a Permanent

Establishment and Assets Pertaining to a Fixed Base Used for the Performance of Independent Personal Services) (that is, where the decedent or transferor was domiciled in or a national of the United States), then, except in cases to which paragraph (3) applies, double taxation shall be avoided in the following manner:

(a) Where the United Kingdom imposes tax with respect to property in accordance with the said Article 6 or 7 , the United States shall credit against the tax calculated according to its law with respect to that property an amount equal to the tax paid in the United Kingdom with respect to that property.

(b) Where the United Kingdom imposes tax with respect to property not referred to in sub-paragraph (*a*) and the decedent or transferor was a national of the United States and was domiciled in the United Kingdom at the time of the death or transfer, the United States shall credit against the tax calculated according to its law with respect to that property an amount equal to the tax paid in the United Kingdom with respect to that property.

(2) Where under this Convention the United Kingdom may impose tax with respect to any property other than property which the United Kingdom is entitled to tax in accordance with the said Article 6 or 7 (that is, where the decedent or transferor was domiciled in or a national of the United Kingdom), then, except in the cases to which paragraph (3) applies, double taxation shall be avoided in the following manner:

(a) Where the United States imposes tax with respect to property in accordance with the said Article 6 or 7 , the United Kingdom shall credit against the tax calculated according to its law with respect to that property an amount equal to the tax paid in the United States with respect to that property.

(b) Where the United States imposes tax with respect to property not referred to in sub-paragraph (*a*) and the decedent or transferor was a national of the United Kingdom and was domiciled in the United States at the time of the death or transfer, the United Kingdom shall credit against the tax calculated according to its law with respect to that property an amount equal to the tax paid in the United States with respect to that property.

(3) Where both Contracting States impose tax on the same event with respect to property which under the law of the United States would be regarded as property held in a trust or trust equivalent and under the law of the United Kingdom would be regarded as property comprised in a settlement, double taxation shall be avoided in the following manner:

(a) Where a Contracting State imposes tax with respect to property in accordance with the said Article 6 or 7 , the other Contracting State shall credit against the tax calculated according to its law with respect to that property an amount equal to the tax paid in the first-mentioned Contracting State with respect to that property.

(b) Where the United States imposes tax with respect to property which is not taxable in accordance with the said Article 6 or 7 then

(i) where the event giving rise to a liability to tax was a generation-skipping transfer and the deemed transferor was domiciled in the United States at the time of that event,

(ii) where the event giving rise to a liability to tax was the exercise or lapse of a power of appointment and the holder of the power was domiciled in the United States at the time of that event, or

(iii) where (i) or (ii) does not apply and the settlor or grantor was domiciled in the United States at the time when the tax is imposed, the United Kingdom shall credit against the tax calculated according to its law with respect to that property an amount equal to the tax paid in the United States with respect to that property.

(c) Where the United States imposes tax with respect to property which is not taxable in accordance with the said Article 6 or 7 and subparagraph (b) does not apply, the United States shall credit against the tax calculated according to its law with respect to that property an .amount equal to the tax paid in the United Kingdom with respect to that property.

(4) The credits allowed by a Contracting State according to the provisions of paragraphs (1), (2) and (3) shall not take into account amounts of such taxes not levied by reason of a credit otherwise allowed by the other Contracting State. No credit shall be finally allowed under those paragraphs until the tax (reduced by any credit allowable with respect thereto) for which the credit is allowable has been paid. Any credit allowed under those paragraphs shall not, however, exceed the part of the tax paid in a Contracting State (as computed before the credit is given but reduced by any credit for other tax) which is attributable to the property with respect to which the credit is given.

(5) Any claim for a credit or for a refund of tax founded on the provisions of the present Convention shall be made within six years from the date of the event giving rise to a liability to tax or, where later, within one year from the last date on which tax for which credit is given is due. The competent authority may, in appropriate circumstances, extend this time limit where the final determination of the taxes which are the subject of the claim for credit is delayed.

ARTICLE 10 NON-DISCRIMINATION
(1)
(a) Subject to the provisions of sub-paragraph (*b*), nationals of a Contracting State shall not be subject in the other State to any taxation or any requirement connected therewith which is other or more burdensome than the taxation and connected requirements to which nationals of that other State in the same circumstances are or may be subjected.

(b) Sub-paragraph (*a*) shall not prevent the United States from taxing a national of the United Kingdom, who is not domiciled in the United States, as a non-resident alien under its law, subject to the provisions of paragraph (5) of Article 8 (Deductions, Exemptions Etc).

(2) The taxation on a permanent establishment which an enterprise of a Contracting State has in the other Contracting State shall not be less favourably levied in that other State than the taxation levied on enterprises of that other State carrying on the same activities.

(3) Nothing contained in this Article shall be construed as obliging either Contracting State to grant to individuals not domiciled in that Contracting State any personal allowances, reliefs and reductions for taxation purposes which are granted to individuals so domiciled.

(4) Enterprises of a Contracting State, the capital of which is wholly or partly owned or controlled, directly or indirectly, by one or more residents of the other Contracting State, shall not be subjected in the first-mentioned Contracting State to any taxation or any requirement connected therewith which is other or more burdensome than the taxation and connected requirements to which other similar enterprises of the first-mentioned State are or may be subjected.

(5) The provisions of this Article shall apply to taxes which are the subject of this Convention.

ARTICLE 11 MUTUAL AGREEMENT PROCEDURE

(1) Where a person considers that the actions of one or both of the Contracting States result or will result in taxation not in accordance with the provisions of this Convention, he may, irrespective of the remedies provided by the domestic laws of those States, present his case to the competent authority of either Contracting State.

(2) The competent authority shall endeavour, if the objection appears to it to be justified and if it is not itself able to arrive at an appropriate solution, to resolve the case by mutual agreement with the competent authority of the other Contracting State, with a view to the avoidance of taxation not in accordance with the Convention. Where an agreement has been reached, a refund as appropriate shall be made to give effect to the agreement.

(3) The competent authorities of the Contracting States shall endeavour to resolve by mutual agreement any difficulties or doubts arising as to the interpretation or application of the Convention. In particular the competent authorities of the Contracting States may reach agreement on the meaning of the terms not otherwise defined in this Convention.

(4) The competent authorities of the Contracting States may communicate with each other directly for the purpose of reaching an agreement as contemplated by this Convention.

ARTICLE 12 EXCHANGE OF INFORMATION

The competent authorities of the Contracting States shall exchange such information (being information available under the respective taxation laws of the Contracting States) as is necessary for the carrying out of the provisions of this Convention or for the prevention of fraud or the administration of statutory provisions against legal avoidance in relation to the taxes which are the subject of this Convention. Any information so exchanged shall be treated as secret and shall not be disclosed to any persons other than persons (including a court or administrative body) concerned with the assessment, enforcement, collection, or prosecution in respect of the taxes which are the subject of the Convention. No information shall be exchanged which would disclose any trade, business, industrial or professional secret or any trade process.

ARTICLE 13 EFECT ON DIPLOMATIC AND CONSULAR OFFICIALS AND DOMESTIC LAW

(1) Nothing in this Convention shall affect the fiscal privileges of diplomatic or consular officials under the general rules of international law or under the provisions of special agreements.

(2) This Convention shall not restrict in any manner any exclusion, exemption, deduction, credit, or other allowance now or hereafter accorded by the laws of either Contracting State.

ARTICLE 14 ENTRY INTO FORCE

(1) This Convention shall be subject to ratification in accordance with the applicable procedures of each Contracting State and instruments of ratification shall be exchanged at Washington as soon as possible.

(2) This Convention shall enter into force immediately after the expiration of thirty days following the date on which the instruments of ratification are exchanged, and shall thereupon have effect:
(a) in the United States in respect of estates of individuals dying and transfers taking effect after that date; and

(b) in the United Kingdom in respect of property by reference to which there is a charge to tax which arises after that date.

(3) Subject to the provisions of paragraph (4) of this Article, the Convention between the Government of the United States of America and the Government of the United Kingdom of Great Britain and Northern Ireland for the Avoidance of Double Taxation and the Prevention of Fiscal Evasion with respect to Taxes on the Estates of Deceased Persons signed at Washington on 16 April 1945 (hereinafter referred to as "the 1945 Convention") shall cease to have effect in respect of property to which this Convention in accordance with the provisions of paragraph (2) of this Article applies.

(4) Where on a death before 27 March 1981 any provision of the 1945 Convention would have afforded any greater relief from tax than this Convention in respect of
(a) any gift inter vivos made by the decedent before 27 March 1974, or

(b) any settled property in which the decedent had a beneficial interest in possession before 27 March 1974 but not at any time thereafter, that provision shall continue to have effect in the United Kingdom in relation to that gift or settled property.

(5) The 1945 Convention shall terminate on the last date on which it has effect in accordance with the foregoing provisions of this Article.

ARTICLE 15 TERMINATION

(1) This Convention shall remain in force until terminated by one of the Contracting States. Either Contracting State may terminate this Convention, at any time after five years from

the date on which the Convention enters into force provided that at least six months' prior notice has been given through the diplomatic channel. In such event the Convention shall cease to have effect at the end of the period specified in the notice, but shall continue to apply in respect of the estate of any individual dying before the end of that period and in respect of any event (other than death) occurring before the end of that period and giving rise to liability to tax under the laws of either Contracting State.

(2) The termination of the present Convention shall not have the effect of reviving any treaty or arrangement abrogated by the present Convention or by treaties previously concluded between the Contracting States.

In witness whereof the undersigned, duly authorized thereto by their respective Governments, have signed this Convention.

Done in duplicate at London this 19th day of October 1978.

For the Government of the United States of America:
  Edward J. Streator

For the Government of the United Kingdom of Great Britain and Northern Ireland:
  Frank Judd

Questions

How do situs style treaties differ from domicile based treaties?

Which countries credit their citizens for payment of U.S. Estate Tax paid on either (i) U.S. assets of the foreign national (non-U.S. resident) or (ii) world-wide assets of the foreign U.S. resident?

How may double estate and/or gift tax be avoided by U.S. individuals with assets in non-treaty jurisdictions?

How may treaty partners fail to prevent double taxation due to different definitions of situs?

How are assets associated with a business abroad often excluded from treaty benefits?

CHAPTER 11
EXCHANGE OF TAX INFORMATION

Treaties

The IRS exchanges tax information with other countries pursuant to both situs and domicile tax treaties.[160] A broad range of Estate Tax and related information is exchanged "as is necessary … for the prevention of fraud or the administration of statutory provisions against tax avoidance …."[161] Information may be exchanged involving a decedent, related family and entities. Information may be related to any tax investigation or attempt to avoid Estate or Gift Tax. Any tax information legally available (under the tax law of the contracting states) may be exchanged.[162]

The IRS generally has three forms of information exchange. The first, "spontaneous" information exchanges, transfers certain tax information without request. The information provided may, for example, arise from an investigation which is likely of interest to a treaty partner. The U.S. engages in spontaneous exchange of information with almost all treaty countries.[163]

The second, "routine" exchanges, are also known as "automatic exchanges of information." Disclosure generally involves income tax return processing. Foreign partners agree to exchange certain tax or financial account-related information on a regular

---

[160] *See, e.g.*, U.S.-Austria Estate and Gift Tax Treaty art. 12 (domicile tax treaty) and U.S.-Greece Estate Tax Treaty (situs tax treaty).

[161] U.S.-Finland Treaty art. VII.

[162] *See, e.g.*, U.S.-Germany Treaty, art. 14. *See generally* U.S. v. Powell, 379 U.S. 48, 57-58 (1964). The test for relevance is whether the summons seeks information "which might throw light upon the correctness of the taxpayer's return." U.S. v. Cox, 73 F. Supp. 2d 751, 758 (S.D. Tex. 1999).

[163] *See, e.g.*, U.S.-Austria Estate and Gift Tax Treaty art. 12(1).

and systematic basis, without the need for a specific request, pursuant to a tax treaty or tax information exchange agreement.[164]

The third, "special" requests for information, are made on a case-by-case basis.[165]

U.S. exchange requests with (foreign tax agencies) are administered by the Program Manager(s) of the Exchange of Information in Washington, DC ("EOI HQ"); the Revenue Service Representative ("RSR") in Plantation, Florida; the overseas Tax Attaché; or the Program Manager of the Joint International Tax Shelter Information Centre ("JITSIC") in Washington, DC.[166]

To obtain information, the IRS may issue an Information Document Request Form 4564.[167] If the response from the recipient country is inadequate or untimely, the IRS[168] may then issue a Formal Document Request (FDR), a pre-summons letter or a summons pursuant to Section 7602 of the Code.[169] If the request is not honored or a petition to quash is filed, the IRS may seek enforcement, after review by Associate Chief Counsel (International), in conjunction with the Tax Division of the Justice Department.[170] To enforce a summons, the IRS must prove its good faith investigation.[171] No statute of limitations restricts the exchange of information. Tax

---

[164] IRM 4.60.1.4 (09-19-14).
[165] IRM 4.60.1.2 (09-19-14) (these exchanges are described as "specific exchanges of information").
[166] IRM 4.60.1.2.1(1), (2) (09-19-14), IRM 4.60.1.2.2(1) (09-19-14).
[167] IRM 4.61.2.2 (5-1-06).
[168] IRM Exhibit 4.46.1-1 (7-22-11), IRM 4.46.4.4.2 (3-1-06), IRM 4.61.2.4 (5-1-06), IRM 35.4.5.2.1 (8-11-04). *See generally* IRM 1.2.43.12 (7-1-10).
[169] IRM 4.61.2.4 (5-01-06).
[170] IRM 34.6.3.6.6(3), (4) (2-1-11).
[171] *See* U.S. v. Stuart, 489 U.S. 353, 356 (1989); See IRM 34.63.6 6 – "Tax Treaty and TIEA Summonses" (02-01-11).

information may therefore be exchanged even if the underlying tax claim cannot be pursued (because too much time has passed).

Tax Information Exchange Agreements

The U.S. and several non-treaty partners have also agreed to share tax information. Tax Information Exchange Agreements ("TIEAs") allow for information sharing with countries with which the U.S. does not have tax treaty.

The U.S. entered into its first TIEA in 1984 with Barbados (the first U.S. tax information exchange arrangement with a non-treaty partner).[172]

The U.S. has signed Tax Information Exchange Agreements with the following countries:

American Samoa

Antigua & Barbuda

Argentina

Aruba

Bahamas

Barbados

Bermuda

Bonaire, Sint Eustatius, & Saba

Brazil

British Virgin Islands

---

[172] *See* Convention Between Barbados and the United States of America for the Avoidance of Double Taxation and the Prevention of Fiscal Evasion with Respect to Taxes on Income, Dec. 31, 1984, U.S.-Barbados, T.I.A.S. (hereinafter "U.S.-Barbados TIEA").

Cayman Islands

Colombia

Costa Rica

Curaçao

Dominica

Dominican Republic

Gibraltar

Grenada

Guernsey

Guyana

Honduras

Hong Kong

Isle of Man

Jamaica

Jersey

Liechtenstein

Marshall Islands

Mauritius

Mexico

Monaco

Netherlands Antilles

Panama

Peru

Saint Maarten

Singapore

St. Lucia

Trinidad & Tobago

Vietnam

The U.S. also has tax information sharing agreements with U.S. possessions. The U.S. offers tax incentives to U.S. possessions to sign tax exchange agreements.

The U.S. Virgin Islands has entered into a "Working Arrangement to deem a return filed with the Virgin Islands by a bona fide resident of the Virgin Islands as a U.S. income tax return,"[173] provided that the U.S. and the Virgin Islands have entered an agreement for the routine exchange of income tax information.[174] The U.S. also has tax coordination agreements (for tax information exchange and mutual assistance to prevent evasion) with American Samoa, Guam, the Commonwealth of the Northern Mariana Islands, Puerto Rico, and the U.S. Virgin Islands.[175]

The Caribbean Basin Economic Recovery Act of 1983 (CBERA) (also known as the "Caribbean Basin Initiative") also provides certain benefits to countries that exchange

---

[173] *See* Tax Implementation Agreement Between the U.S. and the Virgin Islands, Feb. 24, 1984, U.S.-V.I., IRS, www.irs.gov (hereinafter "U.S.-Virgin Islands Agreement").

[174] 2008-1 C.B. 958.

[175] *See* Tax Coordination Agreement Between the United States of America and the Commonwealth of the Northern Mariana Islands, Jan. 30, 2003, U.S.-N. Mar. I., IRS, www.irs.gov (hereinafter "U.S.-Mariana Islands Agreement"); Agreement on Coordination of Tax Administration Between the United States of America and Guam, July 12, 1985, U.S.-Guam, IRS, www.irs.gov (hereinafter "U.S.-Guam Agreement"); Tax Coordination Agreement Between the United States of America and the Commonwealth of Puerto Rico, May 26, 1989, U.S.-P.R., IRS, www.irs.gov (hereinafter "U.S.-Puerto Rico Agreement"); Tax Implementation Agreement Between the United States of America and American Samoa, Jan. 1, 1989, U.S.-Am. Sam., IRS, www.irs.gov (hereinafter "U.S.-American Samoa Agreement"); and U.S.-Virgin Islands Agreement.

tax information with the IRS.[176] As part of the Caribbean Basin Initiative, Section 274(h) was added to the Code.

Section 274(h) generally restricts U.S. income tax deductions for expenses related to a convention, seminar, or similar meeting held outside the "North American area."

The "North American area" includes the United States, its possessions, the Trust Territory of the Pacific Islands, Canada and Mexico. Certain Caribbean countries and Bermuda, which have signed a tax information exchange agreement, are also treated as part of the North American area.[177]

Specifically, the North American area[178] includes the following:

The 50 United States and District of Columbia;

U.S. Possessions: American Samoa, Baker Island, the Commonwealth of Puerto Rico, the Commonwealth of the Northern Mariana Islands, Guam, Howland Island, Jarvis Island, Johnston Island, Kingman Reef, the Midway Islands, Palmyra Atoll, the U.S. Virgin Islands, Wake Island, and other U.S. islands, cays, and reefs not part of the 50 states or the District of Columbia;

Canada,

Mexico,

The Marshall Islands,

---

[176] Pub. L. No. 98-67, §§201–231, 19 U.S.C. §§2701–2707. The Act provides three specific benefits to countries agreeing to exchange tax information. First, the Act makes deductible in the U.S. (Code §274(h)) the costs of hosting conventions, business meetings and seminars. Second, the costs of hosting a foreign sales corporation (as defined in former Code §922) are deductible. Lastly, participating nations may receive loans qualifying for benefits under former Code §936.
[177] IRC §274(h); §274 defines "beneficiary" country to include countries covered by §212(a)(1)(A) of the Caribbean Basin Economic Recovery Act and Bermuda (CBERA) but does not include some later contracting countries with TIEAs such as Peru.
[178] Rev. Rul. 2016-16, 2016-26 I.R.B. 1062.

Micronesia, and

Palau.

Also included within the North American area are the following countries with which the U.S. has entered into a TIEA that meet certain statutory requirements.[179]

Jurisdiction	Effective Date
Antigua and Barbuda	February 10, 2003
Argentina	December 23, 2016
Aruba	September 13, 2004
Bahamas	January 1, 2006
Barbados	November 3, 1984
Bermuda	December 2, 1988
Bonaire, Sint Eustatius, and Saba	March 21, 2007
Brazil	March 19, 2013
British Virgin Islands	March 10, 2006
Cayman Islands	April 14, 2014
Colombia	April 30, 2014
Costa Rica	February 12, 1991
Curaçao	December 23, 2013
Dominica	May 9, 1988
Dominican Republic	October 12, 1989
Gibraltar	December 22, 2009

---

[179] Rev. Rul. 2016-16 (This ruling contains an updated list of all geographical areas included in the North American area for purposes of Section 274 of the Code. Rev. Rul. 2011-26 modified and superseded.).

Grenada	July 13, 1987
Guernsey	January 1, 2006
Guyana	August 27, 1992
Honduras	October 10, 1991
Hong Kong	June 20, 2014
Isle of Man	January 1, 2004
Jamaica	December 18, 1986
Jersey	June 26, 2006
Liechtenstein	January 1, 2009
Mauritius	August 29, 2014
Monaco	March 11, 2010
Panama	April 18, 2011
Peru	March 31, 1993
Saint Lucia	May 5, 2014
Sint Mauritius	March 22, 2007
Trinidad & Tobago	February 8, 1990

CBERA Sections 212(a)(1)(A) and (B) designate the following countries as "beneficiary countries" entitled to additional tax preferences for conventions and conferences: Anguilla, Antigua and Barbuda, Bahamas, Barbados, Belize, Bermuda, Dominica, Grenada, Guyana, Haiti, Jamaica, Saint Lucia, Saint Vincent and the

Grenadines, Surinam, Trinidad and Tobago, Cayman Islands, Montserrat, Netherlands Antilles, St. Kitts and Nevis, Turks and Caicos Islands, and the British Virgin Islands.[180]

Note that entering a TIEA does not guarantee an eligible beneficiary country inclusion in the "North American area." The tax information exchange must be coordinated with and the country designated as a CBERA beneficiary nation.

---

[180] *See also* 19 U.S.C. §2702(a) & (b).

AGREEMENT BETWEEN THE GOVERNMENT OF THE UNITED STATES OF AMERICA AND THE GOVERNMENT OF THE REPUBLIC OF ECUADOR FOR THE EXCHANGE OF INFORMATION RELATING TO TAXES

The Government of the United States of America (the "United States") and the Government of the Republic of Ecuador ("Ecuador"), desiring to facilitate the exchange of information with respect to taxes, have agreed as follows:

ARTICLE 1 Object and Scope of this Agreement

The competent authorities of the Parties shall provide assistance to each other through exchange of information that is foreseeably relevant to the administration and enforcement of the domestic laws of the Parties concerning taxes covered by this Agreement. Such information shall include information that is foreseeably relevant to the determination, assessment and collection of such taxes, the recovery and enforcement of tax claims, or the investigation or prosecution of tax matters. Information shall be exchanged in accordance with the provisions of this Agreement and shall be treated as confidential in the manner provided in Article 10 (Confidentiality).

ARTICLE 2 Jurisdiction

A requested Party shall not be obligated to provide information that is neither held by its authorities nor in the possession or control of persons who are within its territorial jurisdiction. With respect to information held by its authorities or in the possession or control of persons who are within its territorial jurisdiction, however, the requested Party shall provide information in accordance with this Agreement regardless of whether the person to whom the information relates is, or whether the information is held by, a resident or national of a Party.

ARTICLE 3 Taxes Covered

1. This Agreement shall apply to the following taxes imposed by the Parties:

        (a) in the case of the United States, all federal taxes; and
        (b) in the case of Ecuador, all taxes administered by the Internal Revenue Service (Servicio de Rentas Internas - SRI).

2. This Agreement also shall apply to any identical or substantially similar taxes that are imposed after the date of signature of this Agreement in addition to, or in place of, the existing taxes. The competent authorities of the Parties shall notify each other of any significant changes that have been made in their taxation laws or other laws that relate to the application of this Agreement.

ARTICLE 4 Definitions

1. For the purposes of this Agreement, unless otherwise defined:
  (a) the term "Party" means the United States or Ecuador as the context requires;
  (b) the term "competent authority" means:
      (i) in the case of the United States, the Secretary of the Treasury or the Secretary's delegate, and
      (ii) in the case of Ecuador, the Director General of the Internal Revenue Service (Servicio de Rentas Internas - SRI) or the Director General's delegate;
  (c) the term "person" includes an individual, a company and any other body of persons;
  (d) the term "company" means any body corporate or any entity that is treated as a body corporate for tax purposes;
  (e) the term "national" of a Party means any individual possessing the nationality or citizenship of that Party, and any legal person, partnership or association deriving its status as such from the laws in force in that Party;
  (f) the term "publicly traded company" means any company whose principal class of shares is listed on a recognized stock exchange if the purchase or sale of its listed shares is not implicitly or explicitly restricted to a limited group of investors;
  (g) the term "principal class of shares" means the class or classes of shares representing a majority of the voting power and value of the company;
  (h) the term "recognized stock exchange" means any stock exchange agreed upon by the competent authorities of the Parties;
  (i) the term "public collective investment fund or scheme" means any pooled investment vehicle, irrespective of legal form, if the purchase, sale or redemption of the units, shares or other interests in the investment vehicle is not implicitly or explicitly restricted to a limited group of investors;
  (j) the term "tax" means any tax to which this Agreement applies and does not include customs duties;
  (k) the term "applicant Party" means the Party requesting information;
  (l) the term "requested Party" means the Party requested to provide information;
  (m) the term "information gathering measures" means laws and administrative or judicial procedures that enable a Party to obtain and provide the requested information; and
  (n) the term "information" means any fact, statement or record in any form whatever.

2. For purposes of determining the geographic area within which jurisdiction to compel production of information may be exercised:

  (a) the term "United States" means the territory of the United States of America, including American Samoa, Guam, the Northern Mariana Islands, Puerto Rico, the U.S. Virgin Islands and any other U.S. possession or territory; and
  (b) the term "Ecuador" means the territory of the Republic of Ecuador.

3. As regards the application of this Agreement at any time by a Contracting Party, any term not defined therein shall, unless the context otherwise requires or the competent authorities agree to a common meaning pursuant to the provisions of Article 12 (Mutual

Agreement Procedure), have the meaning that it has at that time under the law of that Party, any meaning under the applicable tax laws of that Party prevailing over a meaning given to the term under other laws of that Party.

ARTICLE 5 Exchange of Information Upon Request

1. The competent authority of the requested Party shall provide information for the purposes referred to in Article 1 (Object and Scope of this Agreement) upon request by the competent authority of the applicant Party. Such information shall be exchanged without regard to whether the requested Party needs such information for its own tax purposes or whether the conduct being investigated would constitute a crime under the laws of the requested Party if such conduct occurred in the requested Party.

2. If the information in the possession of the competent authority of the requested Party is not sufficient to enable it to comply with the request for information, the requested Party shall use all relevant information gathering measures to provide the applicant Party with the information requested, notwithstanding that the requested Party may not need such information for its own tax purposes. Privileges under the laws and practices of the applicant Party shall not apply in the execution of a request by the requested Party and the resolution of such matters shall be solely the responsibility of the applicant Party.

3. If specifically requested by the competent authority of the applicant Party, the competent authority of the requested Party shall, to the extent allowable under its domestic laws:
    (a) specify the time and place for the taking of testimony or the production of books, papers, records and other data;
    (b) place the individual giving testimony or producing books, papers, records or other data under oath;
    (c) permit the presence of individuals designated by the competent authority of the applicant Party as being involved in or affected by execution of the request, including an accused, counsel for the accused, individuals charged with the administration or enforcement of the domestic laws of the applicant Party covered by this Agreement or a commissioner or magistrate for the purpose of rendering evidentiary rulings or determining issues of privilege under the laws of the applicant Party;
    (d) provide individuals permitted to be present with an opportunity to question, directly or through the executing authority, the individual giving testimony or producing books, papers, records and other data;
    (e) secure original and unedited books, papers, records and other data;
    (f) secure or produce true and correct copies of original and unedited books, papers, records and other data;
    (g) determine the authenticity of books, papers, records and other data produced, and provide authenticated copies of original books, papers, records and other data;
    (h) examine the individual producing books, papers, records and other data regarding the purpose for which and the manner in which the item produced is or was maintained;

(i) permit the competent authority of the applicant Party to provide written questions to which the individual producing books, papers, records and other data is to respond regarding the items produced;

(j) perform any other act not in violation of the laws or at variance with the administrative practice of the requested Party; and

(k) certify either that procedures requested by the competent authority of the applicant Party were followed or that the procedures requested could not be followed, with an explanation of the deviation and the reason therefor.

4. Each Party shall ensure that its competent authority, for the purposes specified in Article 1 (Object and Scope of this Agreement) of this Agreement, has the authority to obtain and provide upon request:

(a) information held by banks, other financial institutions, and any person acting in an agency or fiduciary capacity including nominees and trustees; and

(b) information regarding the ownership of companies, partnerships, trusts, foundations, "Anstalten" and other persons, including, within the constraints of Article 2 (Jurisdiction), ownership information on all such persons in an ownership chain; in the case of trusts, information on settlors, trustees and beneficiaries; and in the case of foundations, information on founders, members of the foundation council and beneficiaries.

Notwithstanding subparagraph 4(b), this Agreement does not create an obligation on the Parties to obtain or provide ownership information with respect to publicly traded companies or public collective investment funds or schemes unless such information can be obtained without giving rise to disproportionate difficulties to the requested Party.

5. The competent authority of the applicant Party shall provide the following information to the competent authority of the requested Party when making a request for information under this Agreement, with the greatest degree of specificity possible:

(a) the identity of the person or ascertainable group or category of persons under examination or investigation;

(b) a statement of the information sought, including its nature and the form in which the applicant Party wishes to receive the information from the requested Party;

(c) the period of time with respect to which the information is requested;

(d) the matter under the applicant Party's tax law with respect to which the information is sought;

(e) grounds for believing that the information requested is foreseeably relevant to tax administration or enforcement of the applicant Party with respect to the person or group or category of persons identified in subparagraph 5(a);

(f) grounds for believing that the information requested is held in the requested Party or is in the possession or control of a person within the jurisdiction of the requested Party;

(g) to the extent known, the name and address of any person believed to be in possession or control of the requested information;

(h) a statement that the request is in conformity with the law and administrative practices of the applicant Party, that if the requested information was within the jurisdiction of the applicant Party then the competent authority of the applicant Party would be able to obtain the information under the laws of the applicant Party or in the normal course of administrative practice and that it is in conformity with this Agreement; and

(i) a statement that the applicant Party has pursued all means available in its own territory to obtain the information, except those that would give rise to disproportionate difficulties.

ARTICLE 6 Automatic Exchange of Information

The competent authorities may automatically transmit information to each other for the purposes referred to in Article 1 (Object and Scope of this Agreement). The competent authorities shall determine the items of information to be exchanged pursuant to this Article and the procedures to be used to exchange such items of information.

ARTICLE 7 Spontaneous Exchange of Information

The competent authority of a Party may spontaneously transmit to the competent authority of the other Party information that has come to the attention of the first mentioned competent authority and that the first-mentioned competent authority supposes to be foreseeably relevant to the accomplishment of the purposes referred to in Article 1 (Object and Scope of this Agreement). The competent authorities shall determine the procedures to be used to exchange such information.

ARTICLE 8 Tax Examinations Abroad

1. A Party may allow representatives of the other Party to interview individuals and examine records in the territory of the first-mentioned Party with the written consent of the persons concerned. The competent authority of the second mentioned Party shall notify the competent authority of the first-mentioned Party of the time and place of the meeting with the individuals concerned.

2. At the request of the competent authority of one Party, the competent authority of the other Party may allow representatives of the competent authority of the first mentioned Party to be present at the appropriate part of a tax examination in the second-mentioned Party.

3. If the request referred to in paragraph 2 of this Article is acceded to, the competent authority of the Party conducting the examination shall, as soon as possible, notify the competent authority of the other Party about the time and place of the examination, the authority or official designated to carry out the examination and the procedures and conditions required by the first-mentioned Party for the conduct of the examination. All decisions with respect to the conduct of the tax examination shall be made by the Party conducting the examination.

ARTICLE 9 Possibility of Declining a Request

1. The requested Party shall not be required to obtain or provide information that the applicant Party would not be able to obtain under its own laws for purposes of the administration or enforcement of its own tax laws. The competent authority of the requested Party may decline to assist where the request is not made in conformity with this Agreement. The competent authority of the requested Party may decline to assist where the applicant Party has not pursued all means available in its own territory to obtain the information, except those that would give rise to disproportionate difficulties.

2. The provisions of this Agreement shall not impose on a Party the obligation to supply information that would disclose any trade, business, industrial, commercial or professional secret or trade process. Notwithstanding the foregoing, information of the type referred to in Article 5 (Exchange of Information Upon Request), paragraph 4 shall not be treated as such a secret or trade process merely because it meets the criteria in that paragraph.

3. The provisions of this Agreement shall not impose on a Party the obligation to obtain or provide information that would reveal confidential communications between a client and an attorney, solicitor or other admitted legal representative where such communications are:
   (a) produced for the purposes of seeking or providing legal advice; or
   (b) produced for the purposes of use in existing or contemplated legal proceedings.

4. The requested Party may decline a request for information if the disclosure of the information would be contrary to public policy (ordre public).

5. A request for information shall not be refused on the ground that the tax claim giving rise to the request is disputed.

6. A request for information shall not be refused on the ground that the period of limitations in the requested party has expired. Instead, the statute of limitations of the applicant Party pertaining to the taxes to which the Agreement applies shall govern a request for information.

ARTICLE 10 Confidentiality

Any information received by a Party under this Agreement shall be treated as confidential and may be disclosed only to persons or authorities (including courts and administrative bodies) in the jurisdiction of the Party concerned with the assessment, collection or administration of, the enforcement or prosecution in respect of, or the determination of appeals in relation to, the taxes covered by this Agreement, or the oversight of such functions. Such persons or authorities shall use such information only for such purposes. They may disclose the information in public court proceedings or in judicial decisions. The information may not be disclosed to any other person, entity, authority or jurisdiction. Notwithstanding the foregoing:

(a) where the competent authority of the Party that provided the information provides prior, written consent, the information may be disclosed for:

(i) counter-terrorism purposes, but only if the information may be disclosed for such purposes under the domestic laws of the Party that received the information;

(ii) purposes permitted under the provisions of an international agreement governing legal assistance in criminal matters that is in force between the Parties that allows for the exchange of tax information; or

(iii) other purposes, but only when the information may be used for the same or similar such purposes under the domestic laws of both Parties;

(b) the competent authority of a Party may disclose information not relating to a particular person received under this Agreement if it has determined, after consultation with the competent authority of the other Party, that such disclosure would not impair tax administration (including the administration of this Agreement); and

(c) the competent authority of Ecuador may disclose information received under this Agreement to persons or authorities in Ecuador concerned with the oversight of the assessment, collection or administration of, the enforcement or prosecution in respect of, or the determination of appeals in relation to, the taxes covered by this Agreement only with the written consent of the competent authority of the United States.

ARTICLE 11 Costs

Unless the competent authorities of the Parties otherwise agree, ordinary costs incurred in providing assistance shall be borne by the requested Party and extraordinary costs incurred in providing assistance shall be borne by the applicant Party.

ARTICLE 12 Mutual Agreement Procedure

1. Where difficulties or doubts arise between the Parties regarding the implementation or interpretation of this Agreement, the competent authorities shall endeavor to resolve the matter by mutual agreement.

2. The competent authorities may adopt and implement procedures to facilitate the implementation of this Agreement.

3. The competent authorities of the Parties may communicate with each other directly for purposes of reaching a mutual agreement under this Article.

ARTICLE 13 Mutual Assistance Procedure

The competent authorities of the Parties may agree to exchange technical knowhow, develop new audit techniques, identify new areas of non-compliance and jointly study non-compliance areas.

ARTICLE 14 Entry Into Force

This Agreement shall enter into force one month from the date of receipt of Ecuador's written notification to the United States that Ecuador has completed its necessary internal procedures for entry into force of this Agreement. The provisions of this Agreement shall have effect for requests made on or after the date of entry into force, without regard to the taxable period to which the request relates.

ARTICLE 15 Termination

1. The Agreement shall remain in force until terminated by a Party.

2. Either Party may terminate the Agreement by giving notice of termination in writing to the other Party. Such termination shall become effective on the first day of the month following the expiration of a period of six months after the date of the notice of termination.

3. If the Agreement is terminated, both Parties shall remain bound by the provisions of Article 10 (Confidentiality) with respect to any information obtained under the Agreement. In witness whereof, the undersigned, being duly authorized thereto by their respective Governments, have signed this Agreement.

Done at _____ in duplicate, in the English and Spanish languages, both texts being equally authentic, this __ day of _____, 20__.

FOR THE GOVERNMENT OF THE UNITED STATES OF AMERICA:

FOR THE GOVERNMENT OF THE REPUBLIC OF ECUADOR:

Barquero v. U.S.

OPINION

No. 93-7447.

April 20, 1994.

Andy A. Tschoepe, II, John P. Guillory, Akin, Gump, Strauss, Hauer Feld, L.L.P., San Antonio, TX, for plaintiff-appellant.

James P. Springer, Dept. of Justice, Tax Div., Gary R. Allen, Chief, Appellate Section, Charles E. Brookhart, Washington, DC, for appellee.

Appeal from the United States District Court for the Southern District of Texas.

Before HENDERSON, SMITH, and EMILIO M. GARZA, Circuit Judges.

Circuit Judge of the 11th Circuit, sitting by designation.

EMILIO M. GARZA, Circuit Judge:

Plaintiff Julio Roberto Zarate Barquero ("Zarate") and Counter-defendant International Bank of Commerce ("IBC") appeal the district court's order denying their motion to quash an administrative summons issued by the Internal Revenue Service ("IRS") and granting the government's motion to enforce the summons. We affirm.

I

In 1989, the United States and Mexico signed a Tax Information Exchange Agreement ("TIEA"). In 1991, the "competent authority" of Mexico requested pursuant to the TIEA that the IRS provide information regarding Zarate's tax liability under the laws of Mexico. Pursuant to that request, the IRS served IBC with an administrative summons requesting all records in IBC's possession pertaining to bank accounts held or controlled by Zarate. Zarate filed a petition with the district court to quash the summons, which the government answered. The government also filed a counterclaim seeking to enforce the summons and adding IBC as a defendant. Both parties then sought summary judgment. After a hearing, the district court denied the motion to quash and granted the motion to enforce. Zarate and IBC now appeal, arguing that the district court erred in several respects.

As its name suggests, a TIEA is an agreement providing for the exchange between two countries of tax or tax-related information that may otherwise be subject to nondisclosure laws of each country. 26 U.S.C. § 274(h)(6)(C)(i). A TIEA allows both countries to obtain from each other information that "may be necessary or appropriate to carry out and enforce the[ir] tax laws." Id.

Pursuant to a delegation from the Secretary of the Treasury, the IRS is the "competent authority" of the United States. The TIEA charges the competent authorities of each country with carrying out all exchanges of information between the two countries.

II

Zarate initially contends that the United States — Mexico TIEA is unconstitutional because Congress has not authorized the President to enter into such agreements. Section 274(h)(6)(C) of the Internal Revenue Code authorizes the Secretary "to negotiate and conclude an agreement for the exchange of information with any beneficiary country." 26 U.S.C. § 274(h)(6)(C). It is undisputed that Mexico is not a "beneficiary country" as that term is defined by section 212(a)(1)(A) of the Caribbean Basin Economic Recovery Act — 19 U.S.C. § 2702. See 26 U.S.C. § 274(h)(6)(B). Zarate thus concludes that the TIEA between the United States and Mexico is unconstitutional because the President lacked the authority to enter into it.

The Caribbean Basin Economic Recovery Act is also known as the Caribbean Basin Initiative ("CBI"). Beneficiary countries that enter into TIEAs with the United States gain several benefits, the most notable being that they become eligible for project financing under § 936 of the Code.

The government, on the other hand, argues that the 1986 amendments to the Code provided statutory authorization for the U.S. — Mexico TIEA. Specifically, the government points to § 927(e)(3) of the Code, which provides that

The government did not argue in its brief that the President, pursuant to his own constitutional authority, could lawfully enter into the TIEA.

the term ["foreign sales corporation" ("FSC")] shall not include any corporation which was created or organized under the laws of any foreign country unless there is in effect between such country and the United States —

(A) a bilateral or multilateral agreement *described in* <u>*section 274(h)(6)(C)*</u> *(determined by treating any reference to a beneficiary country as being a reference to any foreign country* and by applying such section without regard to clause (ii) thereof). . . .

Clause (ii) of § 274(h)(6)(C) provides:

An exchange of information agreement need not provide for the exchange of qualified confidential information which is sought only for civil tax purposes if —

(I) the Secretary of the Treasury, after making all reasonable efforts to negotiate an agreement which includes the exchange of such information, determines that such an agreement cannot be negotiated but that the agreement which was negotiated will significantly assist in the administration and enforcement of the tax laws of the United States, and

(II) the President determines that the agreement as negotiated is in the national security interest of the United States.

<u>26 U.S.C. § 274(h)(6)(C)(ii)</u>.

26 U.S.C. § 927(e)(3) (emphasis added). While acknowledging that Congress did not explicitly amend § 274(h)(6)(C) by amending § 927(e)(3), the government nonetheless contends that § 927(e)(3) authorizes the President to enter into TIEAs with non-beneficiary countries. We agree.

Prior to 1986, only beneficiary countries that had entered into TIEAs with the United States could serve as host countries for FSCs. However, Congress, through the 1986 amendments, opted to allow any foreign country to enter into a TIEA and become eligible to be a host country:

See 26 U.S.C. § 927(e)(3) (1982).

The 1986 [Tax Reform] Act provided that a country may qualify as a host country for foreign sales corporations (FSCs) by entering into an exchange of information agreement of the type provided for in the Caribbean Basin Economic Recovery Act, *whether or not that country is eligible to be a CBI beneficiary country. . . . [W]here a country other than a CBI beneficiary country enters into a bilateral information exchange agreement* of the type that qualifies it as a FSC host country . . ., the bill provides express protection to individuals who make disclosures in accordance with the terms of the agreement from Code sanctions for unauthorized disclosures. S.Rep. No. 445, 100th Cong., 2d Sess. 332 (1988), *reprinted in* 1988 U.S.C.C.A.N. 4515, 4843-44 (emphasis added). If the Executive lacked the power to enter into TIEAs with non-beneficiary countries, the 1986 amendment to § 927(e)(3) would serve no apparent purpose — an absurd result. Thus, we believe that §§ 274(h)(6)(C) and 927(e)(3), when read together, provide specific congressional authorization for the President's decision to enter into the challenged TIEA. Consequently, the TIEA "is `supported by the strongest of presumptions and the widest latitude of judicial interpretation, and the burden of persuasion would rest heavily upon any who might attack it.'" *Dames Moore v. Regan,* <u>453 U.S. 654</u>, <u>101 S.Ct. 2972</u>, <u>69 L.Ed.2d 918</u> (1981) (quoting *Youngstown Sheet Tube Co. v. Sawyer,* <u>343 U.S. 579, 637</u>, <u>72 S.Ct. 863, 871</u>, <u>96 L.Ed. 1153</u> (1952) (Jackson, J., concurring)). "Under the circumstances of this case, we cannot say that [Zarate] has sustained that heavy burden." *Id.* Accordingly, we find that the U.S. — Mexico TIEA is both constitutional and valid.

The report was promulgated in 1988 when Congress corrected technical errors in the 1986 Tax Reform Act.

Zarate argues that the 1986 amendment to § 927(e)(3) "merely provides that if the Secretary did enter into [TIEAs with non-beneficiary countries], the foreign countries who are party to those agreements could qualify as a host country [sic] for FSCs." In Zarate's opinion, before the Secretary actually could enter into a TIEA with a non-beneficiary country, Congress would need to pass a statute specifically authorizing the proposed TIEA. We disagree. Section 927(e)(3)'s cross-reference to and incorporation of § 274(h)(6)(C) and redefinition of the term "beneficiary country" demonstrates Congress's intent to authorize the Secretary to negotiate and conclude a TIEA with "any foreign country." 26 U.S.C. § 927(e)(3)(A).

See State Dept. Rel. No. 90-85 (noting that the TIEA at issue "was concluded pursuant to section 274(h)(6)(C) of the Code, which is incorporated by reference and implication in section 936(d) of the Code, as amended by . . . the Tax Reform Act of 1986").

This, of course, does not mean that every cross-reference in the Code incorporates and amends the referenced provision.

Although we conclude that §§ 274(h)(6)(C) and 927(e)(3) constitute specific congressional authorization to the President to enter into the TIEA at issue, we alternatively find that these sections of the Code provide "implicit approval" for the President's actions. The Supreme Court has noted that a "failure of Congress specifically to delegate authority does not, `especially . . . in the area of foreign policy . . .,' imply `congressional disapproval' of the action taken by the Executive." *Dames Moore,* 453 U.S. at 678, 101 S.Ct. at 2986 (quoting *Haig v. Agee,* 453 U.S. 280, 291, 101 S.Ct. 2766, 2774, 69 L.Ed.2d 640 (1981)) (some alterations in original). Instead,

See Restatement (Third) of Foreign Relations Law of the United States § 303 cmt. e (stating that "Congress may enact legislation that requires, *or fairly implies,* the need for an agreement") (emphasis added).

The enactment of legislation closely related to the question of the President's authority in a particular case which evinces legislative intent to accord the President broad discretion may be considered to "invite" "measures on independent presidential responsibility." At least this is so where there is no contrary indication of legislative intent and when . . . there is a history of congressional acquiescence in conduct of the sort engaged in by the President.

Id., 453 U.S. at 678-79, 101 S.Ct. at 2986 (quoting *Youngstown,* 343 U.S. at 637, 72 S.Ct. at 871 (Jackson, J., concurring)). Here, the 1986 amendment to § 927(e)(3) constitutes an "invitation" for the President to enter into TIEAs with non-beneficiary countries. *Cf. id.,* 453 U.S. at 680, 101 S.Ct. at 2987 ("By creating a procedure to implement future settlement agreements, Congress placed its stamp of approval on such agreements."). Moreover, there exists a history, albeit a short one, of congressional acquiescence in the President's concluding TIEAs with non-beneficiary countries, and Congress has not questioned the power of the President to conclude such agreements. Indeed, the Senate appears to have given its explicit approval to the TIEA at issue when it ratified the United States — Mexico comprehensive income tax convention in November 1993. Consequently, we believe that the Executive did not exceed its power by entering into the TIEA with Mexico.

See also 26 U.S.C. § 6103(k) ("A return or return information may be disclosed to a competent authority of a foreign government which has . . . [a] convention or bilateral agreement relating to the exchange of tax information with the United States. . . .").

In addition to the U.S. — Mexico agreement, the President has signed TIEAs with Columbia and Peru, both non-beneficiary countries, without any indication of congressional disapproval. *See* Financial Times, Oct. 1993, available in LEXIS, Nexis Library (IRS announces the signing of a TIEA with Columbia); *U.S. Signs Anti-Drug Pacts with Bolivia and Peru,* Reuters, February 1990, available in LEXIS, Nexis Library. At one time, the President also was actively negotiating with Bolivia regarding the possibility of entering into a TIEA. *See Treasury Department Announcement of Status of Negotiations of Income Tax Treaties and Tax Information Exchange Agreements,* Daily Report for Executives, April 5, 1993, available in LEXIS, Nexis Library.

In September 1992, the United States and Mexico signed a comprehensive income tax convention. Article 27 of the convention states that "[t]he competent authorities [of both countries] shall exchange information as provided in the Agreement Between the United States of America and the United Mexican States for the Exchange of Information with Respect to Taxes signed on November 9, 1989." Convention Between the Government of the United States of America and the Government of the United Mexican States for the Avoidance of Double Taxation and the Prevention of Fiscal Evasion with Respect to Taxes on Income, September 18, 1992, U.S. — Mex., art. 27, S. Treaty Doc. No. 7, 103d Cong., 1st Sess. 52 (1993). The President transmitted the convention to the Senate in May 1993, and the Senate advised and consented to the ratification of the convention on November 20, 1993. *See* 139 Cong.Rec. S16857-01 (daily ed. Nov. 20, 1993).

III

Zarate next argues that even if the TIEA is valid, the IRS lacks the authority to issue a summons on behalf of a request by Mexico pursuant to the TIEA. The IRS contends that it may use the powers and authority granted to it under chapter 78 of the Code, 26 U.S.C. § 7601 *et seq.,* to obtain information and documents requested by the competent authority of a country that has a TIEA with the United States. *See United States v. Stuart,* 489 U.S. 353, 109 S.Ct. 1183, 103 L.Ed.2d 388 (1989) (upholding administrative summons issued by IRS pursuant to a request by Canada, which had a tax convention with the United States providing for the exchange of tax information between the countries).

Section 274(h)(6)(D) of the Code provides that the Secretary "may exercise his authority under subchapter A of chapter 78 to carry out any obligation of the United States under an [exchange of information] agreement referred to in [§ 274(h)(6)(C)]." 26 U.S.C. § 274(h)(6)(D). Here, the TIEA with Mexico states:
If information is requested by a Contracting State pursuant to paragraph 4, the requested State shall obtain the information requested in the same manner, and provide it in the same form, as if the tax of the applicant State were the tax of the requested State and were being imposed by the requested State.

Thus, the TIEA obliges the IRS to seek documents from IBC as if the IRS was determining Zarate's American tax liability. Moreover, the TIEA is, pursuant to the cross-reference found in § 927(e)(3)(A), negotiated under § 274(h)(6)(C). Thus, the TIEA obliges the IRS to use its authority under chapter 78 of the Code to obtain the information and documents sought by the Mexican tax authorities. Chapter 78 authorizes the IRS to summon any person the Secretary deems proper "to produce such books, papers, records, or other data . . . as may be relevant to" "ascertaining the correctness of any return, making a return where none has been made, determining the liability of any person for any internal revenue tax . . ., or collecting any such liability." 26 U.S.C. § 7602(a)(2). Accordingly, the IRS possessed the authority to issue the summons on behalf of the competent authority of Mexico.

IV

Zarate next complains that the district court erred in enforcing the summons because the IRS issued it in bad faith. To obtain enforcement of an administrative summons, the IRS must demonstrate that it issued the summons in good faith — i.e.,
that the investigation will be conducted pursuant to a legitimate purpose, that the inquiry may be relevant to the purpose, that the information sought is not already within the Commissioner's possession, and that the administrative steps required by the Code have been followed — in particular, that the [IRS], after investigation, has determined the further examination to be necessary and has notified the taxpayer in writing to that effect.
United States v. Powell, 379 U.S. 48, 57-58, 85 S.Ct. 248, 254-55, 13 L.Ed.2d 112 (1964). Once the IRS has made such a showing, "it is entitled to an enforcement order unless the taxpayer can show that the IRS is attempting to abuse the court's process." *Stuart,* 489 U.S. at 360, 109 S.Ct. at 1188.

The affidavits the IRS submitted in this case "plainly satisfied the requirements of good faith [the Supreme Court] set forth in *Powell.*" *Id.,* 489 U.S. at 360, 109 S.Ct. at 1188; *see also id.* at 370, 109 S.Ct. at 1193 (noting that the summons will be enforced "[s]o long as *the IRS itself* acts in good faith") (emphasis added). The IRS Assistant Commissioner (International) stated under oath that the information sought was not within the possession of American or Mexican tax authorities, that it might be relevant to the determination of Zarate's Mexican tax liabilities, that the same type of information could be obtained by Mexican tax authorities under Mexican law, and that Mexican tax authorities had requested that the IRS seek such information. She further noted that any exchanged information could be disclosed only "as required in the normal administrative or judicial process operative in the administration of the tax system" in Mexico and that improper use of exchanged information would be protested. Moreover, the IRS issued the summons in conformity with applicable statutes and duly informed Zarate by certified or registered mail of its issuance.

Finally, Zarate has failed to adduce any facts indicating that the IRS was trying to use the district court's process for some improper purpose, "such as harassment or the acquisition of bargaining power in connection with some collateral dispute." *Id.* at 360-61, 109 S.Ct. at 1188. Accordingly, the IRS was entitled to an enforcement order. *See id.* (where the Supreme Court upheld IRS summonses issued on behalf of Canada where the supporting affidavits were virtually identical to the supporting affidavits supplied here); *United States v. Linsteadt,* 724 F.2d 480, 482 (5th Cir. 1984) (noting that "the requisite showing [of relevance] may be made by a simple affidavit filed with the petition to enforce by the agent who issued the summons").

Zarate, without citing any authority, complains that the IRS did not issue the summons in conformity with applicable statutes because the TIEA was not published in "a compilation entitled `United States Treaties and Other International Agreements,'" 1 U.S.C. § 112a, and was not transmitted to Congress within sixty days after the TIEA "entered into force," 1 U.S.C. § 112b. However, Zarate did not contend before the district court that these facts demonstrated that the IRS issued the summons in bad faith. Accordingly, we need not address these issues. *See Alford v. Dean Witter Reynolds, Inc.,* 975 F.2d 1161, 1163 (5th Cir. 1992) (noting that we need not consider issues raised on appeal if they were not raised before the district court). While Zarate did raise these issues below regarding the validity of the TIEA, he does not argue on appeal that the TIEA is unconstitutional or invalid for these reasons. *See United States v. Valdiosera-Godinez,* 932 F.2d 1093, 1099 (5th Cir. 1991) ("Any issues not raised or argued in the appellant's brief are considered waived and will not be entertained on appeal."), *cert. denied,* ___ U.S. ___, 113 S.Ct. 2369, 124 L.Ed.2d 275 (1993).

V

Zarate next argues that because the IRS failed to comply with the Right to Financial Privacy Act ("RFPA") when issuing the summons to IBC, the summons is unenforceable. Zarate points out that Article 4(4)(b) of the TIEA specifically imposes upon the IRS the duty to comply with the RFPA when seeking information on behalf of the Mexican government:

If the United States is requested to obtain the types of information covered by section 3402 of the Right to Financial Privacy Act of 1978 [12 U.S.C. § 3402] as in effect at the time of signing this agreement, it shall obtain the requested information pursuant to that provision.

Thus, the plain language of the TIEA requires the IRS to comply with § 3402 of RFPA. *See Stuart,* 489 U.S. at 365, 109 S.Ct. at 1191 (noting that the clear import of treaty language controls). Section 3402 provides that the government may not obtain from any financial institution the financial records of any person, "except as provided by section . . . 3413" of the RFPA. Section 3413, in turn, provides that "[n]othing in [the RFPA] prohibits the disclosure of financial records in accordance with procedures authorized by Title 26." Because Zarate does not argue that the summons failed to comply with the examination and inspection procedures set out in Title 26, *see* 26 U.S.C. § 7601 *et seq.,* we find that the IRS issued the summons in compliance with both § 3402 of the RFPA and Article 4 of the TIEA.

VI

Zarate, again without citing any authority, contends that the summons is unenforceable to the extent the IRS seeks to obtain documents created before the TIEA took effect. The government, on the other hand, argues that "information may be requested and provided for tax periods prior to the effective date of the TIEA." Initially, we note that "the Supreme Court has consistently declined to circumscribe the breadth of the summons authority that Congress intended to grant the IRS, absent unambiguous directions from Congress." *United States v. Barrett,* 837 F.2d 1341, 1349 (5th Cir. 1988) (en banc), *cert. denied,* 492 U.S. 926, 109 S.Ct. 3264, 106 L.Ed.2d 609 (1989). For example, the Court has refused to read into the Code requirements that summons, to be enforceable, be founded upon probable cause, *Powell,* 379 U.S. at 53-54, 85 S.Ct. at 253, that the summons authority be limited to case where no criminal prosecution was pending, *Donaldson v. United States,* 400 U.S. 517, 533, 91 S.Ct. 534, 544, 27 L.Ed.2d 580 (1971), and that the IRS did not have the authority to issue "John Doe" summonses to determine the identity of unknown individuals who might be liable for unpaid taxes, *United States v. Bisceglia,* 420 U.S. 141, 150, 95 S.Ct. 915, 921, 43 L.Ed.2d 88 (1975). Moreover, it is clear that an IRS summons can require the production of records for years that are time-barred from investigation so long as the material from those years is relevant for the years under investigation that are not time-barred. *Dunn v. Ross,* 356 F.2d 664, 666 (5th Cir. 1966). Furthermore, "the evident purpose behind [the TIEA] — the reduction of tax evasion by allowing signatories to demand information from each other — counsels against interpreting [the agreement] to limit inquiry in the manner [Zarate] desire[s]." *Stuart,* 489 U.S. at 368, 109 S.Ct. at 1192. Accordingly, because neither the TIEA nor Congress circumscribes the breadth of the summons authority that Congress granted the IRS, we find that the IRS may use that authority to obtain documents generated before the TIEA went into effect.

VII

Zarate's final contention is that the summons — by requesting "[a]ll records in [IBC's] possession, custody, or control relative to all accounts . . . held or controlled by or on behalf of Julio Roberto Zarate Barquero" — is overbroad because it does not identify with "reasonable particularity" the documents that IBC is to produce. "An overbreadth summons . . . is simply a summons which does not advise the summoned party what is required of him with sufficient specificity to permit him to respond adequately to the summons." *United States v. Wyatt,* 637 F.2d 293, 302 n. 16 (5th Cir. 1981). Because the summons identified with sufficient specificity the actions required of IBC in responding to the summons — IBC had to produce all records in its possession that pertained to IBC accounts held by Zarate — we uphold the district court's finding that the summons was not overbroad. *See Linsteadt,* 724 F.2d at 483.

In arguing that the summons was overbroad, Zarate appears to argue that the summons seeks information and documents irrelevant to the determination of his Mexican tax liability, although he confuses the concept of overbreadth with that of relevance. *See Wyatt,* 637 F.2d at 301 (noting that "overbreadth and relevance are two separate inquiries"). As we already have determined that the information sought is relevant to the determination of Zarate's Mexican tax liabilities, *see* part IV *supra,* we reject Zarate's argument that it is not.

We note that neither Zarate nor IBC argued that the summons was overly burdensome. *See Wyatt,* 637 F.2d at 302 n. 16 (noting that the concept of burdensome is distinct from the concept of overbreadth).

Zarate further argues that the district court erred both by examining *in camera* the Mexican competent authority's request that the IRS obtain the information at issue and a letter from Mexican authorities demonstrating that their investigation into Zarate's tax liability was not barred by any Mexican statute of limitations and by denying Zarate the opportunity to conduct discovery. However, "the method and scope of discovery allowed in summons enforcement proceedings are committed in large part to the discretion of the district court." *United States v. Johnson,* 652 F.2d 475, 476 (5th Cir. 1981). Here, the challenged actions do not constitute an abuse of its discretion by the district court. *See id.; cf. Barrett,* 837 F.2d at 1349 (noting that summons enforcement "proceedings are intended to be summary in nature").

VIII

For the foregoing reasons, we AFFIRM the judgment of the district court.

Case No. 13-00441-01-CR-W-GAF

03-17-2016

UNITED STATES OF AMERICA, Plaintiff, v. VERNA CHERYL WOMACK,
Defendant.

SARAH W. HAYS UNITED STATES MAGISTRATE JUDGE

REPORT AND RECOMMENDATION

This matter is currently before the Court on Defendant Verna Cheryl Womack's Motion to Dismiss the Indictment for Conduct in Violation of the Due Process Clause (docs #75 and #76). For the reasons set forth below, it is recommended that defendant's motion to dismiss be denied.

Doc #75 is a redacted version of the motion and doc #76 is an unredacted version filed under seal. Defendant redacted portions of the motion at the request of the government until ruling by the Court on the United States' Ex Parte Motions for Protective Order (docs #41 and #50). On March 31, 2015, the Court granted the motions for protective order to the extent that the subject TIEA applications and related correspondence shall not be disclosed to any third parties outside of this criminal action and denied the motions to the extent that they request that any pleading which references the content of the subject documents be filed under seal. (Doc #84)

I. INTRODUCTION

"The level of outrageousness needed to prove a due process violation is quite high, and the government's conduct must shock the conscience of the court." United States v. Pardue, 983 F.2d 843, 847 (8th Cir.)(per curiam)(citation and internal quotations omitted), cert. denied, 509 U.S. 925 (1993). The defense is reserved for a "narrow band of the most intolerable government conduct." Id. In United States v. Bugh, 701 F.3d 888 (8th Cir. 2012), cert. denied, 133 S.Ct. 2012 (2013), the Eighth Circuit Court of Appeals provided the following explanation:

Law enforcement agents' conduct is so outrageous that due process principles bar the Government from using the judicial process to obtain a conviction only when agents' conduct violates "that fundamental fairness, shocking the universal sense of justice, mandated by the Due Process Clause of the Fifth Amendment." United States v. Russell, 411 U.S. 423, 432 (1973)(internal quotation marks omitted).

701 F.3d at 894. Aggressive and persistent government conduct does not equate to outrageous conduct that shocks the conscience. Id.

Defendant Womack argues that the indictment should be dismissed because of these alleged violations of due process:

• Searching for and seizing documents, without a warrant, off of electronic evidence stolen by Defendant Brandy Wheeler, a former employee of Ms. Womack's, who was convicted of felony bank fraud for embezzling more than one million dollars from Ms. Womack; and then subsequently utilizing the tainted evidence to execute a Tax Information Exchange Agreement on the Cayman Islands, and obtain statements from Ms. Womack.

• Evidence and statements the government obtained in violation of statutory rights conferred on Ms. Womack by virtue of her statutory designation by the government as the crime victim under the Crime Victims' Rights Act ("CVRA"), 18 U.S.C. § 3771.

• Illegally and improperly utilizing civil IRS and DOJ Civil Tax attorneys to aid in the criminal investigation; and compelling Ms. Womack to testify in the district to obtain venue and in violation of her Fifth Amendment rights, despite a valid Protective Order in a civil case prohibiting their use outside of that case.

• Abuse of the Tax Information Exchange Agreement (TIEA) with the Cayman Islands; and detention of a resident of the Cayman Islands in circumcision of the TIEA.

• The government's unlawful disclosures of Ms. Womack's tax return information in violation of 26 U.S.C. § 6103(a).

• The government's unwarranted *ex parte* communications with the Court.

• Withholding exculpatory <u>Brady</u> material.

(Defendant Verna Cheryl Womack's Motion to Dismiss the Indictment for Conduct in Violation of the Due Process Clause (docs #75 and #76) at 4) The Court will address each of defendant's claims.
Defendant withdrew the manufactured venue argument at the hearing held on July 24, 2015. (Tr. at VIII-3 to VIII-4)

This alleged violation of due process was made in defendant Womack's reply brief (doc #96).

Many of the claims of due process violations already have been addressed by the Court in other Reports and Recommendations regarding defendant's various motions to suppress. The Court will not repeat the Findings of Fact which relate to those claims, but will make Findings of Fact with respect to claims which have not otherwise been addressed.

II. <u>DISCUSSION</u>

A. <u>The Electronic Evidence</u>

Defendant Womack filed a Motion to Suppress Illegally Searched and Seized Electronic Evidence (doc #67) which is the subject of a separate Report and Recommendation. In that separate Report and Recommendation, the Court recommends the denial of defendant's motion to suppress electronic evidence. Thus, given the Court's recommendation that there was no unconstitutional search and seizure of electronic evidence, there can be no due process violation in the government's searching for and seizing of documents from the electronic evidence and the subsequent use made of those documents.

B. <u>The Crime Victims' Rights Act</u>

The Crime Victims' Rights Act, provides in part:

(a) Rights of crime victims. A crime victim has the following rights:

(1) The right to be reasonably protected from the accused.

(2) The right to reasonable, accurate, and timely notice of any public court proceeding, or any parole proceeding, involving the crime or of any release or escape of the accused.
(3) The right not to be excluded from any such public court proceeding, unless the court, after receiving clear and convincing evidence, determines that testimony by the victim would be materially altered if the victim heard other testimony at that proceeding.

(4) The right to be reasonably heard at any public proceeding in the district court involving release, plea, sentencing, or any parole proceeding.

(5) The reasonable right to confer with the attorney for the Government in the case.

(6) The right to full and timely restitution as provided in law.

(7) The right to proceedings free from unreasonable delay.

(8) The right to be treated with fairness and with respect for the victim's dignity and privacy. **(9)** The right to be informed in a timely manner of any plea bargain or deferred prosecution agreement. **(10)** The right to be informed of the rights under this section and the services described in section 503(c) of the Victims' Rights and Restitution Act of 1990 (42 U.S.C. 10607(c)) and provided contact information for the Office of the Victims' Rights Ombudsman of the Department of Justice.

(b) Rights afforded.

(1) In general.--In any court proceeding involving an offense against a crime victim, the court shall ensure that the crime victim is afforded the rights described in subsection (a). Before making a determination described in subsection (a)(3), the court shall make every effort to permit the fullest attendance possible by the victim and shall consider reasonable alternatives to the exclusion of the victim from the criminal proceeding. The reasons for any decision denying relief under this chapter shall be clearly stated on the record.

(c) Best efforts to accord rights.

(1) Government.--Officers and employees of the Department of Justice and other departments and agencies of the United States engaged in the detection, investigation, or prosecution of crime shall make their best efforts to see that crime victims are notified of, and accorded, the rights described in subsection (a).

(d) Enforcement and limitations.--

(6) No cause of action.--Nothing in this chapter shall be construed to authorize a cause of action for damages or to create, to enlarge, or to imply any duty or obligation to any victim or other person for the breach of which the United States or any of its officers or employees could be held liable in damages. Nothing in this chapter shall be construed to impair the prosecutorial discretion of the Attorney General or any officer under his direction.

18 U.S.C. § 3771.

In support of her motion to dismiss, defendant Womack claims that rather than treat her with "fairness," "the government actually used Ms. Womack's victim status as a ruse to interview Ms. Womack [on December 15, 2008] without a lawyer present in the hopes that she would incriminate herself." (Motion to Dismiss the Indictment for Conduct in Violation of the Due Process Clause (docs #75 and #76) at 8) Defendant Womack filed a Motion to Suppress Illegally Obtained Evidence of Her Statements at the December 2008 Interview and Her May 2009 Civil Deposition in U.S. v. Davison (doc #71) which is the subject of a separate Report and Recommendation. In that separate Report and Recommendation, the Court recommends the granting of defendant's motion to suppress as it relates to statements made by defendant at the December 15, 2008 interview. The Court found that Special Agent Witt affirmatively and intentionally misled defendant Womack to obtain the December 15, 2008 interview in violation of defendant's due process rights.

Other than the December 15, 2008 interview, defendant Womack claims that her victim rights have been abused in that Brandy Wheeler is only required to pay Womack $150.00 per month in restitution, that the government has made no effort to obtain or liquidate the assets Wheeler purchased with Womack's money, and that Womack's civil tax case relating to her 2001 through 2004 tax years has been put on hold. (Motion to Dismiss the Indictment for Conduct in Violation of the Due Process Clause (docs #75 and #76) at 7 n.7 and 8) Defendant Womack argues for dismissal to counter the current message to crime victims "that cooperating with the government will not only hinder the administration of justice in their own circumstances, but could result in the government surreptitiously abusing the CVRA to *bring charges against* cooperative victims." (Id. at 8)

The Court first notes that the Honorable Fernando J. Gaitan, Jr., found that V. Cheryl Womack was not the "victim" for purposes of the Crime Victim's Rights Act in the criminal matter of United States v. Brandy M. Wheeler; VCW Holding Company, LLC was the "victim." (See Order (doc #29) in Case No. 08-00216-01-CR-W-FJG) Further, Judge Gaitan found defendant Wheeler's ordered restitution was not in violation of VCW Holding Company, LLC's victim rights. (Id.) Womack's motion for reconsideration of Judge Gaitan's Order was denied. (See Order (doc #34) in Case No. 08-00216-01-CR-W-FJG) This Court will not address further defendant Womack's claims of victim's rights violations with respect to restitution. With respect to the government's decision to put any civil tax cases against defendant Womack on hold pending the resolution of this criminal prosecution, the Court finds that this decision does not appear unreasonable, let alone a violation of defendant's due process. Finally, the Court declines defendant's invitation to dismiss the charges against her to counter the purported message to other crime victims. The Court has recommended the suppression of defendant's statements made at the December 15, 2008 interview. This appears to be a sufficient sanction for a violation of defendant Womack's rights.

C. Civil Investigation of Allen Davison

As set forth above, defendant Womack filed a Motion to Suppress Illegally Obtained Evidence of Her Statements at the December 2008 Interview and Her May 2009 Civil Deposition in U.S. v. Davison (doc #71) which is the subject of a separate Report and Recommendation. In that separate Report and Recommendation, the Court recommends the denial of defendant's motion to suppress as it relates to statements made by defendant in the civil investigation of Allen Davison. The Court found that the attorneys handling the Davison civil injunction case did not know that Womack was under criminal tax investigation when she was deposed and did not affirmatively mislead Womack about a criminal investigation in order to obtain information from her or use her deposition in the Davison case to develop evidence for the criminal case. With respect to the protective order, the Court found that Womack's deposition testimony was never designated "Confidential" and, thus, was not subject to the protective order. Thus, given the Court's recommendation, there can be no due process violation with respect to defendant's involvement in the civil investigation of Allen Davison.

D. The Tax Information Exchange Agreement (TIEA)

Defendant Womack filed a Motion to Suppress Evidence Obtained Pursuant to the Tax Information Exchange Agreement (docs #69 and #70) which is the subject of a separate Report and Recommendation. In that separate Report and Recommendation, the Court recommends the denial of defendant's motion to suppress as it found no violations of the TIEAs with respect to document requests. Given the Court's recommendation, there can be no due process violation with respect to the TIEA document requests.

However, defendant's due process argument goes beyond the issues addressed in the separate Report and Recommendation in that defendant claims her due process rights were violated by the detention of Stephen Gray, a resident of the Cayman Islands, in circumcision of the TIEA. The Court makes the following Findings of Fact with respect to this issue:

1. On October 8, 2010, Revenue Service Representative Raul Pertierra sent a request for documents under the TIEA to the Cayman Islands Competent Authority. (Tr. at II-47; Government's Ex. 58) The purpose of the request was to obtain information from Butterfield Bank (Cayman) Limited; Caledonia Bank, Trust and Fund Services Limited; Walkers Global; and Willis Management Limited regarding Verna Cheryl Womack. (Government's   Ex.   58)

2. Stephen Gray is a Director and Vice President of Willis Management (Cayman), Ltd., a licensed Cayman Islands Insurance Manager. (Government's Ex. 188) Mr. Gray provided records in connection with a Notice to Produce Information issued by the Tax Information Authority on January 28, 2011 to Willis Management (Cayman), Ltd. (Government's Ex. 188) These records related to JoJoDi Insurance Company, Ltd., DAR Holdings, Lucy Limited, Future Strategies Consulting, Tenth Trust, Eleventh Trust, Twelfth Trust, Thirteenth Trust and Emerald Star Trust. (Government's Ex. 188)

3. On March 15, 2011, the Cayman Islands Competent Authority provided the affidavits and documents received pursuant to the Notices to Produce Information served on Caledonian Bank Limited, Willis Management (Cayman) Ltd. and Walkers Corporate Services Limited to the United States Competent Authority. (Tr. at II-54; Government's Ex. 65)

4. In 2012, Mr. Pertierra was contacted about a second request in this case. (Tr. at II-54 to II-55) Special Agent Joe Schmidt requested assistance with interviews of people who live in the Cayman Islands. (Tr. at II-55) A TIEA request for voluntary interviews was made on May 2, 2012. (Government's Ex. 67) One of the persons from whom an interview was sought was Stephen Gray. (Government's Ex. 67)

5. Special Agent Schmidt travelled to the Cayman Islands to conduct interviews on May 7 and 8, 2012. (Tr. at II-57 and VII-35; Defendant's Ex. 26) Special Agent Schmidt testified that he had been told that Stephen Gray and others would be willing to speak with him in voluntary interviews. (Tr. at VII-35) The day of the interviews, Special Agent Schmidt was advised that the interviews would not take place as the witnesses did not consent to be interviewed. (Tr. at II-57 and VII-35; Defendant's Ex. 26) The Cayman Islands Competent Authority agreed to leave the request open. (Tr. at II-58) The Cayman Islands Competent Authority proposed that written questions could be served on the witnesses under a notice to produce information. (Tr. at II-58 and VII-36) The United States ultimately decided not to serve those questions. (Tr. at II-58)

6. Special Agent Schmidt testified that he wanted to ask Stephen Gray about who had control and ownership of those Cayman Islands entities for which Gray had provided documents to the Tax Information Authority. (Tr. at VII-34 to VII-36) Special Agent Schmidt wanted spontaneous answers to the questions, not something where people could sit and review the questions. (Tr. at VII-36)

7. Special Agent Schmidt received information that Stephen Gray was going to have a five-hour layover in the Miami Airport on a flight from Cayman to Toronto. (Tr. at VII-36) Special Agent Schmidt reached out to an agent in Miami and asked him to contact Customs and Border Patrol ("CBP") to try and set up a witness interview. (Tr. at VII-37) Special Agent Schmidt testified that CBP has authority to stop and speak with people as they come into the country. (Tr. at VII-37) On May 20, 2013, Special Agent Schmidt and Agent Skinner went to the Miama Airport. (Tr. at VII-38) Special Agent Schmidt and Agent Skinner met with CBP officers and then went to an interview room and waited for Mr. Gray to get into the country. (Tr. at VII-38) After Mr. Gray unboarded from the plane, CBP officers asked him to come back and speak with the agents. (Tr. at VII-38) When Mr. Gray entered the interview room, Special Agent Schmidt asked him if he would be willing to answer some questions. (Tr. at VII-38) Special Agent Schmidt testified that Mr. Gray seemed mildly annoyed as he said that he had been going to try and catch an earlier flight to Toronto. (Tr. at VII-38) Special Agent Schmidt told Mr. Gray that if he wanted to go try and catch that flight, he could, but asked him to take down Special Agent Schmidt's information so that they could do the interview at another time. (Tr. at VII-38) Mr. Gray said that he was no longer going to be able to catch the earlier flight. (Tr. at VII-38)

8. Special Agent Schmidt testified that Stephen Gray was free to leave at any time. (Tr. at VII-39) Mr. Gray was in no way a target himself. (Tr. at VII-39) Special Agent Schmidt testified that Mr. Gray did not appear to be reluctant to speak, rather he was very friendly. (Tr. at VII-39) Mr. Gray described Willis' relationship with Cheryl Womack. (Tr. at VII-39) Special Agent Schmidt and Mr. Gray discussed entities that are a part of this case. (Tr. at VII-39) Mr. Gray never stated that he wanted more time to think about his answers or that he wanted to have a lawyer present. (Tr. at VII-40) Special Agent Schmidt did not tell Mr. Gray that he had to talk to him. (Tr. at VII-41) Mr. Gray never said that he did not want to talk to Special Agent Schmidt. (Tr. at VII-41)

9. Special Agent Schmidt testified that he was aware that it would be improper to try to interview Stephen Gray in the Cayman Islands. (Tr. at VII-60) However, Special Agent Schmidt testified that he was not aware of any way that the TIEA was violated in asking Stephen Gray questions while Gray was in the United States. (Tr. at VII-41) Mr. Pertierra testified that there is nothing in the TIEAs that would prohibit a person from being

interviewed in the United States after they have declined to be interviewed in their host country. (Tr. at II-111)

While defendant Womack would have the Court find that border patrol officers detained and interrogated Mr. Gray in violation of federal law (see Motion to Dismiss the Indictment for Conduct in Violation of the Due Process Clause (docs #75 and #76) at 18), no evidence was presented at the hearing to support these allegations. Defendant would also have the Court find that the Cayman Tax Competent Authority expressly prohibited the interview of Mr. Gray (id.), despite again the lack of evidence to support this allegation. Finally, defendant would have the Court find that Special Agent Schmidt violated federal law by making disclosures of information to Mr. Gray. (Id.) Again, no evidence was presented at the hearing to support this allegation.

No evidence or case law has been presented to indicate that the TIEA was violated by Special Agent Schmidt's interview of Stephen Gray while Mr. Gray was present in the United States. No case law has been presented that would indicate that defendant Womack's due process rights were violated by the interview. While Special Agent Schmidt's actions may have been aggressive, the Court does not find them to be outrageous conduct that shocks the conscience. There is no basis for a dismissal based on a due process violation with respect to the TIEAs.

E. Disclosure of Defendant's Tax Return Information

Defendant Womack claims that IRS and FBI agents made numerous disclosures of her and her family members' tax returns and return information to third parties. (Motion to Dismiss the Indictment for Conduct in Violation of the Due Process Clause (docs #75 and #76) at 20) Specifically, defendant cites the following disclosures as violations of her due process rights:

• On March 31, 2009, a civil attorney for the IRS, David Flassing, sent to defendant Wheeler a disk containing a set of approximately 60 documents he obtained in a case pending in Tax Court against VCW Holdings and one of its subsidiaries, CARD Aeronautics, LLC. The documents were sensitive and confidential as the disk was encrypted and password protected. Attorney Flassing provided Defendant Wheeler with the password the previous day so that she could view the files on the disk. Mr. Flassing asked her to "authenticate" the documents on the disk or indicate whether they were "not familiar" to her, indicating that he had no knowledge as to whether Defendant Wheeler had ever previously reviewed or accessed these documents.

• Mr. Flassing sent another package of materials to Defendant Wheeler on or about April 10, 2009. That package included tax returns for Ms. Womack's company, VCW, for other companies owned by Ms. Womack or VCW called Mysis, Inc., CARD Aeronautics, R&A Properties, and Ms. Womack's own personal returns. Wheeler kept the documents.

• On July 30, 2012, the local IRS case agent Joseph Schmidt sent to Defendant Wheeler return information for both Ms. Womack and her husband, including their respective social security numbers, information about specific tax deductions and income, their annual purchases and sales, retirement plan contributions, and other information about itemization of potential deductions from federal income tax.

• In December 2012, IRS Agent Schmidt asked Defendant Wheeler to come [to] his office so that she could review tax returns in person. She did so on January 2, 2013 and was interviewed by both IRS Agent Schmidt and IRS Agent Jaime Seematter. During the interview, she was shown, at a minimum, tax returns and return information for companies called PAS, and Mysis, Inc., as well as Ms. Womack's personal returns.

• [G]overnment agents unlawfully disclosed that Ms. Womack was under criminal investigation to at least 18 identified witnesses in the course of their investigation. In just one example, on July 29, 2013, a business associate of Ms. Womack's named Mario Chalmers was hosing his annual charity golf tournament at the

Alvamar Golf Club in Lawrence, Kansas. Local IRS Agent Schmidt approached Mr. Chalmers and his father, Ronnie Chalmers, at the golf course, and disclosed that he wanted to talk to them about Ms. Womack, whom Agent Schmidt disclosed was under criminal investigation. Ronnie Chalmers informed Agent Schmidt that a phone interview at a later date would be more appropriate, as he and his son were in the middle of hosting a charity event. On August 9, 2013, Agent Schmidt and Tax Fraud Investigative Assistant, Heather Dutzel, placed a phone call to Ronnie Chalmers, and again disclosed that Womack was the target of a criminal investigation.

(Id. at 21-23)

The government disagrees that there has been an improper disclosure of defendant Womack's tax return information. (Response in Opposition to Defendant's Pretrial Motion to Dismiss on Due Process Grounds (doc #83) at 7) However, the government argues that even if one assumes that there was an improper disclosure, that conduct does not warrant a dismissal of the indictment. (Id. at 7-8)

While testimony was taken at the hearings held in this case to suggest that Mr. Flassing and Special Agent Schmidt did provide Brandy Wheeler with return information relating to defendant Womack, the Court does not find it necessary to ascertain whether or not these disclosures violated 26 U.S.C. § 6103. The only case cited by defendant Womack in support of her argument is Snider v. United States, 468 F.3d 500 (8th Cir. 2006), which involved a civil action brought by taxpayers against the IRS for the illegal disclosure of return information wherein the taxpayers were found to be entitled to an award of damages. No case law has been presented to the Court which would suggest that a criminal defendant is entitled to a dismissal of a criminal action based on a due process violation relating to the disclosure of return information to a third party. The fact that IRS agents and attorneys looked to Brandy Wheeler, the person who had served for years as VCW Holding's controller, who described her duties to Womack as "anything and everything related to Cheryl Womack's personal finances, all of the businesses that she would invest in, ... anything pretty much that would fall underneath a financial umbrella" (Tr. at VI-62) and who was actively cooperating against defendant Womack, to answer questions that they had with respect to Womack's return information for purposes of their investigations, does not appear to be outrageous conduct that shocks the conscience of the Court. There is no basis for a dismissal based on a due process violation with respect to the disclosure of defendant's tax return information.

The Court does not believe that any testimony was presented at the hearings regarding any disclosure to Mario or Ronnie Chalmers.

The Court notes that section 6103(k)(6) does allow for the disclosure of return information for investigative purposes. The statute provides:

An internal revenue officer or employee ... may, in connection with his official duties relating to any audit, collection activity, or civil or criminal tax investigation or any other offense under the internal revenue laws, disclose return information to the extent that such disclosure is necessary in obtaining information, which is not otherwise reasonably available, with respect to the correct determination of tax, liability for tax, or the amount to be collected or with respect to the enforcement of any other provision of this title.

26 U.S.C. § 7431 provides for civil damages for the unauthorized disclosure of return information.

F. Ex Parte Communications

Defendant Womack claims that the government has engaged in due process violations by twice attempting to communicate with the Court ex parte. (Motion to Dismiss the Indictment for Conduct in Violation of the Due Process Clause (docs #75 and #76) at 24) Specifically, defendant cites the following ex parte communications as violations of her due process rights:

• After the government indicted Ms. Womack, on New Year's Eve 2013, after the U.S. Attorney's Office was closed, the U.S. Attorney's Office Criminal Chief sent alleged information about Ms. Womack in an e-mail to the U.S. Magistrate judge who had presided over her arraignment and bond hearing. After returning to the office after the New Year's holiday, the Court immediately forwarded the attempted *ex parte* communication and information supplied to the Court by the

government to counsel for Ms. Womack.

• In another instance, on November 12, 2014, one day after Ms. Womack filed a motion for leave to file a motion to compel the government's TIEA application discovery, unbeknownst to Ms. Womack, the government attempted a second *ex parte* contact with the Court. The government filed an *ex parte* motion for a protective order covering the TIEA application in question. Ms. Womack was not aware that the papers were submitted to the court, as they did not appear even as a sealed entry on ECF. On December 10, 2014, the Court ordered the Court ordered the government to provide Ms. Womack with a copy of the *ex parte* pleading to give Ms. Womack an opportunity to respond to the government's arguments and to file the motion publicly.

(Id. at 24-25)

With respect to the first ex parte communication, the Court notes that the communication consisted of an email which stated: "a news item that may be of interest to you," and attached a news article entitled, "Court bans US businesswoman from Cayman trip." (See doc #14-3) The article referenced a detention decision which had already been made by the Court. No detention issue was still pending before the Court. While it certainly would have been preferable for the government attorney to have copied defense counsel on the email, this is hardly the sort of conduct that is so outrageous that it shocks the conscience of the Court. The Court quickly provided the government's ex parte communication to defense counsel. Defendant suffered no prejudice from the original ex parte nature of the communication.

With respect to the second ex parte communication, the Court notes that the Federal Rules of Criminal Procedure provide: "The court may permit a party to show good cause [for a protective order] by a written statement that the court will inspect ex parte." Rule 16(d)(1). The government filed an Ex Parte Motion for Protective Order (doc #41). The Court denied the government's request to proceed ex parte and directed the parties to proceed with publicly filed papers on the issue. There was no due process violation.

G. Brady Material

In her reply brief, defendant Womack claims that the government withheld two items of exculpatory material from her until March 2015: (1) an IRS report of an interview of Roland Louie, a Senior Finance Analyst in the Reinsurance Unit for Fireman's Fund Insurance Company, prepared in March 2014, that explains why a reinsurance company would incorporate in the Cayman Islands; and (2) an FBI memorandum of an interview of defendant Womack in 2001 which shows that Womack never intended to hide her relationship with JoJoDi or her business dealings in the Cayman Islands. (Reply to the Government's Response to Ms. Womack's Motion to Dismiss the Indictment for Conduct in Violation of the Due Process Clause (doc #96) at 14-16)

While the Court does not have the benefit of a government response as this issue was first presented in defendant's reply brief, it is the Court's experience in cases where investigations have spanned several years and involved different agencies that reports are sometimes discovered by government counsel as counsel prepares the case for trial and the government then provides these reports to defense counsel after other materials have been provided. The Court finds that there is nothing outrageous or shocking about the somewhat untimely disclosure to defense counsel of the two instant reports, especially when those reports were provided approximately one year before the actual commencement of the trial. There is no due process violation.

III. <u>CONCLUSION</u>

Based on the foregoing, the conduct of the government in this case cannot be said to be outrageous or to shock the conscience of the Court, looking both at the cited individual incidents and at the cumulative impact of all the cited incidents. Therefore, it is

RECOMMENDED that the Court, after making an independent review of the record and applicable law, enter an order denying Defendant Verna Cheryl Womack's Motion to Dismiss the Indictment for Conduct in Violation of the Due Process Clause (docs #75 and #76).

Counsel are reminded they have fourteen days from the date of receipt of a copy of this Report and Recommendation within which to file and serve objections to same. A failure to file and serve timely objections shall bar an attack on appeal of the factual findings in this Report and Recommendation which are accepted or adopted by the district judge, except on the grounds of plain error or manifest injustice.

/s/ Sarah W . Hays

SARAH W. HAYS

UNITED STATES MAGISTRATE JUDGE

Collection of U.S. Tax Abroad

The U.S. cannot generally force another country to collect an IRS debt. One country is not required to take action to collect tax owed to a foreign country.[181]

Situs treaties, however, typically permit each country to collect tax covered by the treaty.[182] Domicile treaties do not address or alter the general rule that neither country may force the other to collect tax.

Practically speaking, cooperation among (even situs treaty) countries is necessary. Typically, the country attempting to enforce collection must seek assistance from the treaty partner to collect assets inside the borders of the partner nation.[183]

---

[181] *See, e.g.*, Moore v. Mitchell, 30 F. 2d 600 (2d Cir. 1929), *aff'd on other grounds*, 281 U.S. 18 (1930); Her Majesty Queen in Right of British Columbia v. Gilbertson, 597 F2d 1161, 1164 (9th Cir. 1979) ("[a]pparently ... the first time ... that a foreign nation has sought enforcement of a tax judgment in a court of the United States"); U.S. v. Boots, 80 F. 3d 580, 587 (1st Cir. 1996).
[182] U.S.-Finland Estate Tax Treaty art. VIII.
[183] The 2003 OECD Model Income Tax Convention added Article 27 "Assistance in the Collection of Taxes" Article 27(1) and (2) provide that the Contracting States shall lend assistance to each other in the collection of revenue claims.

Questions

Does the IRS have the right to collect tax in a foreign country?

How do members of the Caribbean Basin benefit by sharing tax information with the IRS?

CHAPTER 12
FOREIGN TRUSTS

Income Tax

General

A foreign trust is generally treated as a NRNC for U.S. income tax purposes. Foreign trusts are therefore subject to U.S. income tax only on U.S. source income.[184] Trust distributions to U.S. citizens and income tax residents carry out taxable "distributable net income" to the beneficiary.[185] Additional tax may be recognized for accumulated income, unless the trust qualifies as a "grantor trust." Grantor trusts (generally controlled by the founder) are ignored for income tax purposes. Grantor trust assets are deemed owned by the grantor[186] with all U.S. income taxed to the grantor.

---

[184] IRC §§641(b), 872(a).
[185] IRC §652; §662.
[186] IRC §§671-679.

<u>Income Tax Consequences of Creation</u>
<u>and Funding by U.S. Persons</u>

Understanding the tax impact on U.S. citizens and resident grantors and beneficiaries of foreign trusts is helpful to understand the corresponding impact on NRNCs. There are no income tax consequences for a U.S. citizen or resident upon creating a foreign trust. Under certain circumstances, income tax may be imposed on the transfer of property to the foreign trust. Internal Revenue Code §684 generally treats the gratuitous transfer of property by a U.S. person to a foreign trust (with no U.S. beneficiary) as a sale or exchange of the assets contributed.

Section 684 deems the grantor to sell the assets transferred for fair market value, triggering taxable gain (but not loss) on the excess of fair market value over tax basis in the transferred property.[187] In determining whether fair market value is received, if the transferor is the grantor or a trust beneficiary (or a related person within the meaning of I.R.C. §643(i)(2)(B)), any obligation issued by the trust to the transferor (or by certain related persons) is generally disregarded (and treated as a gift of the assets transferred).[188]

Transfers by U.S. persons to entities owned by a foreign trust are treated as transfers to the foreign trust (followed by a transfer of the asset by the trust to the controlled entity).[189] The deemed funding of an entity applies unless the U.S. contributor is not related to a trust beneficiary or proves that the transfer is attributable to his independent ownership

---

[187] IRC §684(a).
[188] *See* IRC §679(a)(3)(A)(i); *See also* Treas. Reg. §1.679-4(d) providing that certain "qualified obligations" (generally any bond, note, debenture, certificate, bill receivable, account receivable, note receivable, open account, or other evidence of indebtedness, and to the extent not previously described, any annuity contract as defined under Notice 97-34, IRB 1997-25 and IRC. §6048) will be recognized as consideration.
[189] Treas. Reg. §1.679-3(f).

in the entity. For example, if a foreign trust and a U.S. contributor jointly fund a corporation, each taking back stock proportionate to their transfers, the funding is not gratuitous and Code §679 is not applicable.

The §684 deemed sale of trust assets does not, however, apply to "grantor" trusts (disregarded for income tax purposes, with trust assets deemed owned by the grantor).[190]

If a foreign trust has a U.S. beneficiary, Code §679 deems the trust a grantor trust. The funding of a foreign trust by a U.S. citizen or resident grantor, for any U.S. beneficiary (including himself), therefore has no immediate U.S. income tax implications.

Grantor status ends upon the earlier of (1) the foreign trust no longer having a U.S. beneficiary or (2) the death of the grantor.[191]

Income Tax Treatment Upon Death of U.S. Grantor

Upon the death of the U.S. settlor (resident or citizen) of a foreign grantor trust, grantor status terminates.[192] Death of the grantor triggers two possible tax outcomes.[193] If trust assets are not includable in the gross estate of the U.S. grantor, they are subject to a deemed sale under Code §684 (deemed as transferred to the foreign trust immediately prior to U.S. grantor's death).[194] Following the deemed sale, trust assets receive a basis step-up, based on the recognized gain (but no loss).[195]

---

[190] IRC §684(b).
[191] Treas. Reg. §§1.684-2(e) (death of grantor); 1.679-2(c)(2) (no U.S. beneficiary for foreign trust).
[192] Treas. Reg. §1.684-2(e).
[193] IRC §684(c); Treas. Reg. §1.684-3(c)(1); Treas. Reg. §1.684-2(e).
[194] IRC §684(c).
[195] Treas. Reg. §1.684-1(a).

Foreign trust assets includable in the U.S. grantor's gross estate are not subject to deemed sale under Code §684 upon the grantor's death. Instead, trust assets (which avoid the deemed sale) are subject to Estate Tax and receive a fair market value step-up in basis on the grantor's death.[196] See p. 5 above.

After trust assets are deemed sold or subject to Estate Tax, the trust is treated as an independent foreign non-grantor trust for federal income tax purposes.

<u>Income Tax Treatment of Foreign Trusts Created by NRNC</u>

As a general rule, non-grantor foreign trusts incur taxable income like NRNC individuals (with certain limitations on credits and deductions, unique to trusts).[197] Neither Code §684(a) (deemed sales provisions) nor Code §679 (deemed grantor status) apply to transfers by a NRNC to a foreign trust (with no U.S. beneficiaries). U.S. source income is generally treated (for U.S. income tax purposes) as earned by the foreign non-grantor trust.[198]

U.S. gross income of a foreign non-grantor trust consists only of (1) income derived from sources within the U.S. (not effectively connected with the conduct of a trade or business in the U.S.) and (2) income effectively connected with the conduct of a trade or business within the U.S.[199]

Accordingly, foreign non-grantor trusts are subject to U.S. income tax on the following types of income:

---

[196] Treas. Reg. §1.684-1.
[197] IRC §§641(b), §872(a). See IRC §§642, 643, 651, and 661 regarding special rules for credits and deductions for trusts.
[198] Unless IRC §672(f) (grantor status) applies to the trust.
[199] See IRC §872(a).

i.   Income Effectively Connected with a U.S. Trade or Business.[200]

ii.   Disposition of U.S. Real Property Interests.[201]

iii.   Fixed or determinable annual or periodic income ("FDAPI") from U.S. sources (i.e. interest, dividends, rents, annuities, etc.).[202]

If a NRNC funds a trust for the benefit of a U.S. person, the trust will be treated as a grantor trust as to the U.S. beneficiary (for that portion of the trust benefitting the U.S. beneficiary).[203] The U.S. beneficiary is taxed on worldwide income earned by that portion of trust assets.[204] To avoid having U.S. beneficiaries recognize taxable income (and tax on accumulated income), NRNCs should generally attempt to organize foreign trusts as grantor trusts. In such event, the NRNC grantor is responsible for all U.S. source income recognized by the foreign trust. Since 1996, NRNCs are, however, subject to certain restrictions on establishing a foreign grantor trust.[205] There are three exceptions to non-grantor status of foreign trusts formed by a NRNC:

1.   The Grantor has full power to revoke the trust without the consent of any person, or with the consent of a subservient third-party.[206]

2.   The Grantor or the Grantor's spouse is the sole beneficiary of the trust during the life of the Grantor.[207]

---

[200] IRC §871(b).
[201] IRC §897(a).
[202] IRC §871(a).
[203] Treas. Reg. §1.672(f)-1.
[204] Treas. Reg. §1.671-3.
[205] *See* IRC §672(f).
[206] IRC §672(f)(2)(A)(i).
[207] IRC §672(f)(2)(A)(ii).

3.   The trust was created before September 19, 1995 (regarding assets in trust as of such date) if the trust qualified as a grantor trust, pursuant to Code §676 or Code §677.[208]

Internal Revenue Code §672(f) thus denies NRNC settlors grantor trust status for trusts formed after 1995 unless (i) the grantor retains the right (exercisable either unilaterally or with the consent of a related or subordinate person), to revoke the trust; or (ii) distributions from the trust during the grantor's life are distributable only to the grantor or his spouse. One strategy to avoid attribution of trust income to U.S. children is for the NRNC grantor (and the grantor's spouse) to fund a foreign trust pursuant to which distributions are limited to husband and wife.

Foreign assets distributed to the grantor may be given (tax-free) to a U.S. relative.[209] See page 89. Note that the U.S. donee must still report receipt of significant gifts (even if such gifts are not taxable). See page 253.

Upon the death of the NRNC grantor, the offshore trust loses its grantor trust status. Trust income from U.S. sources is then recognized by the trust (an independent taxpayer).

Foreign Tax Credit

A foreign non-grantor trust engaged in a U.S. trade or business which pays foreign income tax on income effectively connected to the U.S. business may generally offset such foreign tax against its U.S. income tax liability.[210] Alternatively, the trust may potentially deduct (from U.S. taxable income) such taxes.[211]

---

[208] Treas. Reg. §§1.672(f)-3(a)(3); 1.672(f)-3(b)(3).
[209] *See* IRC §672(f)(2)(A)(ii).
[210] *See* IRC §§901(b)(4), 906(a).
[211] *See* IRC §164(a)(3).

Tax Rates

All U.S. source income earned by a foreign trust is subject to the tax rates applicable to trusts under Code § 1(e). The rates are as follows:

Taxable Income	Tax Due
$0 - $2,600	10% of taxable income
$2601 - $9,300	$260 + 24% of the amount over $2,600
$9,301 - $12,750	$1,868 + 35% of the amount over $9,300
$12,751 +	$3,705.50 + 37% of the amount over $12,750

Tax Treaties

Applicable tax treaties may reduce U.S. income tax on foreign (non-grantor) trusts, if the trust is resident of a treaty partner country. For example, most U.S. income tax treaties reduce the tax imposed on passive dividends from 30% to 15%.[212]

---

[212] *See* Convention Between the United States of America and Canada with Respect to Taxes on Income and on Capital, Sep. 26, 1980, U.S.-Canada, T.I.A.S. (hereinafter "U.S.-Canada Income Tax Treaty").

Estate and Gift Tax

Funding by U.S. Persons

The lifetime gratuitous transfer of property by a U.S. citizen or resident is generally subject to Gift Tax, for value above the annual $15,000 exclusion per donee. NRNCs are subject to Gift Tax on completed gifts of U.S. situs tangible property. Incomplete gifts (including gifts to trusts) are disregarded for Estate and Gift Tax purposes. Incomplete gifts remain in the estate of the grantor. (See Completed Gifts, page 60).[213]

Foreign trusts created by U.S. persons are typically "self-settled" (i.e., benefitting the grantor), to utilize the asset protection laws of a foreign jurisdiction. The U.S. settlor typically retains rights to trust income during his lifetime (subject to the foreign trustee's discretion). The Settlor also typically reserves certain powers over trust corpus (i.e., the ability to add or remove new beneficiaries and the right to receive income or principal from the trust, subject to trustee discretion). The Code treats such retained rights as preventing completion of the gift to trust (for Gift Tax Purposes).

Such retained rights permit the Settlor to obtain the benefits of foreign protection yet avoid Gift Tax (on the "incomplete" gift). To the extent lifetime gifts to an irrevocable trust remains incomplete, Gift Tax is not triggered (and trust assets remain in the grantor's taxable estate).

Incomplete gifts to foreign trusts have no immediate U.S. Estate or Gift Tax consequences. Planning may, however, be required to avoid Estate Tax and the "mark-to-

---

[213] Treas. Reg. §25.2511-2(c).

market" deemed sale of trust assets upon the grantor's death (as death causes loss of grantor status). See page 197 above.

Funding by NRNCs

U.S. Gift Tax is imposed on NRNCs only upon the transfer of U.S. situs property to a foreign trust (assuming the transfer is a completed gift).[214] The general strategy of purchasing U.S. assets in a foreign corporation allows for the avoidance of direct U.S. taxable gifts and bequests. Limiting trust contributions to equity in a foreign corporation (itself owning U.S. situs assets) thus avoids Gift Tax. See page 109 above. Transfers of foreign situs property by an NRNC to a foreign trust have no legal nexus to (and are not taxed by) the U.S.

Pre-Immigration Trusts

All NRNCs intending to immigrate to the U.S. should consider planning to avoid recognizing U.S. income, Estate and Gift Tax on worldwide assets. Planning (before establishing U.S. residency) generally involves completing gifts before U.S. residency.

Given the worldwide reach of U.S. income, Estate and Gift Tax on U.S. residents, clear and irrevocable asset transfers prior to U.S. residency is the the most effective tax planning for NRNCs contemplating a permanent move to the U.S.

The funding of an irrevocable foreign trust with foreign assets prior to moving to the United States effectively avoids Estate and Gift Tax. If structured properly, non-U.S. assets transferred to the foreign trust will never (under current law) be subject to Gift or Estate Tax.

---

[214] See IRC §684.

If, however, the NRNC grantor establishes U.S. residency within five years of funding the foreign trust, trust assets may be exposed to U.S. income tax (under the Code §684 deemed sale and the Code §679 deemed grantor trust rules).

Five-Year "Taint" of NRNC Funded Foreign Trust

NRNCs intending to immigrate to the U.S. should take great care to avoid U.S. residency within five years of transferring property to a foreign trust. Internal Revenue Code §679 applies to trusts funded by an NRNC grantor who becomes a U.S. resident within five years of funding.[215]

The immigrant grantor (who becomes a U.S. resident within five years of funding a foreign trust) is treated as having re-transferred property to the foreign trust on the date of establishing residency, triggering either (i) the deemed sale rules of Code §684 (if the trust has no U.S. beneficiaries) or (ii) grantor status under Code §679 (if the foreign trust has a U.S. beneficiary). In the event of deemed grantor status under Code §679, either deemed sale of trust assets (under Code §684) or exposure to the Estate Tax will be triggered upon the death of the immigrating grantor.

---

[215] *See* IRC §679(a)(4); Treas. Reg. §1.679-5(a).

<u>Reporting</u>

Immigrants deemed by Code §679 to own (for income tax purposes) property transferred to a foreign trust within five years of U.S. residency must report such transfers (deemed or actual) on IRS Form 3520.[216] The U.S. residency starting date triggers the filing requirements necessary to inform the IRS of facts potentially causing the deemed sale of assets held by a foreign trust. Trust income accruing before U.S. residency is not subject to U.S. tax and not reportable (except to the extent of U.S. source income).

<u>Five-Year Period to Determine U.S. Beneficiaries</u>

The determination of whether a foreign trust has U.S. beneficiaries (making the trust disregarded as "grantor" under Code §679) is made annually. A foreign trust created by a U.S. resident as non-grantor (with no U.S. beneficiaries) may become grantor if a beneficiary obtains U.S. residency within 5 years of the grantor funding the trust.[217] The U.S. grantor must recognize all accumulated trust income in the taxable year the NRNC beneficiary becomes a U.S. resident.[218] The U.S. grantor recognizes all income of the foreign trust for each subsequent year the foreign trust remains grantor.

Note that, if a foreign trust ceases to have a U.S. beneficiary, the U.S. grantor is treated as having made a transfer to the foreign trust on the first day of the first taxable year following the last taxable year the trust was treated as having a U.S. beneficiary. The deemed transfer by a U.S. grantor to a foreign trust with no U.S. beneficiary triggers the

---

[216] *See* IRS Form 3520, Annual Return to Report transactions with Foreign Trusts and Receipt of Certain Foreign Gifts.
[217] *See* Treas. Reg. §1.679-2(a)(3).
[218] *See* Treas. Reg. §1.679-2(c)(1).

deemed sale by the grantor or trust assets under Code §684. Trust assets are deemed sold at fair market value (including appreciation since contribution to the trust).[219]

No U.S. Beneficiaries

Deemed grantor status under Code §679 does not apply to foreign trusts without U.S. beneficiaries. Potential U.S. beneficiaries and future beneficiaries are, however, counted. For example, if a foreign trust may be amended to add a U.S. person as a beneficiary, trust assets will be deemed recontributed by an immigrating grantor upon U.S. residency. The trust is then deemed a foreign grantor trust, with all income taxable to the immigrant grantor.[220] However, if a foreign beneficiary first becomes a U.S. resident more than five years after the trust is funded, the trust is not treated as having a U.S. beneficiary for purposes of Code §679. The exception is not available if the beneficiary was previously a U.S. resident.[221]

Indirect Transfers

Internal Revenue Code §679 applies to direct as well as indirect transfers.[222] For example, consider a proposed immigrant "A" who gives assets to his brother "B" before moving to the U.S. If B funds a trust for A and his family less than 5 years before A moves to the U.S., A will be treated as the owner of the trust assets for income tax purposes. A's only defense would require proof that B was not acting as an intermediary.[223]

---

[219] *See* Treas. Reg. §1.679-2(c)(2).
[220] Treas. Reg. §1.679-2(a)(4)(ii)(A).
[221] *See* Treas. Reg. §1.679-2(a)(3), Ex. 2.
[222] Treas. Reg. §1.679-3(c).
[223] Treas. Reg. §1.679-3(c).

No Transfer Taxes Upon Funding

As noted on page 89 above, with the exception of transfers of U.S. situs tangible property to a foreign trust, U.S. Estate and Gift Tax (unlike the applicable U.S. income tax provisions) does not apply to NRNC contributions to a foreign trust. The Estate and Gift Taxes are not triggered by transfer by a NRNC of foreign property to a foreign trust, even in anticipation of U.S. immigration.[224] The trust is generally treated like an individual NRNC.

Five-Year Lookback Does Not Apply to Transfer Taxes

When an NRNC becomes a U.S. resident within five years of transferring property to a foreign trust, the NRNC grantor is treated (for income tax purposes) as owning the property so transferred (if such trust has a U.S. beneficiary). This provision, however, does not alter the immigrant's avoidance of Estate or Gift Tax (governed under Subtitle B of the Code). When summarizing Code §679, the U.S. House of Representatives confirmed that:

"an inter vivos trust which is treated as owned by a U.S. person under this provision [Section 679)] is not treated as owned by the estate of that person upon his death. These rules [only] apply for income tax purposes. Whether the corpus of the inter vivos trust is included in the estate for the U.S. person depends on the estate tax provisions of the Code. Such provisions, as well as the gift tax provisions of the Code, are unaffected by this amendment."[225]

---

[224] Text refers to Code §§2001, 2501, 2601. This assumes a completed gift.

[225] *See* P.L. 94-455, Tax Reform Act of 1976, HR. Rpt. No. 658, 94th Cong., 1st Sess. At 209 (Nov. 12, 1975). The Senate Report contains the same language. P.L. 94-455, Tax Reform Act of 1976, S. Rpt. No. 938, 94th Cong., 2nd Sess. At 218 (June 10, 1976). Furthermore, this interpretation was affirmed when the IRS quoted the same language in PLR 9332006 (1992).

Furthermore, in 2000, the U.S. Treasury issued proposed regulations under Code §679, including Proposed Regulation 1.679-5 for Code §679(a)(4). The proposed regulation is titled "Pre-Immigration Trusts." The preamble to the proposed regulation affirms the original legislative history of the statute, and provides that:

"Section 679 applies only for income tax purposes. The estate and gift tax provisions of the Code determine whether a transfer to a foreign trust is subject to the federal gift tax, or whether the corpus of a foreign trust is included in the gross estate of the U.S. transferor."[226]

The 5-year "deemed owner" rule (of Code §679(a)(4)) does not therefore apply for U.S. Estate and Gift Tax purposes. Completed gifts by the NRNC grantor to a foreign trust (removing foreign assets from exposure to U.S. Estate Tax) are therefore respected for Estate and Gift Tax purposes (without regard to the grantor's later U.S. residency).

---

[226] *See* Preamble to Prop. Reg. §1.679-5, 65 F.R. 48185-02 (Aug. 7, 2000).

Questions

What is a "foreign trust"?

Under what circumstances may a trust (formed in a U.S. state) be considered a foreign trust for U.S. Estate Tax purposes?

When should such a foreign trust be domesticated to the U.S.?

Under what circumstances may a foreign trust be deemed "grantor" (solely due to its "foreign trust" status)?

Why would such a deemed grantor (of a grantor/foreign trust) avoid completing a taxable gift (of appreciating assets) to a foreign trust?

How may a foreign trust (funded by and benefitting an NRNC) be considered grantor (for income tax purposes)?

If gift tax is paid on an irrevocable/taxable gift to a foreign trust by a U.S. grantor, may Estate Tax ever become owing on such assets?
- Income tax?

Under what circumstances should a U.S. grantor complete a taxable gift to a foreign trust

- with U.S. beneficiaries?
- with no U.S. beneficiaries?
- if the grantor has children citizens / U.S. residents?
- if the grantor has children /non-citizens /non-U.S. residents?

When should a U.S. citizen fail to complete a gift to a foreign trust (benefitting the grantor and his or her family)?

How may a foreign trust be utilized to avoid Estate and Gift Tax by an NRNC contemplating immigration to the U.S.?

How may U.S. income tax be incurred by the grantor of such a trust upon U.S. residency?

CHAPTER 13
PRE-IMMIGRATION PLANNING

Gifting Assets Prior to Residency

U.S. citizens and residents are subject to Estate and Gift Tax on their worldwide assets (without regard to the location of the property). Individuals planning to move to the U.S. should consider avoiding U.S. Estate and Gift Tax by giving assets to non-U.S. based family and foreign trusts prior to relocating. Lifetime gifts of foreign property and intangible U.S. property to non-U.S. persons remove the property from Estate Tax forever. Only gifts of U.S. tangible property subject NRNCs to Gift Tax. Pre-immigration gifts remove property from the NRNC's taxable estate and (if properly effected) avoid Gift Tax.

Gifts by NRNCs (before relocation) may be made to irrevocable foreign trusts. Once assets are properly transferred, all trust assets avoid any later Gift or Estate Tax. If the trust is structured to exclude U.S. beneficiaries and avoid characterization as a "grantor trust," U.S. income tax may also potentially be avoided on future trust income.[227]

Although potentially not as efficient from an income tax perspective, the NRNC anticipating a permanent move to the U.S. should also consider gifts to U.S. residents and citizens. Once given, appreciating assets (if properly transferred, either outright or in trust) avoid any later Gift or Estate Tax.

Note that gifting property to a foreign trust in which the grantor retains an interest may not function to avoid Estate Tax. A retained interest (generally allowing the grantor

---

[227] *See* IRC §672(f)(5)(B).

access to property contributed) may bring trust assets into the immigrant's taxable estate. See page 60 regarding "incomplete" gifts.

Selling Appreciated Assets

Although this book covers only certain aspects of the Estate Tax and Gift Tax, one trap for the unwary immigrant is the U.S. capital gains tax. The tax is incurred by U.S. residents and citizens when gain is realized on the sale of appreciated assets (wherever located). NRNCs are not generally subject to capital gains tax on the sale of U.S. securities. Gains should be incurred (U.S. tax-free) before entering the U.S. Before establishing U.S. residency (or spending at least 130 days in the U.S. during any year), all appreciated liquid securities and (if feasible) other appreciated assets should be sold or gifted (free of U.S. capital gains tax). Upon becoming a U.S. income tax resident, the immigrant is taxed on gains realized on the sale of all property wherever located.

To the extent feasible (and defendable), potential immigrants should consider selling appreciated property to related parties. The foreign sales may often be structured to increase the basis held in the property to current fair market value (avoiding future U.S. capital gains tax).

Questions

Prior to immigration, what types of assets should be gifted to beneficiary NRNCs?

- to U.S. citizens?
- to U.S. resident non-citizens?
- to a spouse NRNC?

When should gifts by a NRNC (potentially contemplating a move to the U.S.) be made to a foreign trust?

CHAPTER 14
EXPATRIATION

<u>General</u>

Long-term residents who abandon U.S. residency may face the web of tax provisions applicable to U.S. citizens who expatriate. Non-citizen residents who leave the U.S. may be liable for an "Exit Tax" on the deemed sale of all assets worldwide as well as an "Inheritance Tax.".

U.S. citizens may expatriate by renouncing their U.S. nationality at a U.S. embassy or consulate. [228] Non-citizen long-term permanent residents may similarly terminate residency. Certain long-term resident non-citizens who exit after at least eight of the last fifteen taxable years in the U.S. are subject to the same tax imposed on expatriating citizens (Code §§877(e)(2) or 877(A)).

---

[228] 8 USC §1481.

The "Exit Tax"

The "Exit Tax" is an income tax on (i) gain from the deemed sale of worldwide assets on the day prior to expatriation and (ii) the deemed taxable distribution of IRAs, 529 plans and health savings accounts.

A long-term permanent resident is defined as any individual lawful resident green-card holder during eight of the fifteen years prior to abandonment of the green card.[229] If a green card holder "expatriates" before this "8 of 15" year test is met, the tax on expatriation does not apply. A non-green card resident alien (living in the U.S. and taxed on worldwide income) is not subject to the expatriation tax.

Two actions are required to abandon long-term U.S. residency. First, long-term residency by a non-citizen is abandoned for immigration purposes upon formal relinquishment of the resident's green card (after having enjoyed permanent U.S. residency for eight of the fifteen tax years ending with the year of renunciation). A green card holder may abandon permanent U.S. resident status by signing and submitting Form I-407[230] to a U.S. consulate or U.S. Citizenship and Immigration Services (USCIS) and relinquishing the green card. The application is included in Form I-407 or may be made by certified letter of abandonment, submitted with the permanent resident card. Although green cards generally expire after ten years, the holder must formally relinquish permanent resident status to avoid remaining a "long-term" U.S. resident for tax purposes.

Long-term residents abandoning residency after June 3, 2004 must also file a tax information statement with the IRS (for any taxable year in which Code Sections 877(b) or

---

[229] *See* IRC §7701(b)(6), §877-A(g)(5) and §877(e)(2).
[230] *See* USCIS Form I-407, Record of Abandonment of Lawful Permanent Resident Status.

877A[231] applies) on Form 8854 (*Expatriation Information Statement*).[232] Failure to file Form 8854 for the year in which the green card was abandoned and for any tax year to which the expiration tax rules apply could result in fines as high as $10,000 per year.[233]

Expatriation for immigration purposes does not relieve the expatriate from the obligation to file U.S. tax returns and report worldwide income as a citizen or U.S. resident.[234] Until the expatriated individual files Form 8854 and notifies the Department of State or the Department of Homeland Security of his or her expatriating act, the U.S. will continue to tax the expatriate for income tax purposes. The applicable Treasury Regulation provides that resident status is deemed "abandoned" only when it is "administratively or judicially determined to have been abandoned."[235]

Thus, it may be possible for an expatriate to remain a citizen or resident for tax purposes, taxable on worldwide income, for years after citizenship/residency has been lost for nationality/immigration law purposes.[236] A former long-term resident who fails to notify the IRS of loss of residency could potentially continue to be taxed as a resident in perpetuity (even after surrendering his or her green card to the Department of Homeland

---

[231] IRC §6039G(a), amended by P.L.108-357, §804 and P.L. 110-245, §301(e)(1).

[232] *See* Notice 2009-85, 2009-45 I.R.B 598 (HEART Act Guidance); Notice 2005-36.

[233] IRC §6039G(c). Such penalties may be abated if the taxpayer shows that the failure to file is due to reasonable cause and not to willful neglect.

[234] *See* IRS Instructions for Form 8854.

[235] *See* Treas. Reg. §301.7701(b)-1(b)(3); *See also* Topsnik v. Comm'r, 146 T.C. 1 (2016) (holding that expatriation date was the date on which former lawful permanent resident completed Form I-407 and surrendered his green card); and Topsnik v. Comm'r, 143 T.C. 240 (2014) (stating that permanent resident status for Federal income tax purposes turns on Federal income tax law and is only indirectly determined by immigration law; recognizes that the Internal Revenue Code and Regulations circumscribe the means by which a permanent resident may abandon that status for federal income tax purposes).

[236] *Id.*; Former IRC §7701(n), effective for any expatriate between 2004-2008.

Security).[237] Moreover, at death, worldwide assets of the expatriate may be subject to U.S. Estate Tax.[238]

Interestingly, a green-card holder may make an unintended expatriation. An unintended expatriation may occur if the green-card holder becomes a resident of a country which has an income tax treaty with the U.S. If the individual files his or her U.S. income tax return, and, on that return, takes a treaty-based position (as a foreign resident) for tax relief, expatriation (for U.S. tax purposes) occurs.[239] The green card holder is deemed to abandon U.S. permanent residency under Code §7701(b)(6), triggering an expatriation event.

Depending on the year of renunciation, the expatriate may incur U.S. tax under Code §§877 or 877A. The expatriation date determines which set of expatriation tax rules apply. Individuals who expatriated after June 3, 2004 and before June 17, 2008 are subject to a ten-year transition rules under Code §877. The Heroes Earnings Assistance and Relief Tax Act of 2008 (the "HEART Act") added Section 877A, effective for individuals who expatriate on or after June 17, 2008. The HEART Act imposes the newer expatriation tax under Code §877A. As the prior law has waned in relevance, Code §877A is discussed below.

---

[237] *See* former §7701(n)(2).

[238] *Id.*

[239] John L. Campbell & Michael J. Stegman, ACTEC L. J. 266 (2009) (citing IRC §7701(b)(6)). IRC §7701(b)(6) provides that "An individual shall cease to be treated as a lawful permanent resident of the U.S. if such individual commences to be treated as a resident of a foreign country under the provisions of a tax treaty between the United States and the foreign country, does not waive the benefits of such treaty applicable to residents of the foreign country, and notifies the Secretary of the commencement of such treatment."

Generally, a nonresident alien becomes a "resident alien" for U.S. tax purposes on the "Residency Start Date" ("RSD"). Pre-immigration tax planning (whether for Estate, Gift or U.S. income tax purposes) cannot generally be accomplished after the RSD. Regarding the U.S. income tax, the RSD is the earlier of (i) the first day the person is present in the U.S. during the year of "substantial presence" (explained below); or (ii) the first day the individual is physically present in the U.S. as a green card holder. For the Estate and Gift Tax, the RSD is the date the individual becomes "domiciled" in the U.S. (i.e., the day a foreign individual relocates to the U.S. with the intent to remain in the U.S. permanently).

For U.S. income tax purposes, the "substantial presence test" classifies a non-citizen as "resident" or "nonresident" (under §7701(b) of the Code and regulations), based on a weighted average of the number of days present in the U.S. in the current and the two preceding years. Any foreign individual is deemed a "resident" for income tax purposes for any calendar year if present in the U.S. for (i) at least 31 days in the current calendar year and (ii) an average of 183 or more days during the current and two prior years. In calculating the average of the current calendar year and the two preceding calendar years, days during current year are counted at full value, days present during the immediately preceding calendar year are counted as 1/3 of a day, and days present during the second preceding calendar year are counted as 1/6 of a day. To avoid "resident" alien status for U.S. income tax purposes, presence in the U.S. must be less than a weighted annual average presence of 183 days.

Deemed Sale

Internal Revenue Code §877A(a) imposes a "mark-to-market" tax regime on "covered expatriates." Under Section 877A(a)(1), all property of a covered expatriate is treated as being sold on the day before his or her expatriation date for its fair market value.[240]

Section 877(a)(2)(A) provides that any gain arising from the deemed sale is taken into account for the taxable year of the deemed sale (at fair market value).[241]

Thus, the "mark to market" regime imposes an income tax on the unrealized gain (on the covered expatriate's worldwide assets). The deemed gain applies to the extent exceeding a safe harbor threshold ($737,000 for 2020).[242] The rates of tax differ with the type of asset involved. Long-term capital gain assets and qualified dividends receive preferential rates. The unrealized gain in a life insurance contract is generally taxed at ordinary income rates.

The "exit" tax is generally payable immediately (i.e., April 15 following the close of the tax year in which expatriation occurs). Because the Exit Tax deems the taxpayer as either having sold his property or received a distribution of retirement accounts (without actually having sold any property), it may create a liquidity shortage (as no actual sales proceeds are available to pay the tax). Under certain circumstances, payment of the tax may be deferred until actual sale (or death).

---

[240] Topsnik v. Commissioner, 146 T.C. 1, 12 (2016).
[241] Id.
[242] See IRC §877A(a)(1) - (3) (calculating the $600,000 safe harbor with yearly inflation).

"Covered Expatriate" Status of §877A   3 Tests

Section 877A applies to only "covered expatriates" who meet at least one of the three requirements, or "tests," set out in Section 877(a)(2)(A) – (C).[243]

The Net Worth Test. A person is a "covered expatriate" if his or her net worth is $2,000,000 or more on the date of expatriation. The threshold considers all assets worldwide. For purposes of determining an individual's net worth, all assets subject to Gift Tax (Chapter 12 of the Code) are included.

The Average Annual Income Tax Liability Test. A person is a "covered expatriate" if his or her average annual net income tax for the five years ending before the date of expatriation is more than $171,000 (for 2020), adjusted for inflation. An individual who files a joint tax return must take into account the net income tax reflected on the joint return.[244]

Failure to Certify Tax Compliance. A person is a covered expatriate if "such individual fails to certify (under penalty of perjury) that he or she has met the requirements of this title for the five preceding taxable years or fails to submit evidence of such compliance as the Secretary may require."[245] Although courts (including the U.S. Tax Court) are not legally bound by the current IRS Notice 2009-85, it is an official statement of the IRS' position, requiring certification of U.S. tax compliance during the five years

---

[243] Note that statutory exceptions may apply to exclude certain persons from "covered expatriate" status (even if the tests are otherwise satisfied). These statutory exceptions pertain to certain persons who are dual citizens at birth and minors who have relinquished U.S. citizenship prior to reaching age 18 ½ years old and have been income tax residents of the U.S. for no more than 10 years within the 15-year period ending with the taxable year of the expatriation.

[244] Section 2(B) of Notice 2009-85, referencing §III of Notice 97-19.

[245] *Topsnik*, 146 T.C. at 13 (quoting IRC §877A(a)(2)(C)).

prior to expatriation (on Form 8854). The Notice may be considered persuasive authority a court may consider in ruling on compliance with Section 877A.[246]

Even if an individual does not meet either of the two financial tests (the "Net Worth Test" and the "Average Annual Income Tax Liability" test), the failure to file Form 8854 may (at least from the IRS perspective) results in covered expatriate status. Persons without considerable assets or income may nonetheless become exposed to Section 877A by failing to certify tax compliance.

The "Mark to Market" Calculation

A covered expatriate is deemed to have sold any interest in property other than property described in Section 877A(c) (deferred compensation, specified tax-deferred accounts and any interest in a non-grantor trust (discussed below)), as of the day before the expatriation date.[247] The property subject to the mark-to-market regime of §877A(a) is of a type whose value would be includible in the value of a decedent's U.S. gross taxable estate (as if the covered expatriate had died on the day before his expatriation date).[248] A covered expatriate is thus considered to own (for the Exit Tax purposes) and sell the property includable in his or her taxable U.S. estate.

Tax Basis

Section 877A(a) requires "proper adjustments" for any gain or loss realized with respect to an asset that is deemed sold under the Exit Tax. Basis is adjusted upward ("stepped up") by the amount of gain attributable to the deemed sale (to avoid double

---

[246] *Topsnik*, 146 T.C. at 13.

[247] Deferred compensation, specified tax-deferred accounts and interest in non-grantor trusts are taxed independently of the mark-to-market tax, under §877A(c).

[248] *Topsnik*, 146 T.C. at 15.

taxation upon the later actual sale of the property). Similarly, basis is reduced to the extent of a deemed loss.[249] Certain types of property held by a long-term resident are ineligible for the step up. Assets which would have been taxed if the individual had never become a permanent resident (*e.g.*, U.S. real property interests or property used in connection with a U.S. trade or business) are not eligible for the step-up.[250]

Gains Taxed

Under §877A(a)(3), if an expatriate's deemed gain is less than an (adjusted for inflation) the annual threshold amount, there is no tax due. For 2020 expatriates, the exemption amount is $744,000. Gain exceeding the exemption must be allocated pro rata among all appreciated property.[251] Such allocation typically involves a complicated process of allocating the exclusion amount among each gain asset (based on the gain applicable to each asset) over the total built-in gain in all gain assets.[252]

---

[249] IRC §877A(a), (h)(2).
[250] Notice 2009-85 at Section 3.D.
[251] *See* Robert W. Wood, *Expatriating and Its U.S. Tax Impact*, 2011 BNA DAILY TAX REPORT (Jan. 26, 2011).
[252] *Id.*

The "Inheritance Tax"

(IRC Section §2801)

In addition to the Exit Tax (triggering the deemed sale of assets upon expatriation), the HEART Act added the "Inheritance Tax" to the Internal Revenue Code. The Inheritance Tax imposes a transfer tax (in addition to the Estate Tax, Gift Tax and U.S. Generation Skipping Tax) on lifetime or testamentary gifts by covered expatriates.

The "Inheritance Tax" generally applies to all property held by "covered expatriates," in additional to the U.S. "Exit Tax." Appreciated property already taxed by the mark-to-market expatriation tax of §877A is thus also subject to the §2801 Inheritance Tax (imposed at the highest Estate and Gift Tax rate).

The Inheritance Tax is imposed on U.S. citizens and residents who receive (from expatriates) property that would otherwise have escaped U.S. Estate or Gift Tax (as a consequence of the donor's expatriation). U.S. donees are taxed on gifts or bequests by "covered expatriates." Donees subject to the Inheritance Tax include U.S. citizens or residents, domestic trusts, charitable remainder trusts, foreign trusts electing to be treated as domestic trusts for the purposes of §2801 and migrated foreign trusts.[253] The intent of Section 2801 is to ensure that expatriates cannot avoid U.S. transfer tax (as NRNCs) on property transferred (after-expatriation) to U.S. citizens or residents.

Section 2801 imposes what practically amounts to a second expatriation tax on gifts and bequests by expatriates. Unlike NRNCs, who may gift foreign property to U.S. residents tax-free, gifts by "covered expatriates" are taxed on assets held worldwide (even

---

[253] IRC §2801(b), Prop. Treas. Reg. §28.2801-4(a).

if acquired after expatriation). Section §2801 is triggered when a "covered expatriate" makes a "covered gift" or "covered bequest." The Inheritance Tax (unlike the Estate Tax and Gift Tax) is imposed on the U.S. recipient. The Tax therefore saddles the donee with what amounts to U.S. Estate or Gift Tax (otherwise avoided by the expatriate).

Section 2801 does not expire. Thus, a gift or bequest made by a covered expatriate decades after expatriating may trigger the Inheritance Tax. Currently, the Inheritance Tax rate is 40% of the gross value of the "covered gift" or "covered bequest."[254]

The U.S. recipient (liable for the tax) does not receive an increased tax basis for Inheritance Tax paid. Note, however, that property subject to the mark-to-market regime of §877A (triggered by expatriation) does receive a fair market value tax basis. The increased basis transfers to the donee.[255]

Definitions

A few definitions integral to understanding §2801 are as follows:

"Citizen or Resident of the United States." A citizen or resident of the U.S. (subject to the Inheritance Tax) is an individual who is a citizen or non-citizen Estate and Gift Tax resident of the U.S. at the time of the covered gift or covered bequest.[256] U.S. citizen also includes domestic trusts (as defined under §7701(a)(30)(E)), as well as foreign trusts electing to be treated as a domestic trust.[257]

---

[254] §2801(a); Prop. Treas. Reg. §28.2801-4(b).
[255] §877A(a); *See also* Paragraph C of Section 3, IRS Notice 2009-85 (November 9, 2009).
[256] Accordingly, whether an individual is a "resident" is based on domicile (presence in the United States and an intent to remain), notwithstanding that §877A adopts the income tax definition of the term.
[257] Prop. Treas. Reg. §28.2801-2(b); Prop. Treas. Reg. §28.2801-5(d).

"Covered Gift or Bequest." A gift by an expatriate generally becomes a "covered gift or bequest" if (i) acquired, directly or indirectly, from an individual who, at the time of such acquisition, is a "covered expatriate" (even if mark-to-market tax is paid under §877A) when received by a U.S. citizen or resident or (ii) property acquired directly or indirectly by reason of the death of an individual who, at death (even if mark-to-market tax is paid under §877A), was a "covered expatriate." The determination of whether a gift is a covered gift is made without regard to the situs of the property and whether such property was acquired by the covered expatriate before or after expatriation.[258] Note that a gift of intangible assets (otherwise exempt from Estate and Gift Tax, if made by NRNCs) and gifts of value less than the annual $15,000 Gift Tax exclusion are not excluded from the definition of a "covered gift" under §2801.[259]

Exemptions

Under proposed regulations, the following transfers are exempt from the application of the §2801 Inheritance Tax:

Reportable Taxable Gifts. A taxable gift reported on the donor's timely filed Form 709 Gift Tax Return is not a "covered gift" under §2801.

Property Subject to the Estate Tax. Property included in the gross estate of the "covered expatriate" and timely reported and paid is not subject to Inheritance Tax.

Transfers to Charities. Charitable gifts (described in §2522(b) of the Code) and bequests (described in §2055(a)) are not "covered gifts" or "covered bequests," to the extent a charitable deduction under §2522 or §2055 of the Code would have been allowed

---

[258] Prop. Treas. Reg. §28.2801-2(f).
[259] Prop. Treas. Reg. §28.2801-3(c)(1).

if the "covered expatriate" had been a U.S. citizen or resident at the time of transfer.[260]

Charitable giving may therefore be a viable strategy to avoid the Inheritance Tax.

Transfers to Spouse. A transfer from a "covered expatriate" to the covered expatriate's spouse is not a "covered gift" or "covered bequest," to the extent a marital deduction under §2523 or §2056 would have been allowed if the "covered expatriate" had been a U.S. citizen or resident at the time of the transfer.[261]

Qualified Disclaimers. A transfer pursuant to a qualified disclaimer of property by a "covered expatriate" (defined in §2518(b) of the Code), is not a "covered gift" or "covered bequest."[262] A qualified disclaimer is a written refusal of a gift or bequest by the designated beneficiary (i.e., the recipient expatriate) within nine months of the intended transfer to the beneficiary. To be effective, the designated beneficiary must not accept the interest or any of its benefits, and the interest must pass without any direction on the part of the expatriate disclaiming.[263]

Calculation

The §2801 Inheritance Tax is calculated by multiplying the "net covered gifts and covered bequests" received by a U.S. recipient during the calendar year by the highest Estate Tax or Gift Tax rate for the applicable calendar year.[264] "Net covered gifts and covered bequests" include all such gifts and bequests received by the U.S. recipient during

---

[260] Prop. Treas. Reg. §28.2801-3(c)(3); IRC §2801(e)(3).
[261] Prop. Treas. Reg. §28.2801-3(c)(4).
[262] Prop. Treas. Reg. §28.2801-3(c)(5).
[263] IRC §2518(b).
[264] Prop. Treas. Reg. §28.2801-4(b)(1).

the calendar year, less the §2801(c) annual exclusion amount per-donee (currently $15,000).[265]

For example, in Year 1, A, a U.S. citizen, receives a $50,000 covered gift from B and an $80,000 covered bequest from C. Both B and C are covered expatriates. In Year 1, the highest Estate and Gift Tax rate is forty percent and the Code Section 2801(c) annual exempt amount is $15,000. A's Inheritance Tax for Year 1 is computed by multiplying A's net covered gifts and covered bequests by forty percent. A's net covered gifts and covered bequests for Year 1 are $115,000, which is determined by reducing A's total covered gifts and covered bequests received during Year 1 ($130,000) by $15,000 (the §2801(c) exemption amount for 2020). A's §2801 tax liability is then reduced by any foreign estate or gift tax paid under §2801(e). Assuming A, B, and C paid no foreign estate or gift tax on the transfers, A's §2801 tax liability for Year 1 is $46,000 ($115,000 x 40%).

Determining Tax Basis for Payment of §2801 Inheritance Tax

The U.S. recipient's basis in a "covered gift" or "covered bequest," remains governed by Code Sections 1015 and 1014.[266] As property forming a "covered bequest" is technically not included in the expat's taxable gross estate, the property acquired by the U.S. recipient will not receive a tax basis step-up to fair market value (regardless of the §2801 Inheritance Tax paid).[267] "Covered gifts" are governed by the gift tax basis rules and maintain a carryover basis from the expat donor.[268] While Code §1015(d) generally

---

[265] Prop. Treas. Reg. §28.2801-4(b)(2).
[266] Prop. Treas. Reg. §28.2801-6(a).
[267] Treas. Reg. §1.1014-2(b)(2) – the fair market value basis step-up under §1014(a) does not apply for "property not includible in the decedent's gross estate such as property not situated in the United States acquired from a nonresident who is not a citizen of the United States."
[268] Treas. Reg. §1.1015-1(a).

permits a basis step-up on the amount of gift tax paid, it does not apply for any tax paid under §2801 for "covered gifts."[269]

§2801 Tax Treatment of Foreign Trusts

A foreign trust (absent an election to be treated as a domestic trust) which receives a "covered gift" or "covered bequest" is not liable for the Inheritance Tax. U.S. beneficiaries of the trust are, however, liable for the Inheritance Tax upon receipt of distributions from the foreign trust, to the extent attributable[270] to a "covered gift" or "covered bequest." Trust beneficiaries therefore incur Inheritance Tax upon receipt of covered gifts initially contributed to the foreign trust.[271]

Distributions to U.S. beneficiaries may be partially attributable to covered gifts. In such case the covered portion (subject to §2801 tax) is determined by multiplying the fair market value of the distribution, as of December 31 of the preceding tax year, by a §2801 tax ratio which generally apportions the distribution based on the ratio of "covered gift" to non-covered gift property in the trust.[272] If valid records are not available, the §2801 Inheritance Tax is imposed on the entire trust corpus.[273]

Domestic trusts are treated as U.S. citizens under §2801, immediately liable for tax upon receipt of a covered gift.[274] If a foreign trust elects to be treated as a domestic trust under §2801, the Inheritance Tax is due on all "covered gifts" and "covered bequests"

---

[269] Treas. Reg. §1.1015-5.
[270] As determined by Prop. Treas. Reg. §28.2801-5(b) and (c).
[271] Prop. Treas. Reg. §28.2801-4(a)(3); Prop. Treas. Reg. §28.2801 – 4(a)(3).
[272] *Id.*
[273] *Id.*
[274] IRC §2801(e)(4)(A).

received in the calendar year of the election (i.e. the year Form 708 is filed).[275] If the

electing foreign trust received "covered gifts" or "covered bequests" during years prior to

electing domestic trust status, it must also report and pay Inheritance Tax on such

property's fair market value.[276]

---

[275] Prop. Treas. Reg. §28.2801-5(d).
[276] Prop. Treas. Reg. §28.201-5(d)(3)(iii).

Potential Planning Strategies

Gifting Assets to Fall Below $2,000,000 Net Worth Threshold.

Outright Gifts – To Spouse and Others. The proposed expatriate may gift assets sufficient to reduce net worth below the $2,000,000 net worth test for characterization as a covered expatriate. For example, before expatriation, an expatriate may use the §2503(b) annual exclusion (currently $15,000 per donee) to make non-taxable gifts, or larger gifts, utilizing the unified Estate and Gift tax credit. Before doing so, the donor should establish the value of the assets through formal appraisal.[277] To ensure characterization and value of gifts, the expatriate should consider filing an informational Form 709 with the Internal Revenue Service.

Gifts should be made at least three years prior to expatriation, to avoid §2035. Section 2035 adds the value of gifts made within three years of a decedent's death (or deemed expatriation "death")[278] to the deceased's taxable estate (if the value of such property gifted would have been included in the decedent's gross estate under section 2036, 2037, 2038, or 2042, had such property been held at death). Unless an exception applies (i.e., the expatriate was taxed on the gifts),[279] all gifts made during the three years prior to expatriation are not only included in net worth but are also likely included in calculating the Inheritance Tax.

A potential expatriate may also make unlimited tax-free gifts to a U.S. citizen spouse (prior to expatriation).[280] Interspousal gifts are not subject to the 3-year "clawback"

---

[277] Campbell and Stegman, Confronting the New Expatriation Tax: Advice for the U.S. Green Card Holder, at pg. 35,36 (herein the "Campbell Article").
[278] IRS Notice 2009-85
[279] *See*, e.g. IRC § 2053(b) – (e).
[280] IRC § 2523.

of §2035.[281] If, however, the spouse is also expatriating, marital gifting may function only if the spouse is not a "covered expatriate" (or would become a "covered expatriate" due to the gifts). In other words, gifts from the wealthier spouse should be avoided to the extent causing the recipient spouse's net worth to exceed the $2,000,000 covered expatriate threshold.

General Transfer Tax Strategies.   As a permanent legal resident (green card holder), the future "covered" expatriate (domiciled in the U.S.) may take advantage of a full unified estate and gift tax credit ($11,700,000 in 2021) by implementing general U.S. transfer tax avoidance strategies at least three years before expatriation. These include utilizing lack of marketability and lack of control valuation discounts for potential transfers, gifts to domestic irrevocable trusts (such as grantor retained annuity trusts, qualified personal residence trusts, intentionally defective grantor trusts (with a toggle off of grantor trust status), charitable lead trusts, charitable remainder trusts, etc.

Domicile Planning. Another strategy (to avoid U.S. Transfer Tax on foreign assets) is for a green card holder to depart the U.S. permanently (while retaining U.S. income tax residence (via the green card)). After domicile is established abroad, the green card holder makes gift transfers of non-situs U.S. assets and U.S. intangibles, reducing net worth. Thus, although the green card holder remains a U.S. resident for U.S. income tax purposes, the green card holder is not a U.S. resident for U.S. Transfer Tax purposes [282] as Estate and Gift Taxes (Chapters 11 and 12 of Subtitle B of the Code), apply only to citizens and

---

[281] IRC § 2035(c)(3).
[282] See discussion at pages 7 and 16 above regarding the establishment of domicile; See Treas. Reg. §25.2501-1(b).

domiciliaries. The non-domiciled green card holder may therefore gift non-U.S. situs assets Estate and Gift Tax free. Domicile (the standard for residence for Estate and Gift Tax purposes), depends on physical presence and intent to remain in the U.S. There is no quantitative "substantial presence test" or "green card test" deeming the non-citizen a resident for Estate and Gift Tax purposes. Domicile may therefore be transferred outside the U.S. by leaving the U.S. and intending to remain abroad permanently.[283]

Transfers made while as a non-resident non-citizen, for Estate and Gift Tax purposes reduce net worth but are not subject to U.S. Transfer Tax (unless the property gifted is tangible and located in the U.S.).[284] For a resident alien with substantial non-U.S. assets and U.S. situs intangibles, U.S. Transfer Tax may be avoided. Following the passage of three years from such transfers, Section 877A does not deemed sold (upon expatriation) to the assets transferred.[285] This strategy may also permit the potential expatriate to completely avoid the Exit Tax (if transfers bring net worth below $2 million) assuming the net income test doesn't apply.[286]

Use of an Expatriation Trust. As an alternative to outright gifts, a potential expatriate may fund an irrevocable trust for his spouse and/or descendants.[287] Gifts to a properly structured "Expatriation Trust" may lower net worth, to avoid the $2,000,000 net worth test.

---

[283] See discussion regarding the establishment of domicile; See Treas. Reg. §25.501-1(b).
[284] IRC §2501; Treas. Reg. §25.2501-1(a).
[285] Id.
[286] IRC §2501; Treas. Reg. §25.2501-1(a).
[287] Campbell Article at pg. 35.

An Expatriation Trust utilizes a discretionary U.S. domestic trust. An Expatriation Trust may retain flexibility by, for instance, permitting the settlor to replace the independent trustee. The potential expatriate may lower net worth (below $2,000,000) by transferring assets to the Expatriation Trust (utilizing the unified credit, to avoid Gift Tax). The Expatriation Trust should also qualify as "non-grantor" trust for U.S. income tax purposes (with trust income taxed to the trust). To avoid potential inclusion under Section 877A, the potential expatriate should also release any powers over trust assets (i.e. powers of appointment). As this vehicle remains a domestic trust under Section 7701, Section 684 (deemed mark to market sale) would not apply to the transfer of assets into the trust. The potential expatriate may retain the ability to remove and replace independent trustees. Following the passage of three years from funding, Section 877A would not apply to the assets held in such a trust.[288] Moreover, future distributions from the Expatriation Trust to U.S. beneficiaries (or the expatriate) would also avoid the Section 2801 "Inheritance Tax" (discussed below).

The Settlor may also consider making incomplete gifts (for transfer tax purposes) while the grantor remains a U.S. resident (to avoid imposition of Gift Tax). The gift to the Expatriation Trust may be completed after establishing domicile in a new country and allowing at least 3 years to elapse prior to expatriation.[289]

Although a properly structured Expatriation Trust may potentially remove assets when calculating the "Net Worth" test under § 877A, there are some potential drawbacks to this structure. For example, under the "interest in non-grantor trusts" exception to the

---

[288] IRC § 2035(a); Treas. Reg. § 25.2501-1(b), IRS Notice 2009-85.
[289] See Campbell Article, pg. 35.

mark-to-market tax (discussed above), the trustee must withhold 30% (imposed by FIPTA) of the taxable portion of any distribution (as determined under normal tax accounting principles applicable to trusts) as if the covered expatriate were still a U.S. citizen or resident.[290] In such event, a covered expatriate may not claim treaty benefits to reduce withholding tax.

Note that the IRS may attempt to include in the expatriate's net worth the value of the grantor's retained "beneficial interest" in an Expatriation Trust. The IRS may consider (among other factors) the terms of the trust, any letter of wishes submitted by the grantor, historical patterns of trust distributions, and the power of any trust protector or advisor.[291] The claim is similar to an IRS assertion of a decedent's retention of beneficial interests under §2036. Several family limited partnership cases hinge on the same issue.[292]

Sale of Personal Residence. The sale of the expatriate's personal home (prior to expatriation (for cash)), removes any built-in-gain from the market-to-market tax.[293] Sale should be made before expatriation, as the popular §121 income tax exclusion (excluding gain from the sale of a personal residence) is likely not available to a "covered expatriate", to shield deemed gain triggered by expatriation.

Mitigating "Inheritance Tax". If "covered expatriate" status cannot be avoided, the potential expatriate must also be mindful of the potential exposure (to donees of gifts) to liability under §2801.

---

[290] Campbell Article at pg. 35 (citing IRC § 877A(f)(1) & (2)).
[291] Campbell Article pg. 35 (citing IRS Notice 97-19).
[292] Estate of Powell v. Commissioner, 148 T.C. 18 (2017); Bongard v. Commissioner, 124 T.C. 95 (2005); Estate of Strangi v. Commissioner, TC Memo 2003-145.
[293] Estate tax principles are used to determine what property is subject to the mark-to-market tax. *See also Topsnik v. Comm'r*, 146 T.C. 1 (U.S. Tax Ct., 2016) at *16.

The §2801 "Inheritance Tax" is triggered upon a "covered expatriate" making a "covered gift or bequest" to a "covered beneficiary". A "covered beneficiary", as noted above, is a U.S. citizen, a U.S. domiciliary, a domestic trust, an electing foreign trust, and "the U.S. citizen resident shareholders, partners, members, or other interest-holders, as the case may be (if any) of a domestic entity that receives a covered gift or covered bequest". Where possible, a covered expatriate should consider coordinating gifting to non-U.S. recipient beneficiaries.

Also, charitable donations that qualify for the estate or gift tax charitable deduction are not "covered gifts or bequests". Charitable giving may therefore be a potentially viable strategy for mitigating tax under §2801.

Questions

What was the original purpose of the Exit Tax?

How may deemed sale (triggered by the Exit Tax) be avoided by a potential expatriate?

What tax avoidance strategy is addressed by the Inheritance Tax?

How may an individual income tax resident (but non-resident for Estate Tax purposes) incur capital gains liability by deemed sale of

- U.S. business stock?
- Foreign business stock?
- World-wide investments?

CHAPTER 15
TAX REPORTING

Both resident and non-resident non-citizens are subject to a number of IRS reporting requirements. Several significant filing requirements are outlined below.

Residents

Schedule B of Form 1040. The Internal Revenue Code generally requires U.S. citizens and resident non-citizens to report all worldwide income, including income from foreign trusts and foreign bank and securities accounts on Form 1040. Part III of Schedule B (Foreign Accounts and Trusts) requires specific disclosure of foreign accounts, including the country in which each account is held.

Interest and Ordinary Dividends

▶ Go to *www.irs.gov/ScheduleB* for instructions and the latest information.
▶ Attach to Form 1040 or 1040-SR.

OMB No. 1545-0074

2020

Attachment
Sequence No. **08**

Name(s) shown on return

Your social security number

Part I **Interest** (See instructions and the instructions for Forms 1040 and 1040-SR, line 2b.) **Note:** If you received a Form 1099-INT, Form 1099-OID, or substitute statement from a brokerage firm, list the firm's name as the payer and enter the total interest shown on that form.	1	List name of payer. If any interest is from a seller-financed mortgage and the buyer used the property as a personal residence, see the instructions and list this interest first. Also, show that buyer's social security number and address ▶		**Amount**
			1	
	2	Add the amounts on line 1	2	
	3	Excludable interest on series EE and I U.S. savings bonds issued after 1989. Attach Form 8815	3	
	4	Subtract line 3 from line 2. Enter the result here and on Form 1040 or 1040-SR, line 2b . . . . ▶	4	
		Note: If line 4 is over $1,500, you must complete Part III.		**Amount**
Part II **Ordinary** **Dividends** (See instructions and the instructions for Forms 1040 and 1040-SR, line 3b.) **Note:** If you received a Form 1099-DIV or substitute statement from a brokerage firm, list the firm's name as the payer and enter the ordinary dividends shown on that form.	5	List name of payer ▶		
			5	
	6	Add the amounts on line 5. Enter the total here and on Form 1040 or 1040-SR, line 3b . . . . ▶	6	
		Note: If line 6 is over $1,500, you must complete Part III.		

Part III **Foreign** **Accounts** **and Trusts** **Caution:** If required, failure to file FinCEN Form 114 may result in substantial penalties. See instructions.	You must complete this part if you **(a)** had over $1,500 of taxable interest or ordinary dividends; **(b)** had a foreign account; or **(c)** received a distribution from, or were a grantor of, or a transferor to, a foreign trust.	**Yes**	**No**
	7a At any time during 2020, did you have a financial interest in or signature authority over a financial account (such as a bank account, securities account, or brokerage account) located in a foreign country? See instructions		
	If "Yes," are you required to file FinCEN Form 114, Report of Foreign Bank and Financial Accounts (FBAR), to report that financial interest or signature authority? See FinCEN Form 114 and its instructions for filing requirements and exceptions to those requirements		
	b If you are required to file FinCEN Form 114, enter the name of the foreign country where the financial account is located ▶		
	8 During 2020, did you receive a distribution from, or were you the grantor of, or transferor to, a foreign trust? If "Yes," you may have to file Form 3520. See instructions		

For Paperwork Reduction Act Notice, see your tax return instructions.   Cat. No. 17146N   Schedule B (Form 1040) 2020

<u>Form 709, United States Gift (and Generation-Skipping Transfer) Tax Return.</u> A U.S. citizen or resident who transfers money or property to an individual or trust may be required to file Form 709.

Form **709**

Department of the Treasury
Internal Revenue Service

United States Gift (and Generation-Skipping Transfer) Tax Return

▶ Go to *www.irs.gov/Form709* for instructions and the latest information.
(For gifts made during calendar year 2020)
▶ See instructions.

OMB No. 1545-0020

2020

Part 1—General Information

			Yes	No
1	Donor's first name and middle initial	2 Donor's last name		
		3 Donor's social security number		
4	Address (number, street, and apartment number)	5 Legal residence (domicile)		
6	City or town, state or province, country, and ZIP or foreign postal code	7 Citizenship (see instructions)		
8	If the donor died during the year, check here ▶ ☐ and enter date of death _____			
9	If you extended the time to file this Form 709, check here ▶ ☐			
10	Enter the total number of donees listed on Schedule A. Count each person only once ▶			
11a	Have you (the donor) previously filed a Form 709 (or 709-A) for any other year? If "No," skip line 11b			
b	Has your address changed since you last filed Form 709 (or 709-A)?			
12	**Gifts by husband or wife to third parties.** Do you consent to have the gifts (including generation-skipping transfers) made by you and by your spouse to third parties during the calendar year considered as made one-half by each of you? (See instructions.) (If the answer is "Yes," the following information must be furnished and your spouse must sign the consent shown below. **If the answer is "No," skip lines 13–18.**)			
13	Name of consenting spouse	14 SSN		
15	Were you married to one another during the entire calendar year? See instructions			
16	If line 15 is "No," check whether ☐ married ☐ divorced or ☐ widowed/deceased, and give date. See instructions ▶			
17	Will a gift tax return for this year be filed by your spouse? If "Yes," mail both returns in the same envelope			
18	**Consent of Spouse.** I consent to have the gifts (and generation-skipping transfers) made by me and by my spouse to third parties during the calendar year considered as made one-half by each of us. We are both aware of the joint and several liability for tax created by the execution of this consent.			

Consenting spouse's signature ▶   Date ▶

19	Have you applied a DSUE amount received from a predeceased spouse to a gift or gifts reported on this or a previous Form 709? If "Yes," complete Schedule C		

Part 2—Tax Computation

1	Enter the amount from Schedule A, Part 4, line 11	1	
2	Enter the amount from Schedule B, line 3	2	
3	Total taxable gifts. Add lines 1 and 2	3	
4	Tax computed on amount on line 3 (see *Table for Computing Gift Tax* in instructions)	4	
5	Tax computed on amount on line 2 (see *Table for Computing Gift Tax* in instructions)	5	
6	Balance. Subtract line 5 from line 4	6	
7	Applicable credit amount. If donor has DSUE amount from predeceased spouse(s) or Restored Exclusion Amount, enter amount from Schedule C, line 5; otherwise, see instructions	7	
8	Enter the applicable credit against tax allowable for all prior periods (from Sch. B, line 1, col. C)	8	
9	Balance. Subtract line 8 from line 7. Do not enter less than zero	9	
10	Enter 20% (0.20) of the amount allowed as a specific exemption for gifts made after September 8, 1976, and before January 1, 1977. See instructions	10	
11	Balance. Subtract line 10 from line 9. Do not enter less than zero	11	
12	Applicable credit. Enter the smaller of line 6 or line 11	12	
13	Credit for foreign gift taxes (see instructions)	13	
14	Total credits. Add lines 12 and 13	14	
15	Balance. Subtract line 14 from line 6. Do not enter less than zero	15	
16	Generation-skipping transfer taxes (from Schedule D, Part 3, col. G, total)	16	
17	Total tax. Add lines 15 and 16	17	
18	Gift and generation-skipping transfer taxes prepaid with extension of time to file	18	
19	If line 18 is less than line 17, enter **balance due.** See instructions	19	
20	If line 18 is greater than line 17, enter **amount to be refunded**	20	

Sign Here

Under penalties of perjury, I declare that I have examined this return, including any accompanying schedules and statements, and to the best of my knowledge and belief, it is true, correct, and complete. Declaration of preparer (other than donor) is based on all information of which preparer has any knowledge.

May the IRS discuss this return with the preparer shown below? See instructions. ☐ Yes ☐ No

▶ _____
Signature of donor   Date

Paid Preparer Use Only

Print/Type preparer's name	Preparer's signature	Date	Check ☐ if self-employed	PTIN
Firm's name ▶			Firm's EIN ▶	
Firm's address ▶			Phone no.	

Attach check or money order here.

For Disclosure, Privacy Act, and Paperwork Reduction Act Notice, see the instructions for this form.   Cat. No. 16783M   Form **709** (2020)

SCHEDULE A	Computation of Taxable Gifts (Including transfers in trust) (see instructions)

A Does the value of any item listed on Schedule A reflect any valuation discount? If "Yes," attach explanation . . . . . . Yes ☐ No ☐

B ☐ ◄ Check here if you elect under section 529(c)(2)(B) to treat any transfers made this year to a qualified tuition program as made ratably over a 5-year period beginning this year. See instructions. Attach explanation.

Part 1—Gifts Subject Only to Gift Tax. Gifts less political organization, medical, and educational exclusions. See instructions.

A Item number	B • Donee's name and address • Relationship to donor (if any) • Description of gift • If the gift was of securities, give CUSIP no. • If closely held entity, give EIN	C	D Donor's adjusted basis of gift	E Date of gift	F Value at date of gift	G For split gifts, enter ¹/₂ of column F	H Net transfer (subtract col. G from col. F)
1							

Gifts made by spouse—complete **only** if you are splitting gifts with your spouse and he/she also made gifts.

Total of Part 1. Add amounts from Part 1, column H . . . . ▶

Part 2—Direct Skips. Gifts that are direct skips and are subject to both gift tax and generation-skipping transfer tax. You must list the gifts in chronological order.

A Item number	B • Donee's name and address • Relationship to donor (if any) • Description of gift • If the gift was of securities, give CUSIP no. • If closely held entity, give EIN	C 2632(b) election out	D Donor's adjusted basis of gift	E Date of gift	F Value at date of gift	G For split gifts, enter ¹/₂ of column F	H Net transfer (subtract col. G from col. F)
1							

Gifts made by spouse—complete **only** if you are splitting gifts with your spouse and he/she also made gifts.

Total of Part 2. Add amounts from Part 2, column H . . . . ▶

Part 3—Indirect Skips and Other Transfers in Trust. Gifts to trusts that are indirect skips as defined under section 2632(c) or to trusts that are currently subject to gift tax and may later be subject to generation-skipping transfer tax. You must list these gifts in chronological order.

A Item number	B • Donee's name and address • Relationship to donor (if any) • Description of gift • If the gift was of securities, give CUSIP no. • If closely held entity, give EIN	C 2632(c) election	D Donor's adjusted basis of gift	E Date of gift	F Value at date of gift	G For split gifts, enter ¹/₂ of column F	H Net transfer (subtract col. G from col. F)
1							

Gifts made by spouse—complete **only** if you are splitting gifts with your spouse and he/she also made gifts.

Total of Part 3. Add amounts from Part 3, column H . . . . ▶

(If more space is needed, attach additional statements.)

Form **709** (2020)

Part 4—Taxable Gift Reconciliation

1	Total value of gifts of donor. Add totals from column H of Parts 1, 2, and 3	**1**	
2	Total annual exclusions for gifts listed on line 1 (see instructions)	**2**	
3	Total included amount of gifts. Subtract line 2 from line 1	**3**	

Deductions (see instructions)

4	Gifts of interests to spouse for which a marital deduction will be claimed, based on item numbers _____ of Schedule A	**4**		
5	Exclusions attributable to gifts on line 4	**5**		
6	Marital deduction. Subtract line 5 from line 4	**6**		
7	Charitable deduction, based on item numbers _____ less exclusions	**7**		
8	Total deductions. Add lines 6 and 7		**8**	
9	Subtract line 8 from line 3		**9**	
10	Generation-skipping transfer taxes payable with this Form 709 (from Schedule D, Part 3, col. G, total)		**10**	
11	**Taxable gifts.** Add lines 9 and 10. Enter here and on page 1, Part 2—Tax Computation, line 1		**11**	

Terminable Interest (QTIP) Marital Deduction. (See instructions for Schedule A, Part 4, line 4.)

If a trust (or other property) meets the requirements of qualified terminable interest property under section 2523(f), and:

a. The trust (or other property) is listed on Schedule A; and

b. The value of the trust (or other property) is entered in whole or in part as a deduction on Schedule A, Part 4, line 4, then the donor shall be deemed to have made an election to have such trust (or other property) treated as qualified terminable interest property under section 2523(f).

If less than the entire value of the trust (or other property) that the donor has included in Parts 1 and 3 of Schedule A is entered as a deduction on line 4, the donor shall be considered to have made an election only as to a fraction of the trust (or other property). The numerator of this fraction is equal to the amount of the trust (or other property) deducted on Schedule A, Part 4, line 6. The denominator is equal to the total value of the trust (or other property) listed in Parts 1 and 3 of Schedule A.

If you make the QTIP election, the terminable interest property involved will be included in your spouse's gross estate upon his or her death (section 2044). See instructions for line 4 of Schedule A. If your spouse disposes (by gift or otherwise) of all or part of the qualifying life income interest, he or she will be considered to have made a transfer of the entire property that is subject to the gift tax. See *Transfer of Certain Life Estates Received From Spouse* in the instructions.

12   Election Out of QTIP Treatment of Annuities

☐ ◄ Check here if you elect under section 2523(f)(6) **not** to treat as qualified terminable interest property any joint and survivor annuities that are reported on Schedule A and would otherwise be treated as qualified terminable interest property under section 2523(f). See instructions. Enter the item numbers from Schedule A for the annuities for which you are making this election ►

SCHEDULE B   Gifts From Prior Periods

If you answered "Yes" on line 11a of page 1, Part 1, see the instructions for completing Schedule B. If you answered "No," skip to the Tax Computation on page 1 (or Schedule C or D, if applicable). Complete Schedule A before beginning Schedule B. See instructions for recalculation of the column C amounts. Attach calculations.

A Calendar year or calendar quarter (see instructions)	**B** Internal Revenue office where prior return was filed	**C** Amount of applicable credit (unified credit) against gift tax for periods after December 31, 1976	**D** Amount of specific exemption for prior periods ending before January 1, 1977	**E** Amount of taxable gifts

1	Totals for prior periods **1**			
2	Amount, if any, by which total specific exemption, line 1, column D, is more than $30,000 . . . . **2**			
3	Total amount of taxable gifts for prior periods. Add amount on line 1, column E, and amount, if any, on line 2. Enter here and on page 1, Part 2—Tax Computation, line 2 . . . . **3**			

(If more space is needed, attach additional statements.)   Form **709** (2020)

SCHEDULE C	Deceased Spousal Unused Exclusion (DSUE) Amount and Restored Exclusion

Provide the following information to determine the DSUE amount and applicable credit received from prior spouses. Complete Schedule A before beginning Schedule C.

A Name of deceased spouse (dates of death after December 31, 2010, only)	B Date of death	C Portability election made?		D If "Yes," DSUE amount received from spouse	E DSUE amount applied by donor to lifetime gifts (list current and prior gifts)	F Date of gift(s) (enter as mm/dd/yy for Part 1 and as yyyy for Part 2)
		Yes	No			
Part 1—DSUE RECEIVED FROM LAST DECEASED SPOUSE						
Part 2—DSUE RECEIVED FROM PREDECEASED SPOUSE(S)						

TOTAL (for all DSUE amounts applied from column E for Part 1 and Part 2) . . . . ▶		

1	Donor's basic exclusion amount (see instructions)	**1**	
2	Total from column E, Parts 1 and 2	**2**	
3	Restored Exclusion Amount (see instructions)	**3**	
4	Add lines 1, 2, and 3	**4**	
5	Applicable credit on amount in line 4 (see *Table for Computing Gift Tax* in the instructions). Enter here and on line 7, Part 2—Tax Computation	**5**	

SCHEDULE D	Computation of Generation-Skipping Transfer Tax

Note: Inter vivos direct skips that are completely excluded by the GST exemption must still be fully reported (including value and exemptions claimed) on Schedule D.

Part 1—Generation-Skipping Transfers. List items from Schedule A first, then items to be reported on Schedule D, including any transfers subject to an Estate Tax Inclusion Period (ETIP).

A Item number (from Schedule A, Part 2, col. A, then ETIP transfers, if any)	B Description (only for ETIP transfers)	C Value (from Schedule A, Part 2, col. H, or close of ETIP described in col. B)	D Nontaxable portion of transfer	E Net transfer (subtract col. D from col. C)
1				
Gifts made by spouse (for gift splitting only)				

(If more space is needed, attach additional statements.)   Form **709** (2020)

Part 2—GST Exemption Reconciliation (Section 2631) and Section 2652(a)(3) Election

Check here ▶ ☐ if you are making a section 2652(a)(3) (special QTIP) election. See instructions.

Enter the item numbers from Schedule A of the gifts for which you are making this election ▶ --------------------------------

1	Maximum allowable exemption (see instructions)	**1**	
2	Total exemption used for periods before filing this return	**2**	
3	Exemption available for this return. Subtract line 2 from line 1	**3**	
4	Exemption claimed on this return from Part 3, column C, total below	**4**	
5	Automatic allocation of exemption to transfers reported on Schedule A, Part 3. To opt out of the automatic allocation rules, you must attach an "**Election Out**" statement. See instructions	**5**	
6	Exemption allocated to transfers not shown on line 4 or line 5 above. **You must attach a "Notice of Allocation."** See instructions	**6**	
7	Add lines 4, 5, and 6	**7**	
8	Exemption available for future transfers. Subtract line 7 from line 3	**8**	

Part 3—Tax Computation

A Item number (from Schedule D, Part 1)	B Net transfer (from Schedule D, Part 1, col. E)	C GST exemption allocated	D Divide col. C by col. B	E Inclusion ratio (Subtract col. D from 1.000)	F Applicable rate (multiply col. E by 40% (0.40))	G Generation-skipping transfer tax (multiply col. B by col. F)
1						

Gifts made by spouse (for gift splitting only)

Total exemption claimed. Enter here and on Part 2, line 4, above. May not exceed Part 2, line 3, above . . .		**Total generation-skipping transfer tax.** Enter here; on page 3, Schedule A, Part 4, line 10; and on page 1, Part 2—Tax Computation, line 16	

(If more space is needed, attach additional statements.)　　　　　　　　　　　　　　　　Form **709** (2020)

<u>FinCEN Form 114, Report of Foreign Bank and Financial Accounts ("FBAR").</u>

The Bank Secrecy Act requires U.S. persons (any U.S. citizen, green card holder or any individual that satisfies the Code's substantial presence test for residents) to disclose any financial interest in or signature authority over a foreign financial account, including a bank account, brokerage account, mutual fund, trust, or other type of foreign financial account with a value exceeding $10,000. The Act requires the U.S. person to annually report the account to the IRS on FinCEN Form 114. This "FBAR" is not filed with any tax return. The FBAR is filed on or before April 15 following the tax year during which the account was opened and (thereafter) owned.

<table>
<tr><td>

Form **114a**

Department of the Treasury
Financial Crimes Enforcement
Network (FinCEN)

May 2015

</td><td>

Record of Authorization to
Electronically File FBARs

(See instructions below for completion)

Do not send to FinCEN. Retain this form for your records.
The form 114a may be digitally signed

</td><td>

</td></tr>
</table>

Part I	Persons who have an obligation to file a Report of Foreign Bank and Financial Account(s)

1. Owner last name or entity's legal name	2. Owner first name	3. Owner M. I.

4. Spouse last name (if jointly filing FBAR - see instructions below)	5. Spouse first name	6. Spouse M. I.

I/we declare that I/we have provided information concerning _____ (enter number of accounts) foreign bank and financial account(s) for the filing year ending December 31, _____ to the preparer listed in Part II; that this information is to the best of my/our knowledge true, correct, and complete; that I/we authorize the preparer listed in Part II to complete and submit to the Financial Crimes Enforcement Network (FinCEN) a Report of Foreign Bank and Financial Accounts (FBAR) based on the information that I/we have provided; and that I/we authorize the preparer listed in Part II to receive information from FinCEN, answer inquiries and resolve issues relating to this submission. I/we acknowledge that, notwithstanding this declaration, it is my/our legal responsibility, not that of the preparer listed in Part II, to timely file an FBAR if required by law to do so.

7. Owner signature (Authorized representative if entity)	8 Date ___/___/___ MM DD YYYY	9 Owner or entity TIN	10 TIN type	a ☐ EIN b ☐ SSN/ITIN c ☐ Foreign
11. Spouse signature	12 Date ___/___/___ MM DD YYYY	13 Spouse TIN	14 TIN type	a ☐ EIN b ☐ SSN/ITIN c ☐ Foreign

Part II	Individual or Entity Authorized to File FBAR on behalf of Persons who have an obligation to file.

15. Preparer last name	16. Preparer first name	17. Preparer M.I.	18. Preparer PTIN

19 Address	20 City	21 State	22 ZIP/postal code

23 Country code	24 Preparer's (item 15) employer's (Entity) name	25. Employer EIN	26. Preparer's signature

Instructions for completing the FBAR Signature Authorization Record
This is a fill and print form using Adobe Reader

This record may be completed by the individual or entity granting such authorization (Part I) OR the individual/entity authorized to perform such services. The completed record must be signed by the individual(s)/entity granting the authorization (Part I) and the individual/entity that will file the FBAR. The Preparer/filing entity must be registered with FinCEN BSA E-File system. (See http://bsaefiling.fincen.treas.gov/main.html for registration).

Read and complete the account owner statement in Part I.

To authorize a third party to file the Foreign Bank and Financial Accounts Report (FBAR), the account owner should complete Part I, items 1 through 3 (as required), sign and date the document in Part I, Items 7/8 and complete items 9 and 10. Item 7 may be digitally signed.

Accounts Jointly Owned by Spouses (see exceptions in the FBAR instructions)
If the account owner is filing an FBAR jointly with his/her spouse, the spouse must also complete Part I, items 4 through 6. The spouse must also sign and date the report in items 11/12, (item 11 may be digitally signed) and complete items 13 and 14. A third party preparer may be one of the spouses of the jointly owned foreign account. In this case, both spouses must complete Part I of form 114a in its entirety. The third party preparer (spouse) that will file the FBAR on behalf of both spouses will complete Part II in its entirety (do not use such terms as *see above*, or *same as item number x*).

Complete Part II, items 15 through 18 with the preparer's information. The address, items 19 through 23, is that of the preparer **or** the preparer's employer if the preparer is an employee. Record the employer's information (if any) in items 24 and 25. If the preparer does not have a PTIN, leave item 18 blank. The third party preparer must sign in item 26 (digital signature acceptable) of Part II indicating that the FBAR will be filed as directed by the authorizing authority.
The person(s) listed in Part I, and the person listed in Part II as authorized to file on behalf of the person(s) listed in Part I, should retain copies of this record of authorization and the filing itself, both for a period of 5 years. See 31 CFR 1010. 430(d).
DO NOT SEND THIS RECORD TO FinCEN UNLESS REQUESTED TO DO SO.

Rev. 10.7 May 21, 2015

FATCA Form 8938, Statement of Special Foreign Financial Assets. The Foreign Account Tax Compliance Act requires U.S. citizens, resident aliens and certain nonresident aliens to report specified foreign financial assets on Form 8938, if the aggregate value exceeds certain thresholds. Required reporting includes interests in any (1) financial account maintained by a foreign trust/entity; (2) stock or security issued by other than a U.S. person; (3) foreign entities; or (4) trust instrument or contract that has an issuer or counterpart that is not a U.S. person. Form 8938 must be filed with the individual's U.S. income tax return for the tax year during which the asset was acquired and (thereafter) owned.

Form 8938

Department of the Treasury
Internal Revenue Service

Statement of Specified Foreign Financial Assets

▶ Go to *www.irs.gov/Form8938* for instructions and the latest information.
▶ Attach to your tax return.

For calendar year 2020 or tax year beginning _____ , 2020, and ending _____ , 20 ____

OMB No. 1545-2195

2020

Attachment
Sequence No. 938

If you have attached continuation statements, check here ☐ Number of continuation statements _____

1	Name(s) shown on return	2	Taxpayer identification number (TIN)

3 Type of filer

a ☐ Specified individual   b ☐ Partnership   c ☐ Corporation   d ☐ Trust

4 If you checked box 3a, skip this line 4. If you checked box 3b or 3c, enter the name and TIN of the specified individual who closely holds the partnership or corporation. If you checked box 3d, enter the name and TIN of the specified person who is a current beneficiary of the trust. (See instructions for definitions and what to do if you have more than one specified individual or specified person to list.)

a Name _____   b TIN _____

Part I   Foreign Deposit and Custodial Accounts Summary

1	Number of deposit accounts (reported in Part V) . . . . ▶	
2	Maximum value of all deposit accounts	$
3	Number of custodial accounts (reported in Part V) . . . . ▶	
4	Maximum value of all custodial accounts	$
5	Were any foreign deposit or custodial accounts closed during the tax year?	☐ Yes ☐ No

Part II   Other Foreign Assets Summary

1	Number of foreign assets (reported in Part VI) . . . . ▶	
2	Maximum value of all assets (reported in Part VI)	$
3	Were any foreign assets acquired or sold during the tax year?	☐ Yes ☐ No

Part III   Summary of Tax Items Attributable to Specified Foreign Financial Assets (see instructions)

(a) Asset category	(b) Tax item	(c) Amount reported on form or schedule	Where reported	
			(d) Form and line	(e) Schedule and line
1 Foreign deposit and custodial accounts	a Interest	$		
	b Dividends	$		
	c Royalties	$		
	d Other income	$		
	e Gains (losses)	$		
	f Deductions	$		
	g Credits	$		
2 Other foreign assets	a Interest	$		
	b Dividends	$		
	c Royalties	$		
	d Other income	$		
	e Gains (losses)	$		
	f Deductions	$		
	g Credits	$		

Part IV   Excepted Specified Foreign Financial Assets (see instructions)

If you reported specified foreign financial assets on one or more of the following forms, enter the number of such forms filed. You do not need to include these assets on Form 8938 for the tax year.

1. Number of Forms 3520 _____   2. Number of Forms 3520-A _____   3. Number of Forms 5471 _____
4. Number of Forms 8621 _____   5. Number of Forms 8865 _____

Part V   Detailed Information for Each Foreign Deposit and Custodial Account Included in the Part I Summary (see instructions)

If you have more than one account to report in Part V, attach a continuation statement for each additional account. See instructions.

1	Type of account	☐ Deposit ☐ Custodial	2	Account number or other designation

3 Check all that apply   a ☐ Account opened during tax year   b ☐ Account closed during tax year
c ☐ Account jointly owned with spouse   d ☐ No tax item reported in Part III with respect to this asset

4 Maximum value of account during tax year . . . . $ _____

5 Did you use a foreign currency exchange rate to convert the value of the account into U.S. dollars? . . ☐ Yes ☐ No

6 If you answered "Yes" to line 5, complete all that apply.

(a) Foreign currency in which account is maintained	(b) Foreign currency exchange rate used to convert to U.S. dollars	(c) Source of exchange rate used if not from U.S. Treasury Department's Bureau of the Fiscal Service

For Paperwork Reduction Act Notice, see the separate instructions.   Cat. No. 37753A   Form **8938** (2020)

250

Part V **Detailed Information for Each Foreign Deposit and Custodial Account Included in the Part I Summary** (see instructions) *(continued)*

7a Name of financial institution in which account is maintained	**b** Global Intermediary Identification Number (GIIN) (Optional)

8 Mailing address of financial institution in which account is maintained. Number, street, and room or suite no.

9 City or town, state or province, and country (including postal code)

Part VI **Detailed Information for Each "Other Foreign Asset" Included in the Part II Summary** (see instructions)

If you have more than one asset to report in Part VI, attach a continuation statement for each additional asset. See instructions.

1 Description of asset	**2** Identifying number or other designation

3 Complete all that apply. See instructions for reporting of multiple acquisition or disposition dates.
a Date asset acquired during tax year, if applicable . . . . _____
b Date asset disposed of during tax year, if applicable . . . . _____
c ☐ Check if asset jointly owned with spouse   **d** ☐ Check if no tax item reported in Part III with respect to this asset

4 Maximum value of asset during tax year (check box that applies)
a ☐ $0–$50,000   **b** ☐ $50,001–$100,000   **c** ☐ $100,001–$150,000   **d** ☐ $150,001–$200,000
e If more than $200,000, list value . . . . $ _____

5 Did you use a foreign currency exchange rate to convert the value of the asset into U.S. dollars? . . . ☐ Yes   ☐ No

6 If you answered "Yes" to line 5, complete all that apply.

(a) Foreign currency in which asset is denominated	**(b)** Foreign currency exchange rate used to convert to U.S. dollars	**(c)** Source of exchange rate used if not from U.S. Treasury Department's Bureau of the Fiscal Service

7 If asset reported on line 1 is stock of a foreign entity or an interest in a foreign entity, enter the following information for the asset.
a Name of foreign entity _____   **b** GIIN (Optional) _____
c Type of foreign entity   **(1)** ☐ Partnership   **(2)** ☐ Corporation   **(3)** ☐ Trust   **(4)** ☐ Estate
d Mailing address of foreign entity. Number, street, and room or suite no.

e City or town, state or province, and country (including postal code)

8 If asset reported on line 1 is not stock of a foreign entity or an interest in a foreign entity, enter the following information for the asset.
Note: If this asset has more than one issuer or counterparty, attach a continuation statement with the same information for each additional issuer or counterparty. See instructions.
a Name of issuer or counterparty _____
Check if information is for   ☐ Issuer   ☐ Counterparty

b Type of issuer or counterparty
(1) ☐ Individual   **(2)** ☐ Partnership   **(3)** ☐ Corporation   **(4)** ☐ Trust   **(5)** ☐ Estate

c Check if issuer or counterparty is a   ☐ U.S. person   ☐ Foreign person
d Mailing address of issuer or counterparty. Number, street, and room or suite no.

e City or town, state or province, and country (including postal code)

Form **8938** (2020)

251

(Continuation Statement)

Name(s) shown on return	TIN

Part V Detailed Information for Each Foreign Deposit and Custodial Account Included in the Part I Summary (see instructions)

1 Type of account   ☐ Deposit   ☐ Custodial   **2** Account number or other designation

3 Check all that apply   **a** ☐ Account opened during tax year   **b** ☐ Account closed during tax year
                               c ☐ Account jointly owned with spouse   **d** ☐ No tax item reported in Part III with respect to this asset

4 Maximum value of account during tax year . . . . $

5 Did you use a foreign currency exchange rate to convert the value of the account into U.S. dollars? . . ☐ Yes ☐ No

6 If you answered "Yes" to line 5, complete all that apply.

(a) Foreign currency in which account is maintained	**(b)** Foreign currency exchange rate used to convert to U.S. dollars	**(c)** Source of exchange rate used if not from U.S. Treasury Department's Bureau of the Fiscal Service

7a Name of financial institution in which account is maintained   **b** GIIN (Optional)

8 Mailing address of financial institution in which account is maintained. Number, street, and room or suite no.

9 City or town, state or province, and country (including postal code)

Part VI Detailed Information for Each "Other Foreign Asset" Included in the Part II Summary (see instructions)

1 Description of asset   **2** Identifying number or other designation

3 Complete all that apply. See instructions for reporting of multiple acquisition or disposition dates.
a Date asset acquired during tax year, if applicable . . . . _____
b Date asset disposed of during tax year, if applicable . . . . _____
c ☐ Check if asset jointly owned with spouse   **d** ☐ Check if no tax item reported in Part III with respect to this asset

4 Maximum value of asset during tax year (check box that applies)
a ☐ $0–$50,000   **b** ☐ $50,001–$100,000   **c** ☐ $100,001–$150,000   **d** ☐ $150,001–$200,000
e If more than $200,000, list value . . . . $

5 Did you use a foreign currency exchange rate to convert the value of the asset into U.S. dollars? . . . ☐ Yes ☐ No

6 If you answered "Yes" to line 5, complete all that apply.

(a) Foreign currency in which asset is denominated	**(b)** Foreign currency exchange rate used to convert to U.S. dollars	**(c)** Source of exchange rate used if not from U.S. Treasury Department's Bureau of the Fiscal Service

7 If asset reported on line 1 is stock of a foreign entity or an interest in a foreign entity, enter the following information for the asset.
a Name of foreign entity _____   **b** GIIN (Optional)
c Type of foreign entity   **(1)** ☐ Partnership   **(2)** ☐ Corporation   **(3)** ☐ Trust   **(4)** ☐ Estate
d Mailing address of foreign entity. Number, street, and room or suite no.

e City or town, state or province, and country (including postal code)

8 If asset reported on line 1 is not stock of a foreign entity or an interest in a foreign entity, enter the following information for the asset.
a Name of issuer or counterparty _____
      Check if information is for   ☐ Issuer   ☐ Counterparty

b Type of issuer or counterparty
      (1) ☐ Individual   **(2)** ☐ Partnership   **(3)** ☐ Corporation   **(4)** ☐ Trust   **(5)** ☐ Estate

c Check if issuer or counterparty is a   ☐ U.S. person   ☐ Foreign person
d Mailing address of issuer or counterparty. Number, street, and room or suite no.

e City or town, state or province, and country (including postal code)

Form **8938** (2020)

Form 3520, Annual Return to Report Transactions with Foreign Trusts and Receipt of Certain Foreign Gifts. U.S. citizens and residents must report all gifts received from (i) NRNCs or any foreign estate, if exceeding $100,000 in the aggregate and (ii) foreign companies, if exceeding $16,649 (adjusted annually for inflation) in the aggregate. Gifts from related parties must be aggregated. For example, if a U.S. resident or citizen receives $60,000 from one NRNC and $50,000 from a different NRNC during the same year, and the two NRNCs are related, the U.S. person must report the gifts (as they aggregate to more than $100,000). The disclosure is made in Part IV of Form 3520. Gifts from foreign trusts are treated as trust distributions (reported in Part III of Form 3520). Form 3520 is filed separately from the U.S. income tax return. Form 3520 is due on the fifteenth day of the 4th month following the end of the U.S. person's tax year. If a U.S. person is granted an extension of time to file an income tax return, the due date for filing Form 3520 is the fifteenth day of the 10th month following the end of the U.S. person's tax year. [294]

---

[294] *See* IRC §6039F; IRS Notice 97-43.

Form **3520**	**Annual Return To Report Transactions With Foreign Trusts and Receipt of Certain Foreign Gifts**	OMB No. 1545-0159
Department of the Treasury Internal Revenue Service	▶ Go to *www.irs.gov/Form3520* for instructions and the latest information.	20**20**

Note: All information must be in English. Show all amounts in U.S. dollars. File a **separate** Form 3520 for **each** foreign trust.

For calendar year 2020, or tax year beginning _____, 2020, ending _____, 20____

A	Check appropriate boxes: ☐ Initial return ☐ Final return ☐ Amended return	
B	Check box that applies to person filing return: ☐ Individual ☐ Partnership ☐ Corporation ☐ Trust ☐ Executor	
C	Check if any excepted specified foreign financial assets are reported on this form. See instructions . . . . ☐	

Check all applicable boxes. See applicable instructions.

☐ You are **(a)** a U.S. transferor who, directly or indirectly, transferred money or other property during the current tax year to a foreign trust; **(b)** a U.S. person who (1) during the current tax year, transferred property (including cash) to a related foreign trust (or a person related to the trust) in exchange for an obligation, or (2) holds a qualified obligation from the trust that is currently outstanding; or **(c)** the executor of the estate of a U.S. decedent and (1) the decedent made a transfer to a foreign trust by reason of death, (2) the decedent was treated as the owner of any portion of a foreign trust immediately prior to death, or (3) the decedent's estate included any portion of the assets of a foreign trust. **Complete all applicable identifying information requested below and Part I of the form.**

☐ You are a U.S. owner of all or any portion of a foreign trust at any time during the tax year. **Complete all applicable identifying information requested below and Part II of the form.**

☐ You are **(a)** a U.S. person (including a U.S. owner) or an executor of the estate of a U.S. person who, during the current tax year, received, directly or indirectly, a distribution from a foreign trust; **(b)** a U.S. person who is a U.S. owner or beneficiary of a foreign trust and in the current tax year, you or a U.S. person related to you received (1) a loan of cash or marketable securities, directly or indirectly, from such foreign trust, or (2) the uncompensated use of trust property; or **(c)** a U.S. person who is a U.S. owner or beneficiary of a foreign trust and in the current tax year such foreign trust holds an outstanding qualified obligation of yours or a U.S. person related to you. **Complete all applicable identifying information requested below and Part III of the form.**

☐ You are a U.S. person who, during the current tax year, received certain gifts or bequests from a foreign person. **Complete all applicable identifying information requested below and Part IV of the form.**

1a	Name of U.S. person(s) with respect to whom this Form 3520 is being filed (see instructions)	**b**	Taxpayer identification number (TIN)
c	Number, street, and room or suite no. If a P.O. box, see instructions.	**d**	Spouse's TIN
e City or town	**f** State or province	**g** ZIP or foreign postal code	**h** Country

i	Check the box if you are married and filing a joint 2020 income tax return, and you are filing a joint Form 3520 with your spouse . . . ☐
j	If an automatic 2-month extension applies for the U.S. person's tax return, check this box and attach statement. See instructions . . ▶ ☐
k	If an extension was requested for the tax return, check this box ☐ and enter the form number of the tax return to be filed. ▶

2a	Name of foreign trust (if applicable)	**b**	Employer identification number (EIN), if any
c	Number, street, and room or suite no. If a P.O. box, see instructions.	**d**	Date foreign trust was created
e City or town	**f** State or province	**g** ZIP or foreign postal code	**h** Country

3 Did the foreign trust appoint a U.S. agent (defined in the instructions) who can provide the IRS with all relevant trust information? ☐ **Yes** ☐ **No**
If "Yes," complete lines 3a through 3g. If "No," and you are required to complete Part I, complete lines 15 through 18.

3a	Name of U.S. agent	**b**	TIN, if any
c	Number, street, and room or suite no. If a P.O. box, see instructions.		
d City or town	**e** State or province	**f** ZIP or postal code	**g** Country

4a Name of U.S. decedent (see instructions)	**b** Address		**c** TIN of decedent
d Date of death			**e** EIN of estate

f Check applicable box.
☐ U.S. decedent made transfer to a foreign trust by reason of death.
☐ U.S. decedent treated as owner of foreign trust immediately prior to death.
☐ Assets of foreign trust were included in estate of U.S. decedent.

Part I Transfers by U.S. Persons to a Foreign Trust During the Current Tax Year (see instructions)

5a Name of trust creator	b Address	c TIN, if any

6a Country code of country where trust was created	b Country code of country whose law governs the trust	c Date trust was created

7a Will any person (other than the foreign trust) be treated as the owner of the transferred assets after the transfer? . . . . ☐ Yes ☐ No

b	(i) Name of foreign trust owner	(ii) Address	(iii) Country of residence	(iv) TIN, if any	(v) Relevant Code section

8 Was the transfer a completed gift or bequest? If "Yes," see instructions . . . . ☐ Yes ☐ No
9a Now or at any time in the future, can any part of the income or corpus of the trust benefit any U.S. beneficiary? . . . . ☐ Yes ☐ No
b If "No," could the trust be revised or amended to benefit a U.S. beneficiary? . . . . ☐ Yes ☐ No
10 Reserved for future use . . . . ☐ Yes ☐ No

Schedule A—Obligations of a Related Trust (see instructions)

11a During the current tax year, did you transfer property (including cash) to a related foreign trust in exchange for an obligation of the trust or an obligation of a person related to the trust? See instructions . . . . ☐ Yes ☐ No
If "Yes," complete the rest of Schedule A, as applicable. If "No," go to Schedule B.

b Were any of the obligations you received (with respect to a transfer described in line 11a above) qualified obligations? . . ☐ Yes ☐ No
If "Yes," complete the rest of Schedule A and attach a copy of each loan document entered into with respect to each qualified obligation reported on line 11b. If these documents have been attached to a Form 3520 filed within the previous 3 years, attach only relevant updates.
If "No," go to Schedule B.

(i) Date of transfer giving rise to obligation	(ii) Maximum term	(iii) Yield to maturity	(iv) FMV of obligation

12 With respect to each qualified obligation you reported on line 11b, do you agree to extend the period of assessment of any income or transfer tax attributable to the transfer, and any consequential income tax changes for each year that the obligation is outstanding, to a date 3 years after the maturity date of the obligation? . . . . ☐ Yes ☐ No

Note: You have the right to refuse to extend the period of limitations or limit this extension to a mutually agreed-upon issue(s) or mutually agreed-upon period of time. Generally, if you refuse to extend the period of limitations with respect to each qualified obligation you reported on line 11b, then such obligation is not a qualified obligation and you cannot check "Yes" to the question on line 11b.

Schedule B—Gratuitous Transfers (see instructions)

13 During the current tax year, did you make any transfers (directly or indirectly) to the trust and receive less than FMV, or no consideration at all, for the property transferred? . . . . ☐ Yes ☐ No
If "Yes," complete columns (a) through (i) below and the rest of Schedule B, as applicable. When completing columns (a) through (i) with respect to each nonqualified obligation, enter "-0-" in column (h).
If "No," go to Schedule C.

(a) Date of transfer	(b) Description of property transferred	(c) FMV of property transferred	(d) U.S. adjusted basis of property transferred	(e) Gain recognized at time of transfer, if any	(f) Excess, if any, of column (c) over the sum of columns (d) and (e)	(g) Description of property received, if any	(h) FMV of property received	(i) Excess of column (c) over column (h)
Totals ▶					$			$

14 You are required to attach a copy of each sale or loan document entered into in connection with a transfer reported on line 13. If these documents have been attached to a Form 3520 filed within the previous 3 years, attach only relevant updates.

Are you attaching a copy of any of the following?	Yes	No	Attached Previously	Year Attached
a Sale document	☐	☐	☐	_____
b Loan document	☐	☐	☐	_____
c Subsequent variances to original sale or loan documents	☐	☐	☐	

Form **3520** (2020)

255

| **Part I** | **Schedule B—Gratuitous Transfers** *(continued)* |

Note: Complete lines 15 through 18 only if you answered "No" to line 3, acknowledging that the foreign trust did not appoint a U.S. agent to provide the IRS with all relevant trust information.

15

(a) Name of beneficiary	(b) Address of beneficiary	(c) U.S. beneficiary?		(d) TIN, if any
		Yes	No	

16

(a) Name of trustee	(b) Address of trustee	(c) TIN, if any

17

(a) Name of other person with trust powers	(b) Address of other person with trust powers	(c) Description of powers	(d) TIN, if any

18 If you checked "No" on line 3, you are required to attach a copy of all trust documents as indicated below. If these documents have been attached to a Form 3520-A or Form 3520 filed within the previous 3 years, attach only relevant updates.

Are you attaching a copy of any of the following?	Yes	No	Attached Previously	Year Attached
a Summary of all written and oral agreements and understandings relating to the trust	☐	☐	☐	_____
b Trust instrument	☐	☐	☐	_____
c Memoranda or letters of wishes	☐	☐	☐	_____
d Subsequent variances to original trust documents	☐	☐	☐	_____
e Trust financial statements	☐	☐	☐	_____
f Organizational chart and other trust documents	☐	☐	☐	_____

Schedule C—Qualified Obligations Outstanding in the Current Tax Year (see instructions)

19 Did you, at any time during your tax year, hold an outstanding obligation of a related foreign trust (or a person related to the trust) that you reported as a qualified obligation in the current tax year? . . . . ☐ Yes ☐ No
If "Yes," complete columns (a) through (f) below for each obligation.

(a) Date of original obligation	(b) Tax year qualified obligation first reported	(c) Amount of principal payments made during your tax year	(d) Amount of interest payments made during your tax year	(e) Balance of the outstanding obligation at the end of the tax year	(f) Does the obligation still meet the criteria for a qualified obligation?	
					Yes	No

Form **3520** (2020)

256

Part II	U.S. Owner of a Foreign Trust (see instructions)

20	(a) Name of foreign trust owner	(b) Address	(c) Country of tax residence	(d) TIN, if any	(e) Relevant Code section

21a Country code of country where foreign trust was created	b Country code of country whose law governs the trust	c Date foreign trust was created

22 Did the foreign trust file Form 3520-A for the current year? . . . . ☐ Yes ☐ No

If "Yes," attach the Foreign Grantor Trust Owner Statement you received from the foreign trust.

If "No," to the best of your ability, complete and attach a substitute Form 3520-A for the foreign trust.

See instructions for information on penalties for failing to complete and attach a substitute Form 3520-A.

23 Enter the gross value of the portion of the foreign trust that you are treated as owning at the end of your tax year . ▶ $

Part III	Distributions to a U.S. Person From a Foreign Trust During the Current Tax Year (see instructions)

Note: If you received an amount from a portion of a foreign trust of which you are treated as the owner, only complete lines 24 and 27.

24 Enter cash amounts or FMV of property received, directly or indirectly, during your current tax year, from the foreign trust (exclude loans and uncompensated use of trust property included on line 25).

(a) Date of distribution	(b) Description of property received	(c) FMV of property received (determined on date of distribution)	(d) Description of property transferred, if any	(e) FMV of property transferred	(f) Excess of column (c) over column (e)

Total . . . . ▶ $

25 During your current tax year, did you (or a person related to you) receive a loan or uncompensated use of trust property from a related foreign trust (including an extension of credit upon the purchase of property from the trust)? . . . . ☐ Yes ☐ No

If "Yes," complete columns (a) through (g) below for each such loan or use of trust property.

Note: See instructions for additional information, including how to complete columns (a) through (g) for use of trust property.

(a) FMV of loan proceeds or property	(b) Date of original transaction	(c) Maximum term of repayment of obligation	(d) Interest rate of obligation	(e) Is the obligation a qualified obligation? Yes	No	(f) FMV of qualified obligation	(g) Amount treated as distribution from the trust (subtract column (f) from column (a))

Total . . . . ▶ $

26 With respect to each obligation you reported as a qualified obligation on line 25, do you agree to extend the period of assessment of any income or transfer tax attributable to the transaction, and any consequential income tax changes for each year that the obligation is outstanding, to a date 3 years after the maturity date of the obligation? . . . . ☐ Yes ☐ No

Note: You have the right to refuse to extend the period of limitations or limit this extension to a mutually agreed-upon issue(s) or mutually agreed-upon period of time. Generally, if you refuse to extend the period of limitations with respect to an obligation that you reported as a qualified obligation on line 25, then such obligation is not a qualified obligation and you cannot check "Yes" in column (e) of line 25.

27 Total distributions received during your current tax year. Add line 24, column (f), and line 25, column (g) . . . . ▶ $

28 Did the trust, at any time during the current tax year, hold an outstanding obligation of yours (or a person related to you) that you reported as a qualified obligation? . . . . ☐ Yes ☐ No

If "Yes," complete columns (a) through (f) below for each obligation.

(a) Date of original loan transaction	(b) Tax year qualified obligation first reported	(c) Amount of principal payments made during your tax year	(d) Amount of interest payments made during your tax year	(e) Balance of the outstanding obligation at the end of the tax year	(f) Does the loan still meet the criteria of a qualified obligation? Yes	No

Form **3520** (2020)

257

| Part III | Distributions to a U.S. Person From a Foreign Trust During the Current Tax Year *(continued)* |

29	Did you receive a Foreign Grantor Trust Beneficiary Statement from the foreign trust with respect to a distribution? ☐ Yes ☐ No ☐ N/A
	If "Yes," attach the statement and do not complete the remainder of Part III with respect to that distribution.
	If "No," complete Schedule A with respect to that distribution. Also, complete Schedule C if you enter an amount greater than zero on line 37.
30	Did you receive a Foreign Nongrantor Trust Beneficiary Statement from the foreign trust with respect to a distribution? ☐ Yes ☐ No ☐ N/A
	If "Yes," attach the statement and complete either Schedule A or Schedule B below. See instructions. Also, complete Schedule C if you enter an amount greater than zero on line 37 or line 41a.
	If "No," complete Schedule A with respect to that distribution. Also, complete Schedule C if you enter an amount greater than zero on line 37.

Schedule A—Default Calculation of Trust Distributions (see instructions)

31	Enter amount from line 27		31	
32	Number of years the trust has been a foreign trust (see instructions) ▶	32		
33	Enter total distributions received from the foreign trust during the 3 preceding tax years (or during the number of years the trust has been a foreign trust, if fewer than 3 years)		33	
34	Multiply line 33 by 1.25		34	
35	Average distribution. Divide line 34 by 3.0 (or the number of years the trust has been a foreign trust, if fewer than 3 years) and enter the result		35	
36	Amount treated as ordinary income earned in the current year. Enter the smaller of line 31 or line 35		36	
37	Amount treated as accumulation distribution. Subtract line 36 from line 31. If zero, do not complete the rest of Part III		37	
38	Applicable number of years of trust. Divide line 32 by 2.0 and enter the result here ▶	38		

Schedule B—Actual Calculation of Trust Distributions (see instructions)

39	Enter amount from line 27		39	
40a	Amount treated as ordinary income in the current tax year		40a	
b	Qualified dividends ▶	40b		
41a	Amount treated as accumulation distribution. If zero, do not complete Schedule C, Part III		41a	
b	Amount of line 41a that is tax exempt ▶	41b		
42a	Amount treated as net short-term capital gain in the current tax year		42a	
b	Amount treated as net long-term capital gain in the current tax year		42b	
c	28% rate gain ▶	42c		
d	Unrecaptured section 1250 gain ▶	42d		
43	Amount treated as distribution from trust corpus		43	
44	Enter any other distributed amount received from the foreign trust not included on lines 40a, 41a, 42a, 42b, and 43. (Attach explanation.)		44	
45	Amount of foreign trust's aggregate undistributed net income		45	
46	Amount of foreign trust's weighted undistributed net income		46	
47	Applicable number of years of trust. Divide line 46 by line 45 and enter the result here ▶	47		

Schedule C—Calculation of Interest Charge (see instructions)

48	Enter accumulation distribution from line 37 or line 41a, as applicable	48	
49	Enter tax on total accumulation distribution from line 28 of Form 4970. (Attach Form 4970—see instructions.)	49	
50	Enter applicable number of years of foreign trust from line 38 or line 47, as applicable (round to nearest half year) ▶	50	
51	Combined interest rate imposed on the total accumulation distribution (see instructions)	51	
52	Interest charge. Multiply the amount on line 49 by the combined interest rate on line 51	52	
53	Tax attributable to accumulation distributions. Add lines 49 and 52. Enter here and as "additional tax" on your income tax return	53	

Form **3520** (2020)

Part IV   U.S. Recipients of Gifts or Bequests Received During the Current Tax Year From Foreign Persons (see instructions)

54   During your current tax year, did you receive more than $100,000 that you treated as gifts or bequests from a nonresident alien (including a distribution received from a domestic trust treated as owned by a foreign person) or a foreign estate? See instructions for special rules regarding related donors . . . . ☐ **Yes**   ☐ **No**

If "Yes," complete columns (a) through (c) with respect to each such gift or bequest in excess of $5,000. If more space is needed, attach a statement.

(a) Date of gift or bequest	(b) Description of property received	(c) FMV of property received

Total . . . . ► $

55   During your current tax year, did you receive more than $16,649 that you treated as gifts from a foreign corporation or a foreign partnership (including a distribution received from a domestic trust treated as owned by a foreign person)? See instructions regarding related donors . . . . ☐ **Yes**   ☐ **No**

If "Yes," complete columns (a) through (g) with respect to each such gift. If more space is needed, attach a statement.

(a) Date of gift	(b) Name of foreign donor	(c) Address of foreign donor	(d) TIN, if any

(e) Check the box that applies to the foreign donor		(f) Description of property received	(g) FMV of property received
Corporation	Partnership		

56   Do you have any reason to believe that the foreign donor, in making any gift or bequest described in lines 54 and 55, was acting as a nominee or intermediary for any other person? If "Yes," see instructions . . . . ☐ **Yes**   ☐ **No**

Sign Here

Under penalties of perjury, I declare that I have examined this return, including any accompanying reports, schedules, or statements, and to the best of my knowledge and belief, it is true, correct, and complete.

▶ _____   ▶ _____   ▶ _____
Signature   Title   Date

Paid Preparer Use Only

Print/Type preparer's name	Preparer's signature	Date	Check ☐ if self-employed	PTIN
Firm's name ▶			Firm's EIN ▶	
Firm's address ▶			Phone no.	

Form **3520** (2020)

NRNCs

Form 1040NR, U.S. Non-Resident Alien Income Tax Return.   An NRNC

individual or foreign trust (not disregarded for tax purposes), must file Form 1040NR, to

disclose and pay tax on U.S. source income.[295]

---

[295] *See* Publication 519.

Form 1040-NR Department of the Treasury—Internal Revenue Service (99)
U.S. Nonresident Alien Income Tax Return **2020** OMB No. 1545-0074 IRS Use Only—Do not write or staple in this space

Filing Status	
Check only one box.	☐ Single ☐ Married filing separately (MFS) (formerly Married) ☐ Qualifying widow(er) (QW)
	If you checked the QW box, enter the child's name if the qualifying person is a child but not your dependent ▶

Your first name and middle initial	Last name	Your identifying number (see instructions)
Home address (number and street or rural route). If you have a P.O. box, see instructions.	Apt. no.	Check if: ☐ Individual ☐ Estate or Trust
City, town, or post office. If you have a foreign address, also complete spaces below.	State	ZIP code
Foreign country name	Foreign province/state/county	Foreign postal code

At any time during 2020, did you receive, sell, send, exchange, or otherwise acquire any financial interest in any virtual currency? ☐ Yes ☐ No

Dependents (see instructions):		(1) First name Last name	(2) Dependent's identifying number	(3) Dependent's relationship to you	(4) ✔ if qualifies for (see instr.):	
					Child tax credit	Credit for other dependents
If more than four dependents, see instructions and check here ▶ ☐					☐	☐
					☐	☐
					☐	☐
					☐	☐

Income Effectively Connected With U.S. Trade or Business					
1a	Wages, salaries, tips, etc. Attach Form(s) W-2			1a	
b	Scholarship and fellowship grants. Attach Form(s) 1042-S or required statement. See instructions			1b	
c	Total income exempt by a treaty from Schedule OI (Form 1040-NR), Item L, line 1(e)		1c		
2a	Tax-exempt interest	2a	b Taxable interest	2b	
3a	Qualified dividends	3a	b Ordinary dividends	3b	
4a	IRA distributions	4a	b Taxable amount	4b	
5a	Pensions and annuities	5a	b Taxable amount	5b	
6	Reserved for future use			6	
7	Capital gain or (loss). Attach Schedule D (Form 1040) if required. If not required, check here . ▶ ☐			7	
8	Other income from Schedule 1 (Form 1040), line 9			8	
9	Add lines 1a, 1b, 2b, 3b, 4b, 5b, 7, and 8. This is your **total effectively connected income** . ▶			9	
10	Adjustments to income:				
a	From Schedule 1 (Form 1040), line 22		10a		
b	Charitable contributions for certain residents of India. See instructions		10b		
c	Scholarship and fellowship grants excluded		10c		
d	Add lines 10a through 10c. These are your **total adjustments to income** . ▶			10d	
11	Subtract line 10d from line 9. This is your **adjusted gross income** . ▶			11	
12	**Itemized deductions** (from Schedule A (Form 1040-NR)) or, for certain residents of India, standard deduction. See instructions			12	
13a	Qualified business income deduction. Attach Form 8995 or Form 8995-A		13a		
b	Exemptions for estates and trusts only. See instructions		13b		
c	Add lines 13a and 13b			13c	
14	Add lines 12 and 13c			14	
15	**Taxable income.** Subtract line 14 from line 11. If zero or less, enter -0-			15	

For Disclosure, Privacy Act, and Paperwork Reduction Act Notice, see separate instructions. Cat. No. 11364D Form **1040-NR** (2020)

16	Tax (see instructions). Check if any from Form(s): 1 ☐ 8814 2 ☐ 4972 3 ☐ _____		16	
17	Amount from Schedule 2 (Form 1040), line 3		17	
18	Add lines 16 and 17		18	
19	Child tax credit or credit for other dependents		19	
20	Amount from Schedule 3 (Form 1040), line 7		20	
21	Add lines 19 and 20		21	
22	Subtract line 21 from line 18. If zero or less, enter -0-		22	
23a	Tax on income not effectively connected with a U.S. trade or business from Schedule NEC (Form 1040-NR), line 15	23a		
b	Other taxes, including self-employment tax, from Schedule 2 (Form 1040), line 10	23b		
c	Transportation tax (see instructions)	23c		
d	Add lines 23a through 23c		23d	
24	Add lines 22 and 23d. This is your **total tax** . . . . ▶		24	
25	Federal income tax withheld from:			
a	Form(s) W-2	25a		
b	Form(s) 1099	25b		
c	Other forms (see instructions)	25c		
d	Add lines 25a through 25c		25d	
e	Form(s) 8805		25e	
f	Form(s) 8288-A		25f	
g	Form(s) 1042-S		25g	
26	2020 estimated tax payments and amount applied from 2019 return		26	
27	Reserved for future use	27		
28	Additional child tax credit. Attach Schedule 8812 (Form 1040) . . .	28		
29	Credit for amount paid with Form 1040-C . . . . ▶	29		
30	Reserved for future use	30		
31	Amount from Schedule 3 (Form 1040), line 13	31		
32	Add lines 28 through 31. These are your **total other payments and refundable credits** . . . ▶		32	
33	Add lines 25d, 25e, 25f, 25g, 26, and 32. These are your **total payments** . . . . ▶		33	

Refund	34	If line 33 is more than line 24, subtract line 24 from line 33. This is the amount you **overpaid** . .	34	
	35a	Amount of line 34 you want **refunded to you.** If Form 8888 is attached, check here . . ▶ ☐	35a	
Direct deposit? See instructions.	▶ b	Routing number [ ][ ][ ][ ][ ][ ][ ][ ][ ] ▶ c Type: ☐ Checking ☐ Savings		
	▶ d	Account number [ ][ ][ ][ ][ ][ ][ ][ ][ ][ ][ ][ ][ ][ ][ ][ ][ ]		
	▶ e	If you want your refund check mailed to an address outside the United States not shown on page 1, enter it here. _____		
	36	Amount of line 34 you want applied to your **2021 estimated tax** . . . . ▶	36	
Amount You Owe	37	**Amount you owe.** Subtract line 33 from line 24. For details on how to pay, see instructions . . ▶	37	
	38	Estimated tax penalty (see instructions) . . . . ▶	38	

Third Party Designee (Other than paid preparer)	Do you want to allow another person (other than your paid preparer) to discuss this return with the IRS? See instructions . . . . ▶ ☐ **Yes.** Complete below. ☐ **No**
	Designee's name ▶ _____ Phone no. ▶ _____ Personal identification number (PIN) ▶ [ ][ ][ ][ ][ ]

Sign Here	Under penalties of perjury, I declare that I have examined this return and accompanying schedules and statements, and to the best of my knowledge and belief, they are true, correct, and complete. Declaration of preparer (other than taxpayer) is based on all information of which preparer has any knowledge.
	Your signature ▶ _____ Date _____ Your occupation _____ If the IRS sent you an Identity Protection PIN, enter it here (see inst.) ▶ [ ][ ][ ][ ][ ][ ]
	Phone no. _____ Email address _____

Paid Preparer Use Only	Preparer's name _____ Preparer's signature _____ Date _____ PTIN _____ Check if: ☐ Self-employed
	Firm's name ▶ _____ Phone no. _____
	Firm's address ▶ _____ Firm's EIN ▶ _____

Go to *www.irs.gov/Form1040NR* for instructions and the latest information.   Form **1040-NR** (2020)

Itemized Deductions

► Go to *www.irs.gov/Form1040NR* for instructions and the latest information.
► Attach to Form 1040-NR.
Caution: If you are claiming a net qualified disaster loss on Form 4684, see instructions for line 7.

OMB No. 1545-0074

2020

Attachment
Sequence No. **7A**

Name shown on Form 1040-NR	Your identifying number

Taxes You Paid	1a	State and local income taxes	1a	
	b	Enter the smaller of line 1a or $10,000 ($5,000 if you checked Married filing separately under *Filing Status* on page 1 of Form 1040-NR)	1b	
Gifts to U.S. Charities	2	Gifts by cash or check. If you made any gift of $250 or more, see instructions	2	
Caution: If you made a gift and received a benefit in return, see instructions.	3	Other than by cash or check. If you made any gift of $250 or more, see instructions. Individuals **must** attach Form 8283 if line 3 is over $500 .	3	
	4	Carryover from prior year	4	
	5	Add lines 2 through 4	5	
Casualty and Theft Losses	6	Casualty and theft loss(es) from a federally declared disaster (other than net qualified disaster losses). Attach Form 4684 and enter the amount from line 18 of that form. See instructions	6	
Other Itemized Deductions	7	Other—from list in instructions. List type and amount ►	7	
Total Itemized Deductions	8	Add the amounts in the far right column for lines 1b through 7. Also, enter this amount on Form 1040-NR, line 12	8	

For Paperwork Reduction Act Notice, see the Instructions for Form 1040-NR.   Cat. No. 72749E   Schedule A (Form 1040-NR) 2020

Foreign Trusts

Form 3520, Annual Return to Report Transactions with Foreign Trusts and Receipt of Certain Foreign Gifts. Any U.S. person who creates a foreign trust or who transfers property to a foreign trust (generally excluding independent service providers), must report the trust creation or funding on IRS Form 3520. The "owners" must disclose the taxpayer identification number of the foreign trust, the names of other persons considered "owners" of the trust, the Code section which treats the trust as owned by U.S. person(s), the country in which the trust was created and the date of creation. Form 3520 is due with the reporting U.S. person's income tax return (for the year of trust creation or funding). Failure to file may subject the transferor to a penalty of 35% of the amount transferred to the trust. Form 3520 is required to be filed by any U.S. person who:

- Creates or transfers money or property to a foreign trust.

- Receives (directly or indirectly) any distribution from a foreign trust.

- Receives certain gifts or bequests from foreign entities.

- Is treated as the U.S. owner of a foreign trust. "Owners" include any U.S. person who creates a foreign trust or is treated as the owner of any assets held by the foreign trust under IRC §§671-679.

All gratuitous transfers to a foreign trust are reportable by the owner of the trust under I.R.C. §684 (on Form 3520A). If a U.S. "owner" of a foreign trust transfers property to the foreign trust at his death, or whose estate includes (for estate tax purposes) any portion of a foreign trust, the estate of the U.S. person must report the bequest on Form 3520. Form 3520 is due with decedent's last income tax return. Failure to file may subject the executor to a penalty equal to 35% of the amount transferred.

A U.S. trust that becomes a foreign trust is required to report the change of status on Form 3520, with the trust's income tax return covering the year of the transfer. Failure to file may subject the trust to a penalty equal to 35% of trust assets.

Cost payments, such as trustee fees, are not reportable. A beneficiary who receives a payment for services in excess of the market value of such services is, however, deemed to receive a distribution. Thus, if trustee fees paid to a beneficiary/trustee are excessive, the distribution becomes reportable. The reporting obligation is waived if the payee service provider reports the amount received as taxable compensation for services rendered.

Indirect and constructive distributions are also reportable on Form 3520A. For example, if a beneficiary uses a credit card and the trust guarantees or pays the invoice, the amount charged on the card is considered a distribution.

Form 3520-A, Annual Information Return of Foreign Trust with a U.S. Owner. Form 3520-A provides information about the foreign trust, its U.S. beneficiaries, and any U.S. person treated as an "owner" of the foreign trust. Each U.S. owner is responsible for ensuring that the foreign trust files Form 3520-A and furnishes required annual statements to U.S. owners and beneficiaries. The foreign trust must file Form 3520-A on or before each March 15 following the reporting year.

Form 3520-A Foreign Grantor Trust Beneficiary Statement or a Foreign Non-Grantor Trust Beneficiary Statement.[296] Any U.S. person (including a grantor) who receives, directly or indirectly, any distribution from a foreign trust must report the name

---

[296] See IRS Notice 97-34, describing the required information in detail.

of the trust, the amount of distributions received from the trust, and such other information as the IRS may require.[297]

If Form 3520-A is not filed, the U.S. owner may be liable for a penalty of 5% of the value of trust assets (deemed owned by each such owner).[298]

---

[297] *See* IRC §6048(c).
[298] *See* IRC §6677.

Form **3520-A**

Department of the Treasury
Internal Revenue Service

Annual Information Return of Foreign Trust With a U.S. Owner
(Under section 6048(b))
▶ Go to *www.irs.gov/Form3520A* for instructions and the latest information.

OMB No. 1545-0159

20**20**

Note: All information must be in English. Show all amounts in U.S. dollars.

For calendar year 2020, or tax year beginning _____ , 2020, ending _____ , 20 ____ .

Check appropriate boxes: ☐ Initial return ☐ Final return ☐ Amended return ☐ Extension filed ☐ Substitute Form 3520-A

Check if any excepted specified foreign financial assets are reported on this form. See instructions . . . . ☐

Part I   General Information (see instructions)

1a Name of foreign trust	**b** Employer identification number (EIN)
c Number, street, and room or suite no. If a P.O. box, see instructions.	**d** Date foreign trust was created

e City or town	**f** State or province	**g** ZIP or foreign postal code	**h** Country

2 Did the foreign trust appoint a U.S. agent (defined in the instructions) who can provide the IRS with all the relevant trust information? . . . . ☐ Yes ☐ No

If "Yes," skip lines 2a through 2e and go to line 3.

If "No," you are required to attach a copy of all trust documents as indicated below. If these documents have been attached to a Form 3520-A filed within the previous 3 years, attach only relevant updates.

Are you attaching a copy of any of the following?	Yes	No	Attached Previously	Year Attached
a Summary of all written and oral agreements and understandings relating to the trust . . .	☐	☐	☐	_____
b The trust instrument	☐	☐	☐	_____
c Memoranda or letters of wishes	☐	☐	☐	_____
d Subsequent variances to original trust documents	☐	☐	☐	_____
e Organizational chart and other trust documents	☐	☐	☐	_____

3a Name of U.S. agent	**b** Taxpayer identification number (TIN)

c Number, street, and room or suite no. If a P.O. box, see instructions.

d City or town	**e** State or province	**f** ZIP or postal code	**g** Country

4a Name of trustee	**b** TIN, if any

c Number, street, and room or suite no. If a P.O. box, see instructions.

d City or town	**e** State or province	**f** ZIP or postal code	**g** Country

5 Enter the number of **Foreign Grantor Trust Owner Statements** (pages 3 and 4) included with this Form 3520-A . ▶ _____

6 Enter the number of **Foreign Grantor Trust Beneficiary Statements** (page 5) included with this Form 3520-A . ▶ _____

Sign Here

Under penalties of perjury, I declare that I have examined this return, including any accompanying reports, schedules, or statements, and to the best of my knowledge and belief, it is true, correct, and complete.

▶ _____ Trustee's (or U.S. owner's) signature   ▶ Title _____   Date _____

Paid Preparer Use Only

Print/Type preparer's name	Preparer's signature	Date	Check ☐ if self-employed	PTIN
Firm's name ▶			Firm's EIN ▶	
Firm's address ▶			Phone no.	

For Paperwork Reduction Act Notice, see instructions.   Cat. No. 19595G   Form **3520-A** (2020)

Part II	**Foreign Trust Income Statement**

Enter totals from books and records of foreign trust. See instructions.

Income	1	Interest	**1**	
	2	Dividends	**2**	
	3	Gross rents and royalties	**3**	
	4	Income (loss) from partnerships and fiduciaries	**4**	
	5	Capital gains:		
	a	Net short-term capital gain (loss)	**5a**	
	b	Net long-term capital gain (loss)	**5b**	
	6	Ordinary gains (losses)	**6**	
	7	Other income (attach statement)	**7**	
	8	Total income (add lines 1 through 7)	**8**	
Expenses	9	Interest expense	**9**	
	10a	Foreign taxes (attach statement)	**10a**	
	b	State and local taxes	**10b**	
	11	Amortization and depreciation (depletion)	**11**	
	12	Trustee and advisor fees	**12**	
	13	Charitable contributions	**13**	
	14	Other expenses (attach statement)	**14**	
	15	Total expenses (add lines 9 through 14)	**15**	
	16	Net income (loss) (subtract line 15 from line 8)	**16**	
	17a	Enter the fair market value (FMV) of total distributions (directly or indirectly) from the trust to all persons, whether U.S. or foreign. Attach statement. See instructions ▶	**17a**	
	b	Distributions to U.S. owners:		

(i) Name of owner	(ii) TIN	(iii) Date of distribution	(iv) FMV on date of distribution

c Distributions to U.S. beneficiaries:

(i) Name of beneficiary	(ii) TIN	(iii) Date of distribution	(iv) FMV on date of distribution

Part III	**Foreign Trust Balance Sheet**	**Beginning of Tax Year**		**End of Tax Year**	
	Assets	(a)	(b)	(c)	(d)
1	Cash				
2	Accounts receivable				
3	Mortgages and notes receivable				
4	Inventories				
5	Government obligations				
6	Other marketable securities				
7	Other nonmarketable securities				
8a	Depreciable (depletable) assets				
b	Less: accumulated depreciation (depletion)				
9	Real property				
10	Other assets (attach statement)				
11	Total assets				
	Liabilities				
12	Accounts payable				
13	Contributions, gifts, grants, etc., payable				
14	Mortgages and notes payable				
15	Other liabilities (attach statement)				
16	Total liabilities				
	Net Worth				
17	Contributions to trust corpus				
18	Accumulated trust income				
19	Other (attach statement)				
20	Total net worth (add lines 17 through 19)				
21	Total liabilities and net worth (add lines 16 and 20)				

Form **3520-A** (2020)

2020 Foreign Grantor Trust Owner Statement (see instructions)

Important: *Trustee (or U.S. owner if a substitute Form 3520-A) must prepare a separate statement for each U.S. owner and include a copy of each statement with Form 3520-A. Trustee is also required to send to each U.S. owner a copy of the owner's statement. U.S. owner must attach a copy of its statement to Form 3520.*

1a Name of foreign trust	**b** EIN
c Number, street, and room or suite no. If a P.O. box, see instructions.	**d** Date foreign trust was created

e City or town	**f** State or province	**g** ZIP or foreign postal code	**h** Country

2 Did the foreign trust appoint a U.S. agent (defined in the instructions) who can provide the IRS with all relevant trust information? . . . . ☐ Yes ☐ No
If "Yes," complete lines 3a through 3g.

3a Name of U.S. agent	**b** TIN
c Number, street, and room or suite no. If a P.O. box, see instructions.	

d City or town	**e** State or province	**f** ZIP or postal code	**g** Country

4a Name of trustee	**b** TIN
c Number, street, and room or suite no. If a P.O. box, see instructions.	

d City or town	**e** State or province	**f** ZIP or postal code	**g** Country

5 The first and last day of the tax year of the foreign trust to which this statement relates ▶

6a Name of U.S. owner	**b** TIN
c Number, street, and room or suite no. If a P.O. box, see instructions.	

d City or town	**e** State or province	**f** ZIP or postal code	**g** Country

7 Attach an explanation of the facts and law (including the section of the Internal Revenue Code) that establishes that the foreign trust (or portion of the foreign trust) is treated for U.S. tax principles as owned by the U.S. person.

8 If the trust did not appoint a U.S. agent, list the trust documents attached to Form 3520-A. See instructions.

----

9 Gross value of the portion of the trust treated as owned by the U.S. owner . . . . $

10 Cash amounts or FMV of property distributed, directly or indirectly, during the foreign trust's tax year, from the foreign trust (exclude loans) to the U.S. owner.

(a) Date of distribution	(b) Description of property distributed	(c) FMV of property distributed (determined on date of distribution)	(d) Description of property transferred, if any	(e) FMV of property transferred	(f) Excess of column (c) over column (e)

Total . . . . ▶ $

2020 Statement of Foreign Trust Income Attributable to U.S. Owner (see instructions)

Report each item on the proper form or schedule of your tax return.

Income	1a	Taxable interest	1a	
	b	Tax-exempt interest ▶ _____		
	2a	Total ordinary dividends	2a	
	b	Qualified dividends ▶ _____		
	3	Gross rents and royalties	3	
	4	Income from partnerships and fiduciaries	4	
	5	Capital gains (losses)	5	
	6	Ordinary gains (losses)	6	
	7	Other income (attach statement)	7	
	8	**Total income.** Add lines 1 through 7 . . . . ▶	8	
Expenses	9	Interest expense	9	
	10a	Foreign taxes (attach statement)	10a	
	b	State and local taxes	10b	
	11	Amortization and depreciation (depletion)	11	
	12	Trustee and advisor fees	12	
	13	Charitable contributions	13	
	14	Other expenses (attach statement)	14	
	15	**Total expenses.** Add lines 9 through 14 . . . . ▶	15	

Under penalties of perjury, I declare that I have examined this return, including any accompanying reports, schedules, or statements, and to the best of my knowledge and belief, it is true, correct, and complete.

Trustee's (or
U.S. owner's)
signature ▶ _____   Title ▶ _____   Date ▶ _____

2020 Foreign Grantor Trust Beneficiary Statement

Important: *Trustee (or U.S. owner if a substitute Form 3520-A) must prepare a separate statement for each U.S. beneficiary that received a distribution from the trust during the tax year and include a copy of each statement with Form 3520-A. Trustee is also required to send to each such beneficiary a copy of the beneficiary's statement. Each U.S. beneficiary must attach a copy of its statement to its Form 3520.*

1a	Name of foreign trust	b	EIN
c	Number, street, and room or suite no. If a P.O. box, see instructions.	d	Date foreign trust was created

e	City or town	f	State or province	g	ZIP or foreign postal code	h	Country

2 Did the foreign trust appoint a U.S. agent (defined in the instructions) who can provide the IRS with all relevant trust information? . . . . ☐ Yes   ☐ No
If "Yes," complete lines 3a through 3g.
If "No," do you agree that either the IRS or the U.S. beneficiary can inspect and copy the trust's permanent books of account, records, and such other documents that are necessary to establish that the trust should be treated for U.S. tax purposes as owned by another person? . . . . ☐ Yes   ☐ No

3a	Name of U.S. agent	b	TIN
c	Number, street, and room or suite no. If a P.O. box, see instructions.		

d	City or town	e	State or province	f	ZIP or postal code	g	Country

4a	Name of trustee	b	TIN
c	Number, street, and room or suite no. If a P.O. box, see instructions.		

d	City or town	e	State or province	f	ZIP or postal code	g	Country

5 The first and last day of the tax year of the foreign trust to which Form 3520-A applies ▶

6a	Name of U.S. beneficiary	b	TIN
c	Number, street, and room or suite no. If a P.O. box, see instructions.		

d	City or town	e	State or province	f	ZIP or postal code	g	Country

7 Cash amounts or FMV of property that during the current tax year was (1) distributed directly or indirectly to a U.S. person whether or not the U.S. person is designated as a beneficiary of the trust, (2) loaned (exclude loans treated as qualified obligations) directly or indirectly to the U.S. person who is a beneficiary of the trust or a U.S. person related to that U.S. person, or (3) used by the U.S. person who is a beneficiary of the trust or a U.S. person related to that U.S. person without compensating the trust for the FMV of the use of the property within a reasonable period of time. (See the instructions for Part III of Form 3520 for U.S. tax treatment of these amounts.)

(a) Date of distribution	(b) Description of property distributed	(c) FMV of property distributed (determined on date of distribution)	(d) Description of property transferred, if any	(e) FMV of property transferred	(f) Excess of column (c) over column (e)

Total . . . . ▶ | $

8 Attach an explanation of the facts and law (including the section of the Internal Revenue Code) that establishes that the foreign trust (or portion of the foreign trust) is treated for U.S. tax principles as owned by another person.

9 Owner of the foreign trust is (check one):   ☐ Individual   ☐ Partnership   ☐ Corporation

Under penalties of perjury, I declare that I have examined this return, including any accompanying reports, schedules, or statements, and to the best of my knowledge and belief, it is true, correct, and complete.

Trustee's (or
U.S. owner's)
signature ▶   Title ▶   Date ▶

Form **3520-A** (2020)

Schedule B of Form 1040 (Part III, Foreign Accounts and Trusts). Schedule B must be completed by any U.S. person who receives a distribution from, is grantor of, or a transferor to a foreign trust. Any U.S. person treated as the owner (within the meaning of Code §671) of a foreign trust is required to file an annual income tax return describing all trust activities and operations.[299]

---

[299] *See* IRC §6048(b).

Questions

How must U.S. residents and citizens report assets abroad to the IRS?

What is the purpose of IRS Form 3520?

Cases

Treaties

Tax Information Exchange Agreements

IRS Rulings

IRS Forms

Notes